THE BIBLE AND THE UNIVERSE

THE BIBLE AND THE UNIVERSE

Israel and the Theology of History

by

ÉVODE ⌐BEAUCAMP, O.F.M.

THE NEWMAN PRESS
WESTMINSTER · MARYLAND

This translation of La Bible et le sens religieux de l'Univers
(Les Éditions du Cerf, Paris) was made by DAVID BALHATCHET

NIHIL OBSTAT: HUBERTUS RICHARDS, S.T.L., L.S.S.
CENSOR DEPUTATUS
IMPRIMATUR: E. MORROGH BERNARD
VICARIUS GENERALIS
WESTMONASTERII: DIE 8a DECEMBRIS 1962

CONTENTS

INTRODUCTION

THIS BOOK reproduces in substance a thesis submitted in February 1953 to the University of Lyons Faculty of Theology. Extracts from the thesis have been published in a form designed for a wider public in the following periodicals : *Bible et Vie chrétienne, Liber Annuus Studii Biblici Franciscani, La Vie Spirituelle, Les Cahiers du clergé rural.* In re-arranging these articles, we wish to present a new synthesis of what is now an already dated work. Some forms of expression and the exegesis of certain biblical texts have been brought up to date, but basically the work may be said to have been written in 1952 ; works dealing with this subject since then have not, therefore, been taken into account, although we have considered it necessary to mention them in the bibliography.

The title of this thesis clearly set out its object: *Vision of the Universe and History of Salvation. An Essay in the Theology of Material Realities in the Old Testament.* In it an attempt was made to provide an answer to the ambitious question: What is the rôle played by the universe in the drama of our salvation? Or, to put it differently, what place does it fill in God's plan? The subject is of great present-day interest, but it is one which few had hitherto ventured to tackle.[1] Indeed, it is the human

[1] Mention might be made, for example, of the following two works: Gustave Thils' *Théologie des réalités terrestres*, and E. Rideau's *Consécration, le christianisme et l'activité humaine*, both published by Desclée, Paris. One might also note with, however, some reservation the essay by F. Duquesne: *Cosmos et Gloire. Dans quelle mesure l'univers physique a-t-il part à la chute, à la rédemption et à la gloire finale?*, Paris, 1957.

problem, whether treated from a collective or from an individual angle, which normally attracts the attention of exegetes and theologians; and yet, the progress of science has encouraged modern man to probe the secrets of nature and to discover the significance of the world in which he lives, especially as he feels more deeply his history caught up in the very rhythm of the cosmos and finds that the numerous challenges of a life which grows more difficult each day have impelled him to dominate the material world. Marxism has claimed to give some answer to these preoccupations of modern man, putting forward a philosophy of reality, a living, rational justification of human labour. Must the theologian be condemned merely to let others speak, having no light of his own to throw on the subject?

Various attempts have, indeed, been made to answer this challenge of the present day, a challenge to which Catholic action in particular has not been able to remain indifferent. Some thought has been given to the addition of a new treatise to the already existing ones in theology, for example a treatise on work. It must be confessed that the result has been somewhat disappointing. The reason is that familiar texts alone have been examined in an attempt to find an answer to questions which for us may be provocative but whose interest was never foreseen by the inspired writers.

In order, therefore, to establish a theology of material realities, it would appear fruitless to wonder what the Bible may have thought on the subject. It had no opinion to express in this connexion, for the simple reason that the sacred writers were never confronted with the problem as it stands for us to-day. The only thing we can do is to examine in what way the question was resolved concretely, to analyse the attitude of the chosen people to the world about them and the manner in which they reacted to the universe in conformity with the principles of their religious life. Such an attitude is revealed in the routine of daily life at least as much as in moments of crisis; we shall not, therefore, struggle over the exegesis of those verses which have only too often been subjected to close scrutiny. We have preferred to draw our illustrative material from the inspired text as a whole. In fact it is rather in the less exalted material, in the connective tissue, as it were, of the Bible, that we shall look for matter to strengthen our arguments, choosing those passages which are least often quoted, but which best reflect everyday behaviour. The reader will thus have the advantage of making himself familiar with parts of the Bible he knows less thoroughly, and of discovering an interest he had not formerly recognized.

This attitude of Israel towards the external world, described and exemplified in the way proposed, will, however, prove nothing unless it is seen to be closely dependent on what was original and specific in the revelation made to Moses. Such an examination supposes that we already know exactly wherein lies the originality of the religion of Sinai. Quite on the contrary, our biblical theologies are well able to enumerate certain notions and themes and to follow their progressive development, but they do not seem to be very much concerned with taking us back to the central, initial perception which provides the key to them all and determines their progressive deepening. It is thanks to the work of Mircea Eliade, an authority on religious history, that at last we have been able to glimpse, in the pages of history, the essential novelty and the primary perception of all biblical thought. Throughout the ancient world it was in fact the Hebrew people alone who seemed to regard life as an open adventure, and their own destiny as that of the elect fitting into a transcendent, immutable pattern. Some years ago Emmanuel Mounier had written: "In the whole of antiquity, during that era of world religions which marks the first thousand years before the coming of Christ, one race and one religion alone held with force and earnestness the belief that the world has a single, universal history: the Jewish race and religion."[1] This idea has since been re-stated in many forms until it has come to be almost a commonplace: "The biblical philosophy of human

---

[1] "Le Christianisme et la notion de progrès", in *La Petite Peur du XXᵉ siècle*, Paris, 1958, p. 115.

history may be defined as an unalterable, progressive growth and maturing of humanity as it advances towards a given end."[1]

More and more clearly this discovery of history is seen to be one of the essential and fundamental aspects of the religion of Moses. The God of Israel in particular appears to more recent exegetes as the God of an historical experience.[2] Thus, for Martin Buber, Yahweh is essentially a God who is "invisible, identified by the fact that he appears and disappears, sits down and rises up",[3] differing from all other divinities by the way in which he arrogates to himself the guidance of the course of history: "The God by whom Abraham allows himself to be led in his journeyings . . . is first and foremost different from all the other solar, lunar and stellar divinities in that he is not to be seen regularly appearing in the sky but shows himself to his elect at certain moments only, when and where he chooses."[4] Such a God can be defined only in terms of his historical work, not of his cosmic attributes: "Yahweh who sits enthroned thereon [on

---

[1] Claude Tresmontant, *Études de métaphysique biblique*, Paris, 1955, p. 186. Among the many other recent studies of this biblical conception of history may be mentioned the following: Jean Daniélou, *The Lord of History: Reflections on the Inner Meaning of History*, London, 1958; Edmond Jacob, *La Tradition historique en Israel*, Montpellier, 1946; G. von Rad, "Theologische Geschichte im Alten Testament", in *Theologische Zeitschrift*, 4, pp. 161 ff.; W. Eichrodt, "Offenbarung und Geschichte im Alten Testament", *Th. Z.*, 4, pp. 322-329; E. Meyer, *Geschichte des Altertums*, 2nd ed. 1953, p. 285; Hartmut Gese, "Geschichtliches Denken im Alten Orient und im Alten Testament", in *Zeitschrift für Theologie und Kirche*, Dec. 1958.

[2] In this connexion it must suffice for us to refer our readers to the chapter entitled "The Nature of God" in H. H. Rowley's *The Faith of Israel*, London, 1956. It provides a wealth of bibliographical material on the question. In the present study, we shall often have occasion to refer to the etymology of the name Yahweh; no final solution has yet been given and since 1952 there have been further publications on the subject, for example that of S. D. Goitein, "YHVH the Passionate", *Vetus Testamentum* 1956, pp. 1 ff. It is noteworthy however that all suggested etymologies are agreed on the idea of an actual, historical intervention of the God of the Covenant. We may note that this etymological problem has no connexion with the exegesis of Ex. 3.4: "I am he who is", or "I am who am". In this latter case a subsequent interpretation has been given to the divine name which we shall be discussing several times in the course of this work.

[3] *Moses*, Heidelberg, 1952, p. 190.

[4] *Ibid.*, p. 149.

the ark] visiting his people, sits there not as monarch of the cosmos but as Melek of Israel. The thrones of the Babylonian gods are symbols of nature, the Israelitish throne is a symbol of that history, to which are indissolubly linked the Tables bearing the I AM of the God who led his people out of Egypt."[1]

Since this is an idea which is generally accepted to-day, our starting-point may not perhaps appear to be new. We do not think, however, that our study of the great drama of Israel from a historical standpoint merely goes over old ground, as our own approach is personal in so far as its aim is primarily the analysis of an attitude, not the study of notions and themes. We are not interested, therefore, in the significance of history in itself from a purely theoretical angle, but we shall reveal the consequences of a certain conception of history in the daily life of God's people, watching them living an adventure which strains all their energies as they march on breathlessly, carried forward by a vast hope.

This adventure which gives the destiny of Israel its historical impetus and dynamism is the adventure of the Covenant, of the divine call, of the Election.[2] "Israel's very being resides in its fidelity to the Covenant which establishes its identity, 'emûnāh, and which is its truth, 'emèth. The Covenant is a marriage alliance, and the whole of Sacred Scripture may be considered as the love story wherein the leading parts are played by God and his people."[3] One cannot indeed over-emphasize the symbolic value contained in the expression "conjugal love" which "evokes a love-affair unfolding progressively in time . . . [it] animates and vitalizes the Covenant".[4]

---

[1] *Ibid.*, p. 188.

[2] These two notions of Covenant and Election are in fact quite distinct, though opinions differ as to which is the primary one. Nevertheless, we shall use the words interchangeably, referring to the Election of Israel in the Covenant of Sinai: "The Election is the fundamental event, but for it to become a dynamic reality it is made within the framework of a covenant" (E. Jacob, *Théologie de l'Ancien Testament,* Neuchâtel, 1955, p. 170).

[3] C. Tresmontant, *op. cit.,* p. 191.

[4] A. Neher, "Le Symbolisme conjugal, expression de l'histoire dans l'A. T." in *Revue d'histoire et de philosophie religieuse,* 1954, p. 49 and p. 39 respectively.

The choice which God made when he freely and gratuitously took the initial step in this affair has in reality reversed the terms of the dialogue which man had hitherto attempted to hold with the divinity, for it was not Israel which had chosen Yahweh but Yahweh who chose Israel to be his own. This primary intuition governs the whole development of biblical thought; the Covenant and all that it implies will dominate the teachings of the prophets, the ponderings of the sages, and the prayer of the psalmists.[1]

Recent studies have indeed drawn attention to the importance and significance of the Election;[2] but there is still a good deal of confusion on the subject in the mind of the general public. Treating the Covenant as a theme like any other, certain writers have attempted to trace its origin, development and subsequent extension, comparing, without making the necessary distinctions, the Covenant between Yahweh and Israel with the covenants established between God and various biblical figures such as, Noe, Abraham, Aaron, Phineas and David; and one finds references made quite indiscriminately to the covenants with Noe, Abraham and Moses. But the so-called Mosaic Covenant is not a covenant with Moses directly comparable with any other; it is specifically a covenant with Israel through the instrumentality of Moses. On Sinai God created for himself a people to whom he gave a law, with whom he ushered in a history which was to undergo all the vicissitudes of a love-affair. Nowhere in the whole of the Old Testament is there to be found another covenant of this nature: "It is only in the pact of Sinai and in its subsequent renewals that a *berîth* is to be found between *YHWH* and his people, between him and Israel."[3] In fact

---

[1] Our two books *Sous la Main de Dieu*, Paris, Fleurus, 1956, 1957, made an attempt to demonstrate the truth of this in the Prophetic and Sapiential Books. The same may be said for the Psalms; before they were seen in their true light as a dialogue between the two parties of the Covenant, they were given titles which would have suited just as well many extracts from the liturgies of pagan antiquity.

[2] See especially H. H. Rowley, *The Biblical Doctrine of Election*, London, 1950, and T. C. Vriezen, *Die Erwählung Israels nach dem A. T.*, Zürich, 1953.

[3] M. Buber, *op. cit.*, p. 123.

Ben Sira, though he readily draws attention to the various
covenants concluded with the Patriarchs, from Noe to David,[1]
speaks of the Covenant as if he knows only one, when he
evokes that of Sinai:

> All these things are the book of life,
> and the covenant of the most High,
> and the knowledge of truth.
> Moses commanded a law in the precepts of justices,
> and an inheritance to the house of Jacob (Ecclus 24.32-3).[2]
> Be not ashamed . . . of the law of the most High, and of his
> covenant (ib. 42.1-2).

There is no pact here with a privileged person,[3] for the
partner and eventual beneficiary is the Jewish people and not
Moses himself: "And he gave him commandments before his
face, and a law of life and instruction, that he might teach
Jacob his covenant (translated 'prescriptions' in the *Bible de
Jérusalem*) and Israel his judgments" (ib. 45. 6).

Rather than a mere chapter in biblical theology, and
generally the last, the Covenant-Election should therefore
be seen as one of the most fundamental, specific realities of
Mosaic religion, a reality underlying the whole development
of biblical thought. Consequently it is with this conception
of the Covenant in mind that we shall endeavour to establish
the scriptural authority for a theology of material realities.
For, if the dynamism of the vocation of Israel has given a true
significance to history, then it has also brought with it a new
vision of the whole universe. Only the Bible has succeeded in
discovering a beginning and an end to this cosmos which was
thought to be destined to the inevitable rhythm of an eternal

---

[1] Ecclus 44.18,20; 45.7,15,24,25; 47.1 ff.

[2] (Translator's note: Unless explicitly stated otherwise in a footnote, all
biblical quotations are taken from the Challoner revision of the Douai-
Rheims version).

[3] This is not to say that no connexion exists between the two types of covenant. Covenants with individuals must be considered as extensions into the past
or the future of the central Covenant with Israel: nowhere is it claimed that any
one of them can become a substitution for the latter. The only genuine new
Covenant will be the one which will bring into existence the Church, the new
Israel, with her new commandment.

cyclical recurrence; only the Bible shows how the movement which animates the cosmos is a linear, irreversible movement: "Alongside and behind all human history, there is another vaster history, that of the universe . . . it is therefore permissible to consider the cosmos too as history, involving a sacred history bound up with the history of human endeavour."[1]

It must be admitted that the biblical philosophy of history "would have been incompatible with a theory of the universe not homogeneous with it, such as a cyclical conception of the cosmos. The Bible teaches that the universe is a history and that this history extends into that of mankind. Biblical metaphysics is incompatible with a stoic type of cosmology".[2]

If the universe and history obey the same rhythm, it is essentially because they are governed by the same God who wills that everything should contribute to the fulfilment of a transcendent plan. Some thinkers, it is true, claim to see a discrepancy between the affirmation of God's power over the universe and the acceptance of his mastery over history: "It is only at the time of the setting up of the State, when the theocracy was succeeded by dynastic influence, and the kingship of *YHWH* undergoes a transformation, resolving itself into a completely intangible cosmic notion, it is only then that the symbolization of nature becomes dominant, an attempt being made to deny God's control over human history."[3] Our belief is precisely the opposite and it will form the subject of the second and third chapters of this book, where we shall show how only a more acute sense of the ascendancy over his people of the God of the Covenant made possible their gradual discovery of the cosmic attributes of Yahweh. In doing this, Israel was not seeking to escape from the bond of history by which it felt itself held fast, on the contrary, it sought to rediscover, even in the world of nature around it, the broad outline of the plan to which its own destiny was to conform.

[1] E. Mounier, *op. cit.*, p. 116.
[2] C. Tresmontant, *op. cit.* p. 186.
[3] M. Buber, *op. cit.*, p. 188.

Besides, this universe is an integral part of the drama. Most commentators, mainly interested in the adventurous history of Yahweh's dealings with his people, do not seem to have realized that the gift of the promised land is the central fact of the debate, especially in those books which concentrate on the drama of the Covenant such as Deuteronomy, Osee or Jeremias. The universe, of course, could not form a neutral world between Yahweh and Israel, for there is no place for a third term in the dialectic of the Covenant and the man who belongs entirely to God must of necessity hold all else to be of little value: "For all are yours: and you are Christ's: and Christ is God's" (I Cor. 3. 22-3). The Covenant naturally implies, therefore, the inheritance of the earth, which will be entrusted to the elect not for personal, selfish enjoyment but so that the work of the Creator may be completed. Without this inheritance the Covenant loses its vitality and its significance, becoming nothing more than a simple promise of blessing; so, whereas God promises Ismael only numerous descendants: "I will multiply him exceedingly: he shall beget twelve chiefs, and I will make him a great nation" (Gen. 17. 20; cf. 16. 10), for the race of the Covenant he does not forget to mention the possession of the promised land: "I will establish my covenant between me and thee, and between thy seed after thee in their generations, by a perpetual covenant: to be a God to thee, and to thy seed after thee. And I will give to thee, and to thy seed, the land of thy sojournment, all the land of Chanaan for a perpetual possession, and I will be their God" (Gen. 17. 7-8).

We might extend the problem by trying to reach a more general principle. Does not the course of history itself presuppose that the earth should be conquered, geographical foundations laid, scientific discoveries made and economic development achieved? Would purely human time, uninfluenced by cosmic events, be sufficient to inaugurate the history of the world? Such events seem to provide the friction that makes the wheel move, changing the circle into a cycloid. A Westerner, for example, accustomed to envisage history as a march forward, especially when he thinks of the gradual but slow progress of civilization since the twelfth century, remains bewildered when he contemplates in its entirety the past history of, say, the world of Islam. Here it would appear that empires are created and destroyed without the emergence of anything constructive either politically or economically; time is marked by dynastic successions and genealogies, but there is no progress, no advance. Is this not because Islam lacks the initial dynamism of a world conquest which the Bible alone expresses in its entirety, and because islamic religious thought is concerned solely with the relations between man and God?[1]

In conclusion, we shall show in the following pages that the revelation of a divine plan of salvation, by implanting in the mind of man a consciousness of history, has entailed an entirely new conception of the universe. Through the experience of the Covenant, an experience historically lived in direct contact with cosmic phenomena, Israel was enabled to understand the part played in its destiny by material facts and beings. The God of the Covenant thus gradually asserted himself as God of the universe, a universe which was to usher in history. The impulse which animates the adventure of Israel has its starting-point in a perception anterior to that of the existing realities, and sweeps everything forward and beyond towards a common goal. Given to man as the inheritance promised by the Covenant, the material world is borne along in the wake of history.

---

[1] Which paradoxically enough entails a confusion between the spiritual and temporal planes. It may also be remarked that a similar confusion occurs in those Christian circles also which are particularly diffident about compromising themselves in temporal matters and sublimating the values of the present world.

I

THE BIRTH OF HISTORY

THE COVENANT of Yahweh with Israel created history in the deepest sense of the word. By entering thus upon a dialogue with mortals, God undertakes to guide their destiny, directing their steps towards a goal known only to him. Henceforth the term "history" may be used, because the sequence of events has acquired a certain pattern, traces out a plan which conforms to a definite idea, and because the life of the chosen people is caught up in the rhythm of a movement which has a point of departure and a point of arrival.

To-day we are too familiar with this conception of history for the fact to have gone unnoticed. The now classical viewpoint of the theologian Oscar Cullmann is especially familiar: "We must start from this fundamental perception, that the symbol of time for primitive Christianity as well as for Biblical Judaism and the Iranian religion is the *upward sloping line*, while in Hellenism it is the *circle*."[1] Mircea Eliade, the historian of comparative religion, has shown that this was an original and characteristic aspect of biblical thought as distinct from the rest of ancient thought: "Thus, for the first time, the prophets placed a value on history, succeeded in transcending the traditional vision of the cycle (the conception that ensures all things will be repeated forever), and discovered a one-way time."[2] And the author, in this connexion, insists particularly on the biblical experience of faith: "The classic example of Abraham's

[1] O. Cullmann, *Christ and Time: the Primitive Christian Conception of History*, London, 1955, p. 51.

[2] M. Eliade, *The Myth of the Eternal Return*, London, 1955, p. 104.

1

sacrifice admirably illustrates the difference between the traditional conception of the repetition of an archetypal gesture and the new dimension, *faith*, acquired through religious experience . . . Abraham's religious act inaugurates a new religious dimension: God reveals himself as personal, as a 'totally distinct' existence, that ordains, bestows, demands, without any rational (i.e., general and foreseeable) justification, and for which all is possible."[1]

But this idea has more implications than the authors just quoted seem to suspect; it is no less than a religious revolution plumbing the depths of the soul of Israel and animating all its manifestations; every single event woven into its life becomes naturally incorporated in an overall plan; lamentations and thanksgivings, warnings and promises from the prophets can now call upon the testimony of the past, each claiming to prolong an ever-living tradition. "The insertion of legend is", according to Gunkel,[2] "a specifically Israelitish phenomenon which has no equivalent in either Babylon or Egypt. Together with the presence of eschatology it marks the essential difference between biblical and pagan hymns." Thus, reflexion on the past, on the loving care of Yahweh for his people throughout the course of the centuries, gradually permeated all types of writing found in the Bible, the prayers of the psalmists, the pronouncements of the prophets, the maxims of the men of wisdom.

We shall not, however, spend time here showing the place which the recalling to mind of Yahweh's mighty deeds in history occupies in inspired literature; we shall merely emphasize the extent to which this notion of history succeeded in transforming the psychology of Israel and how, subsequently, the people of the Bible adopted a new, original attitude to life itself. Indeed, because of the Covenant, an extraordinary inward urge gives them the will to live and to survive storms violent enough to sweep all other nations off the political map of the world. They are straining all their energies towards

---

[1] *The Myth of the Eternal Return,* pp. 108-10.
[2] *Einleitung in die Psalmen,* Göttingen, 1933, p. 78.

the fulfilment of a mission, caught up as they are in an adventure which, beginning on Sinai, will find its goal in the coming of God's Kingdom. Thus the Jewish people, and only they, are henceforth free from the fear of the unknown, from that instinctive longing for the warm security of a mother's womb, in short, from the "myth of the eternal return": the consciousness of a call, a vocation, will now enable them to keep their eyes deliberately fixed on the future in the fulfilment of a destiny whose pattern is unchangeable.

When life is envisaged from this point of view, the world takes on a different appearance; nor for the elect does the universe, any more than the world, merely turn upon itself; it is borne forward in a movement which prepares the history of mankind and can even be seen following the way opened up by the drama of salvation. Our first chapter on the birth of history provides the key to this biblical theology of material realities which we shall later attempt to define more precisely.

A. THE DYNAMISM OF THE PEOPLE CALLED BY GOD[1]

The God of Sinai was not content to initiate a dialogue with his creatures, he assumed control of their destiny, sweeping them along behind him in a breath-taking march towards a destination the nature of which he alone knows. Through its very awareness of moving in a certain direction, Israel amasses such reserves of energy that it will survive the harshest blows of fate, catastrophes which no other human community has ever been able to oppose successfully. For if time has finally justified the prophets in their invective against the Gentiles, if nothing now remains of Ammon, Moab, Edom, Assur, Tyre, Babylon, even of the Egypt of the Pharaohs, the chosen people still exists and numbers twelve million; they have withstood political disaster, mass deportation, dispersion into the very heart of vast empires; after twenty-five centuries of humiliation, they have not given up one iota of their claims, rising more vigorously than ever from the abyss

[1] Article published in *La Vie Spirituelle*, December, 1958.

into which they might be thought to have disappeared for ever.

It is the awareness of a vocation which has given the soul of Israel this extraordinary impetus, the working of which we are still witnessing with astonishment to-day. Have not the Jews, whether in the Graeco-Roman world or even our modern society, remained the sons of those proud warriors who formerly, their hair flying in the wind, hurled themselves into the attack (Judges 5. 2 ff.), confident in the irresistible might of their God? Many centuries have indeed passed and yet the initial dynamism has lost none of its vigour, for Israel has never felt that its adventure was over and its goal reached. Its heart is still straining towards the realization of an end which thirty centuries of history have not yet seen it attain; Yahweh has not revealed the secret of the plan he is pursuing: "I am who am."

The onward march of life

In the Bible, life is literally an onward march: "There is but one step between me and death," confided David to his friend Jonathan (1 Kings 20. 3); and when, later, he was told that the child of his sin had died, he asked: "Shall I be able to bring him back any more? I shall go to him rather: but he shall not return to me" (2 Kings 12. 23). Thus Yahweh will reply to the prophet who bewails his fate: "If thou hast been wearied with running with footmen, how canst thou contend with horses?" (Jer. 12. 5).

Furthermore, throughout the whole of Holy Writ there is the idea, amounting almost to an obsession, of having a wide, open space before one so that one may advance freely; as if, in order to live fully, it sufficed to march forward unhindered: "And he brought me forth into a large place: he saved me."[1] Conversely, suffering is most often portrayed as an agonized condition in which the victim feels shut in, obstructed in his forward urge, his route barred: "[Why is life given] to a man whose way is hidden, and God hath surrounded him with

[1] Ps. 17.20; cf. 4.2; 25.12; 26.11; 30.9; etc.

darkness" (Job 3. 23). Like the unfaithful wife whom Yahweh prevents from going after her lovers (Osee 2. 6), the unhappy man cries out: "He hath hedged in my path round about, and I cannot pass, and in my way he hath set darkness" (Job 19. 8; cf. Lam. 3. 7).

Anxious to show what he is capable of in the race to which he finds himself committed, the Israelite lives in constant fear lest his foot be caught in a snare,[1] he has a presentiment that a pit has been dug for him to fall into,[2] he is afraid of the cunning net which the huntsman has spread.[3] Crippled by the base intrigues of his fellows, the unhappy Levite dreams of the blue sky of freedom after vainly trying to scale the walls: "Who will give me wings like a dove, and I will fly and be at rest?" (Ps. 54. 7; cf. Ps. 10. 1). When the clamp has been loosened, energies which have been pent up for too long are released: "Our soul hath been delivered as a sparrow out of the snare of the fowlers. The snare is broken and we are delivered" (Ps. 123. 7).

It will never, of course, be a question of marching merely for its own sake; there must be progress in a certain direction; perpetual movement in itself does not constitute history: "My days have passed away," lamented the holy Job (17. 11), "My days have been swifter than a post: they have fled away and have not seen good" (Job 9. 25). And just as, when the creation of the world was completed, God rested on the seventh day, similarly the people of God aspire to a final "sleep in safety": "The people that were left and escaped from the sword found grace in the desert: Israel shall go to his rest."[4] The vitality of existence can in no way, therefore, be confused with mere empty restlessness. The Jew fears above all else in life being swept away in a blind irresistible whirlwind (Job 27. 20).

[1] Ps. 37.13; 56.7; 63.6; 139.6; 141.4; etc.

[2] Ps. 7.16; 9.16; 34.7; 118.85; Jer. 18.20,22; Prov. 26.27; Eccl. 10.8; etc.

[3] Ps. 9.16; 34.8; Lam. 1.13; Job 18.8; 19.6; etc. (Translator's note: For this footnote and the two previous ones, the Revised Standard Version best reproduces the Hebrew text, to which the author is referring. The numbering here given is, however, that of the Vulgate.)

[4] Jer. 31.2; cf. 6.16; Ps. 94.11; 131.8; see also Ps. 15.9; Prov. 1.33; Deut. 33.12; etc.

His march must have a precise objective even if it remains
beyond the understanding of the marcher; for Israel can
never become accustomed to the idea that life has no particular
import.[1]

The abiding influence of the war chronicles of old

Sometimes this vigorous march forward of life takes on the
appearance of a military expedition: as if the destiny of the
elect were unfolding at the same speed as the conquest of the
promised land. Thus, for example, each of the faithful lets
himself be led to the rich pastures by Yahweh, the Shepherd
(Ps. 22), just like the people whom he led into the land of
Canaan: "In thy mercy thou hast been a leader to the people
which thou hast redeemed: and in thy strength thou hast
carried them to thy holy habitation" (Ex. 15. 13). Besides, the
whole history of Israel reveals itself thus as a march forward
under the guidance of Yahweh: "I will go before thee, and
will humble the great ones of the earth" (Is. 45. 2). "For the
Lord will go before you, and the God of Israel will gather you
together" (Is. 52. 12). And the experience of the nation
becomes the personal experience of each of its members:
will not the angel of Yahweh encamp round about the faithful
(Ps. 33. 8), just as he had appeared at the head of Josue's
armies (Josue 5. 13–14)? The just man will only have to
trust in the Lord to guide him (Ps. 36. 5), and to level his path
(Ps. 5. 9; Is. 26. 7): "With the Lord shall the steps of a man be
directed, and he shall like well his way" (Ps. 36. 23).

Under such leadership, life cannot fail to be given a
tremendous forward impulse: "Through my God I shall go
over a wall" (Ps. 17. 30). But it must be admitted that this
triumphant enthusiasm is scarcely found except on the lips
of kings; in the psalter, those who lament tend to maintain
defensive positions; war is being waged against them and what
they seek is a refuge in an impregnable fortress rather than a

[1] For a discussion of the treatment of this subject in the Book of Ecclesiastes,
see Chapter III, A, "A la poursuite du vent", in our volume *Sous la Main de Dieu*,
II, La Sagesse et le destin des Élus.

triumphant expedition to distant lands: "For thou hast been my hope; a tower of strength against the face of the enemy" (Ps. 60. 4). "Be thou unto me a God, a protector, and a place of strength: that thou mayst make me safe" (Ps. 70. 3). But this difference is immaterial: these images drawn from the art of war and found on every other page[1] give the impression that the Jews remained under arms throughout the whole of their history, even during those times when their State had lost more than a little of its former martial glory. For example, the poor man in the Psalms, a victim of mere calumny, immediately thinks of an enemy sharpening his sword,[2] bending his bow, taking aim and shooting his arrow:[3] "A man that beareth false witness against his neighbour, is like a dart and a sword and a sharp arrow" (Prov. 25. 18). Does this type of language merely indicate the persistence of obsolete and hackneyed literary clichés? It would seem rather to be an indication of Israel's fidelity to its most remote origins. These 'anāwîm who weep profusely on their couch, mourn like a dove, cry like an owl in the waste places (Ps. 101. 7), claim, nevertheless to be sons of Gedeon's soldiers; they will be ready to join with the Machabees in their revolt, to withstand the armies of Titus in one of the bloodiest sieges in history, and twenty centuries later, to regain possession of their own land, defying the hostility of the whole world. Memories of conquest have set an indelible stamp upon the soul of the sons of Israel and give a martial colouring to the idea which each Israelite has of his own destiny.

Prophets and sages point the way

If life is a continual forging ahead, then one cannot think of moral teaching as merely a more or less logically arranged string of categorical imperatives. Divine precepts should serve to mark out the track, aiming not so much at defending an established order as guiding the elect towards a new world.

[1] Ps. 17.3; 26.5; 27.1; 60.3-4; 61.2,3,7; 141.6; 143.1; Prov. 14.26; 18.10; etc.
[2] Ps. 7.13; 36.14; 51.4; 56.5; 58.8; 63.4; 139.4; etc.
[3] Ps. 10.3; 36.14; 56.5; 63.4-5; etc.

Virtues themselves will not remain mere abstractions; they will be seen as wide open paths. Thus the Israelite will have to follow the way of truth (Ps. 118. 30; Tob. 1. 2) and avoid that of falsehood (Ps. 118. 29, 104): "If I have walked in vanity, and my foot hath made haste to deceit . . ." (Job 31. 5).

The Law, in seeking to provide a setting for the forward march of the elect, is always considered in the logic of the Sinai adventure. It does not merely refrain from entangling man in a complex series of edicts which it is difficult not to consider as largely arbitrary, but it seeks to uplift him and to indicate to him the path of his true grandeur. And, just as the nation has Yahweh alone to show it what direction to take: "If Israel had walked in my ways" (Ps. 80. 14), so does each one of the faithful feel like a lost sheep without him (Ps. 118. 176), and ask him to point the way: "Shew, O Lord, thy ways to me, and teach me thy paths" (Ps. 24. 4). "Thy word is a lamp to my feet, and a light to my paths" (Ps. 118. 105). "Bless God at all times: and desire of him to direct thy ways, and that all thy counsels may abide in him", such is the advice given by old Tobias to his son (Tob. 4. 20). Is it not possible to recognize here an echo of the very earliest experience felt by God's people: "Behold I will send my angel, who shall go before thee, and keep thee in thy journey, and bring thee into the place that I have prepared" (Ex. 20. 23)?

If it is to reach the limits of its vocation, Israel must not stray for a single moment from the path traced out by God: "And our heart hath not turned back: neither hast thou turned aside our steps from thy way" (Ps. 43. 19). "My foot hath followed his steps, I have kept his way, and have not declined from it" (Job 23. 11). It is clearly understood that there must be no turning away to right or left from the divine precepts (Josue 1. 7; Deut. 5. 32; 17. 11, 20; 28. 14); just as in the wilderness the Hebrews had followed the king's highway without turning aside to right or left (Num. 20. 17; Deut. 2. 27), or as Asael had hurled himself in pursuit of Abner without turning to the right hand or to the left (2 Kings 2. 19).

The image of the road is, indeed, not particularly original; it can be found elsewhere, especially in Egyptian wisdom literature.[1] What strikes us as interesting is that this image retains throughout the Bible its power of concrete evocation. When, for example, Jeremias thus sums up his prophetic message: "Return ye, every one from his evil way, and from your wicked devices" (Jer. 25. 5), he is not just using an antiquated metaphor, he intends in reality to place his hearers in a whole imagery of walking: "Stand ye on the ways, and see, and ask for the old paths, which is the good way, and walk ye in it: and you shall find refreshment for your souls" (Jer. 6. 16). "My people have forgotten me, sacrificing in vain, and stumbling in their ways, in ancient paths, to walk by them in a way not trodden" (Jer. 18. 15). And he has no hesitation in identifying this theme of conversion with that of a return from exile: "Direct thy heart into the right way wherein thou hast walked. Return, O virgin of Israel, return to these thy cities" (Jer. 31. 21). It would seem that the prophet always sees before him the image of faithless Israel rushing in pursuit of its lovers:

A wild ass accustomed to the wilderness
in the desire of his heart snuffed up the wind of his love:
none shall turn her away . . . .
Keep thy foot from being bare,
and thy throat from thirst (Jer. 2. 24–25).
Why dost thou endeavour to shew thy way good
to seek my love,
thou who hast also taught thy malices
to be thy ways? (Jer. 2. 33).

So, far from being mere moral preachers, our prophets are sentinels of the God of Sinai (Osee 8. 1), posted along the route to stop the people of the Covenant in the mad rush in which they are caught up (Jer. 14. 10) and which can be compared with the headlong plunge of a warhorse into battle (Jer. 8. 6). The

[1] See the article by Fr P. Couroyer, "Le Chemin de la vie en Égypte et en Israël", in *Revue Biblique*, 1949, p. 431.

prophets stand there pointing out the way of Yahweh, desperately beseeching Israel to walk humbly with its God (Micheas 6. 8).

After the exile, Wisdom will take their place at the crossroads where the elect must make their choice (Prov. 8. 1–3). Here too, the road, the famous *dèrèkh* of the sapiential books, must in no way be considered a mere theoretical, abstract norm; it indicates the precise manner in which man is to march forward:

> Three things are hard to me,
> and the fourth I am utterly ignorant of.
> The way of an eagle in the air,
> the way of a serpent upon a rock,
> the way of a ship in the midst of the sea,
> and the way of a man in youth (Prov. 30. 18–19).

The authors of the sapiential books are not preoccupied with working out the rules of practical reason or standards of what is good or beautiful; their mission is solely to show the ignorant the consequences of the choice which lies before them and to tell them where the road they are taking will lead. Here, for example, is how the "strange" woman is described for us:

> Her house inclineth unto death,
> and her paths to hell.
> None that go in unto her, shall return again;
> neither shall they take hold of the paths of life (Prov. 2. 18–19;
> cf. 5. 5).
> Her house is the way to hell,
> reaching even to the inner chambers of death (Prov. 7.27)

Since, then, God has chosen for himself a people and through them has called together all mankind, life is comparable to a march or an expedition. This is an entirely original image and one which is peculiar to the Bible; in eastern antiquity—as with the Greeks—the universe is a closed circle where there is no real development or change, where one has the impression of repeating endlessly the same archetypal pattern. The mere discovery of monotheism would not by itself have been sufficient to alter this conception: the example of Islam shows this only too clearly. For life to possess meaning and direction, it is not sufficient for man to be aware of the existence of God, he must be made to feel that he has been taken in hand by God. With the sealing of the Covenant, mankind has been freed of the great fear of history, that treacherous and persistent hankering after a return to the peace and darkness of a mother's womb; the eyes of humanity now turn fearlessly, at this new call, towards an unknown future, in expectation of the fulfilment of a destiny whose pattern will be new and irrevocable.

The joy of success

History provides us with examples of happy nations such as Ancient Egypt, whose art and literature appear to express nothing but sheer exhilaration and delight in being alive. In the Bible, too, joy has its place but does not derive from the simple fact of living; its true happiness always springs from success. The inspired pages are rarely illuminated with bright clear smiles; there is indeed laughter, but it is usually of the kind that brings a shudder, as when Yahweh laughs at the nations that have risen against him (Ps. 2. 4); it is the laugh of the triumphant enemy: "I will extol thee, O Lord, for thou hast upheld me: and hast not made my enemies to rejoice over me" (Ps. 29. 2), or that of the sceptics, which cuts short any attempt at conversion: "I sat not in the assembly of jesters" (Jer. 15. 17).

Not that the Jewish heart is incapable of leaping up at an image of simple, intimate happiness, such as the happiness of which Jeremias sadly proclaims the imminent end: "And I will take away from them the voice of mirth, and the voice of gladness, the voice of the bridegroom, and the voice of the bride, the sound of the mill, and the light of the lamp" (Jer. 25. 10). Some few sages such as Ben Sira might perhaps accept the notion of a carefree, uneventful existence, but the harsh experiences of the children of Abraham soon destroyed any taste they may have had for joys which come without effort, without a long wait to give them flavour. So for them true joy is that of the barren woman whose womb Yahweh has at last rendered fertile (Ps. 112. 9; Is. 54. 1), of harvest or vintage,[1] of victory and the sharing of the spoils (Is. 9. 3):

> Tell it not in Geth,
> publish it not in the streets of Ascalon:
> lest the daughters of the Philistines rejoice,
> lest the daughters of the uncircumcised triumph (2 Kings 1.20).

There is no doubt that joy in the Bible finds its most characteristic expression in the liturgy. A type of rowdy, somewhat disorderly cheerfulness seems to have been the hallmark of Israel's worship before the Exile; the essentials of this worship are summed up by Deuteronomy as eating, drinking and rejoicing in the presence of Yahweh.[2] This liturgical joy is made manifest on every occasion: the transfer of the ark (2 Kings 6. 15; Ps. 46. 2; 131. 9), processions to the temple (Ps. 41. 5), or royal processions (Ps. 44. 16), and above all else sacrifices in thanksgiving: "Let them sacrifice the sacrifice of praise: and declare his works with joy" (Ps. 106. 22).

The origin of this liturgical exultation may, indeed, be found in the agrarian cults of Canaan;[3] but with the passage of time it will become more and more exclusively joy in the saving power and judgements of Yahweh,[4] the God of Israel bringing joy to his people (Ps. 42. 4; 103. 34) for he is the living God (Ps. 83. 3), in his final triumph as Creator and King:

> Let Israel rejoice in him that made him:
> and let the children of Sion be joyful in their king (Ps. 149.2).

[1] Is. 9.3; 16.10; Jer. 48.33; Joel 1.12; Ps. 4.8; 125.5-7.
[2] Deut. 12.7,18; 14.26; 16.11; 26.11.
[3] Whence the expression "the joy of mountains" (Ez. 7.7). See the article by Paul Humbert: "Laetari et exultare dans le vocabulaire religieux de l'Ancien Testament", in *Rev. d'hist. et de philos. rel.*, 1942.
[4] Ps. 34.9; 47.12; 50.14; 94.1; 95.11-13; 96.8; and the hymns in the Second Isaias.

> Rejoice, and praise, O thou habitation of Sion:
> for great is he that is in the midst of thee,
> the holy One of Israel (Is. 12. 6).

The tribulations which accompanied the Exile were doubtless a partial cause of the seriousness and gravity which temper biblical joy. A very few years of captivity are sufficient to harden a man's features, and there will be no more singing while the Israelites are in Babylon; unable to forget Jerusalem (Ps. 136. 6), they will henceforth recognize only one joy, that of liberation:

> When the Lord brought back the captivity of Sion,
> we became like men comforted.
> Then was our mouth filled with gladness;
> and our tongue with joy.
> The Lord hath done great things for us:
> we are become joyful (Ps. 125. 1–3).

There is, therefore, no risk of confusing joy as evinced in the Bible with the naïve satisfaction of the artless young man who shamelessly sings under the windows of those who suffer: "Sing, friends, life is wonderful." Biblical joy, robust and energetic, comes as an end to long and arduous trials; it is a sky washed and freshened by the storm, or the violent unwinding of a spring which has been held taut for too long: "In the evening weeping shall have place: and in the morning gladness" (Ps. 29. 6). "I will turn their mourning into joy, and will comfort them, and make them joyful after their sorrow" (Jer. 31. 13). True joy, therefore, finally becomes the joy of the resurrection, purified and ennobled by the Cross: "They that sow in tears shall reap in joy" (Ps. 125. 5). "A woman when she is in labour, hath sorrow, because her hour is come; but when she hath brought forth the child, she remembereth no more the anguish, for joy that a man is born into the world" (John 16. 21).

This type of joyful experience is particularly expressive of the tense psychology of Israel. The Jewish world still appears to us to-day as a strangely serious and restricted world; as if the soul of Israel could find its true fulfilment only in the triumph which will mark the end of time. Such is, in fact, the truth; God's people will never find true happiness otherwise than in the conclusion of their astonishing adventure, the adventure of a call which was heard three thousand years ago on Mount Sinai.

The arising

"*Qûm*—Arise!" With this word has man been summoned throughout the course of the Bible to spring into action. He is told to arise and be on his way,[1] to give battle,[2] to hear and proclaim God's oracle,[3] or simply in order to praise Yahweh (Ps. 77. 6; 87. 11). As Yahweh himself is here, as always, the great actor, we shall not be surprised to hear the cry go up to him "Arise, O Lord!":[4] "Now will I rise up, saith the Lord: now will I be exalted, now will I lift up myself" (Is. 33. 10).

The vital impulse not only appears in this initial uprising, it will give the Israelites renewed strength in their steadfast will to hold their heads high. The very act of raising the head or the horn[5] expresses the pride of the man who is conscious of being master of his fate: "And he hath exalted the horn of his people" (Ps. 148. 14)—*Et exaltavit cornu salutaris nostri*. Thus the warrior will be determined to draw himself up to his full height on his triumphant entry into his home town, even if he has first to refresh himself in the brook by the wayside (Ps. 109. 7).

On the other hand, the man in defeat shuffles along with head bowed,[6] as if harnessed beneath the yoke: "Behold, I devise an

---

[1] See, for example, Num. 22.20; 24.25; Judges 19.3,5,7,10; 2 Kings 3.21; 4 Kings 1.3; Jonas 3.2; etc.

[2] See, for example, Judges 4.14; 5.7,12; 7.9,15; 20.18,33; Josue 8.1; Num. 23.24; etc.

[3] Num. 23.18; Jer. 1.17; 3 Kings 19.11; Ez. 2.1; 3.22-3; Deut. 34.10.

[4] Ps. 3.7; 7.7; 9.20,33 (=10.12); 11.6; 16.13; 34.23; 43.23,26; 58.6; 101.14; and contrast Hab. 2.19; Deut. 32.38; etc.

[5] 1 Kings 25.35; 4 Kings 25.27; Amos 2.7; Ps. 3.4; 26.6; etc. For the metaphor of the horn, see P. Dhorme, *L'Emploi métaphorique des noms et parties du corps, en hébreu et en accadien*, 1923, pp. 35-41; cf. Ps. 74.11; 88.18,25; 91.11; 131.17; etc.

[6] Ps. 34.14; 37.7; Is. 58.5; 60.14; Lam. 2.10; Baruch 2.18.

evil against this family: from which you shall not withdraw
your necks, and you shall not walk haughtily" (Micheas 2. 3).
He is a man crushed by too heavy a load (Ps. 37. 5), on whose
neck the enemy shall place his foot;[1] he is reduced to the
level of a worm (Ps. 21. 7; Is. 41. 14) upon which no one will
hesitate to tread (Ps. 65. 12):

> Bow down, that we may go over:
> And thou hast laid thy body as the ground,
> and as a way to them that went over (Is. 51. 23).

If life is felt to be an uprising, death will represent a physical
fall, rather than just absence :

> I went down to the lowest parts of the mountains:
> the bars of the earth have shut me up for ever:
> and thou wilt bring up my life from corruption,
> O Lord my God (Jonas 2. 7).
> Thou hast brought forth, O Lord, my soul from hell:
> thou hast saved me from them that go down into the pit
> (Ps. 29. 4).[2]

It will be essentially a reduction to total, permanent helpless-
ness: "Thou wilt cast them down into the fire: in miseries they
shall not be able to stand" (Ps. 139. 11); thus one day Babylon
will sink, never to rise again from the affliction that Yahweh
will bring upon her (Jer. 51. 64). And it is in this sense that the
symbol for death is dust;[3] not that dust evokes, as it does with
us, what remains of the mortal body when the soul has left it,
but simply because it is a sign of irremediable defeat, of a literally crushing defeat; man reaches the end of his life in the
posture of the vanquished, face to the ground (Ps. 142. 3), his
strength in the dust (Job 16. 16), without having to be deliberately or angrily trampled underfoot:

> Moab shall be trodden down under him,
> as straw is broken in pieces with the wain (Is. 25. 10).

[1] Josue 10.24; 3 Kings 5.3(=17); Baruch 4.25; Ps. 44.6; 71.9; 109.1; etc.
[2] Cf. Ps. 27.1; 39.3; 54.24; 87.5; 142.7; Is. 38.18; Ez. 26.20; etc.
[3] Whence the expression, "They that lie in the dust": Is. 26.19; Dan. 12.2;
Ps. 21.30 (?); cf. Ps. 29.10; Job 7.21; 17.16; 20.11; 21.26; etc.

And I shall beat them as small as the dust before the wind;
I shall bring them to nought, like the dirt in the streets
(Ps. 17. 43).[1]

A struggle against death, an attempt to rise up, to resist
the force of gravity and the centrifugal force of dispersion:
such are the characteristics of life as it appears in the Bible.
It has a kind of dynamism which modern science can but serve
to confirm.   It is as if God's call had been needed for this life
to become fully aware of the strength of its renewed impulse.
In any case, no other people has ever felt existence to be a
road ahead, a unique, irreversible adventure, and that, far
from repeating the same formula for each human being, it has
never ceased to open up new horizons.   What other race has
ever understood that the very fact of raising the head signified
the essential superiority of man over all creation, the ultimate
effort of life towards a transcendental goal? The religion of
Israel is the only religion which has enabled mankind to
gather up and accumulate the momentum inherent in its
past history, because it is the only religion which has caught
the sound of a voice from beyond, calling upon the human
race to draw itself up and march forward.   To be faithful to
this distant past only one solution remains: to stand up and
grasp the hand which God holds out.

B.   HOPE IN THE COMING OF THE KINGDOM OF GOD[2]

Thy kingdom come! We often utter this petition briefly
enough, and without taking any particular interest in it.   It is
difficult to imagine what explosive material was contained in
these three words at the time of Christ.   "The kingdom of
God is at hand," cried John the Baptist, and as though galvan-
ized by an electric charge, the crowds thronged into the desert.
The message had indeed the effect of a sudden shock, for it
expressed the fullest hope of Israel, heavy with the weight of

[1] Cf. Micheas 7.10; Is. 10.6; Lam. 3.34; 4 Kings 13.7; Amos 1.3.
[2] Article published in *La Vie Spirituelle*, June, 1957.

dreams which a thousand years of dramatic history had stored up.[1]

To understand its significance, we must go back to the very origins of the epic of Israel. The God who called Moses in the desert of Madian was not one of the gods whose arbitrary favour had to be coaxed at times. There is no one who can force the hand of God, for it is God who gives the orders and who guides history towards a goal which he alone knows. Moses would have liked very much to know what mysterious force was coming to the help of the Hebrews in their affliction. "I am who am", was the reply (Ex. 3. 14).[2] The name of this unknown God expressed purely and simply this determination to direct with supreme authority the course of history: "It is I, here I am!" Dazzled by the pitiless light of the desert, deafened by the crashing din of a hurricane which calls into question the very structure of creation, the Hebrews felt heavy upon them the hand of him before whom everything trembled and who would recoil before no one.

Stung thus into action by the awareness of God's strength, the Israelitish tribes pressed forward to the conquest of Canaan. Two centuries later their combined forces had completed the subjugation of the whole territory. Had this not proved to be the fulfilment of the promise made on Sinai? To complete the work undertaken, there but remained to establish a monarchy, as for other races. Yahweh would then reign over Israel, uniting all the tribes round his Anointed, reducing to serfdom all the other peoples in the land. The Covenant with David and his dynasty was the first stage in the hope in the coming of the kingdom of God; the establishment of a

[1] The "Kingdom of God" became the central hope of Israel because from the very beginning it was recognized as the crowning fulfilment of the Sinai adventure, the establishment of the Hebrews in a land of their own. The expression, therefore, does not imply only the complete domination of Yahweh over his people which originated in the desert, as certain writers—among them Buber, *Das Königtum Gottes*—appear to believe.

[2] Such is apparently the meaning of these verses, Ex. 3.13-14. A subsequent (Elohistic) interpretation has sought to emphasize the transcendence of divine action, developing the idea implicit in the true etymology of the word Yahweh: "He is".

stable monarchy appeared to complete Yahweh's plan, and to conclude the work of conquest.

In reality the Israelites were committed to follow a route the goal of which was always to recede in proportion as they advanced. They were like travellers who seek to reach the line of the horizon. This kingdom of God which was thought to have materialized did not, in fact, last a century. The kingdom of David was split definitively in two after the death of Solomon. Besides, had Yahweh really intended to grant the Jews the political stability which they desired, the spot was poorly chosen, for Palestine had never been more than a corridor between the two centres of ancient civilization, the Egyptian and the Babylonian. No doubt at the time of entering the land of Canaan the Hebrews might have laboured under a delusion; both great powers had fallen into decadence in face of attacks by the "Peoples from the Sea". But the revival of either civilization would suffice to bring the people of Yahweh back face to face with harsh reality; and in the middle of the eighth century B.C. fierce Assyrian warriors appeared on the horizon. Soon it was all over: the kingdom of Samaria, after Syria, fell in 722, leaving its twin, Jerusalem, to struggle on in a state of semi-dependence until it too finally collapsed in 586. Could there have been a more devastating and complete failure of all hope in the kingdom of Yahweh? But the more the chosen people are overwhelmed by hard trials, the more tense does the psychological spring of Israel become, and the more does their heart throb with hope. For Israel, each disillusionment has been but the turning of yet another page in its history: the kingdom of David had come to an end, the kingdom of God had not yet begun. In the midst of the most dire catastrophes, the people of God at no time had the impression that Yahweh had uttered his final word: "I am who am." When in the depth of distress, the Israelites dreamed all the more earnestly and intensely of vast luminous horizons. At a time when an adverse fate seems to dog their footsteps, when they are reeling from the shock of the captivity, of the disappointments they experienced after their return, of persecution by Antiochus Epiphanes, the former ideal of the kingdom of David gradually resolves itself into an apocalyptic vision of all-embracing dominion over a completely changed universe.

Doubtless the humble supplication of the "poor" Israelite is more acceptable to the modern mind than these far-reaching ambitious dreams. These are, nevertheless, two aspects of the early history of Israel between which there can be no exclusive choice: both are evident in the psalter and are interdependent facts. The full dramatic force of the biblical lamentations derives its power from the dream which inspired the soul of Israel; would Beethoven have suffered to such an extent had he not entertained great ambitions or been aware of his vocation as a genius? Just so does the anguish of the psalmists derive its origin from the contrast between the brilliantly coloured joys of anticipation and the sombre-hued realities of the present. The song of the "poor" Israelites, too, is haunted by dreams and hopes, without ever turning into a fatalistic, resigned lament.

We may have a tendency to underestimate the religious significance contained in this hope in the kingdom of God, feeling perhaps that it is not pure enough to suit our taste. An excessive and to some extent affected spirituality has made us less aware than we should be of the depth of Christian salvation. God does not despise our dreams, however material they may be, for he is able to fulfil the loftiest aspirations of the human heart, far out-reaching them in the process. Let us be careful, therefore, not to offer him through a mistaken sense of modesty only the most exquisitely sharpened point of our soul and that alone: "I have but one soul which I must save!" At a time when humanity is carried away by the violence of Promethean dreams, we deny God if we thus amputate our message of salvation.

The kingdom of God and the kingdom of David

Lift up your gates, O ye princes,
and be ye lifted up, O eternal gates:

and the King of glory shall enter in.
Who is this King of Glory?
The Lord who is strong and mighty:
the Lord mighty in battle (Ps. 23. 7-8).[1]

While to the blaring of trumpets and the shouts of the
crowd, the ark was being borne uphill towards Jerusalem,
David, clad in the traditional loin-cloth worn by the priests of
old, sang and danced with carefree abandon, heedless of the
scornful glances of his wife Michol, the daughter of Saul.
Her protests were, in fact, most untimely, for the king was
fully aware of the importance such a day held for the future
of his monarchy. The Ark of Yahweh was triumphantly
mounting towards this newly conquered Jerusalem, which the
victor dreamed of making his capital.

O clap your hands, all ye nations (tribes):
shout unto God with the voice of joy.
For the Lord is high, terrible:
a great king over all the earth (fatherland).
He hath subdued the people (tribes) under us:
and the nations under our feet.
He hath chosen for us his inheritance,
the beauty of Jacob which he hath loved.
God is ascended with jubilee:
and the Lord with the sound of trumpet.
Sing praises to our God, sing ye:
sing praises to our king, sing ye . . . .
The princes of the people (tribes) are gathered together,
with the God of Abraham (Ps. 46)[2].

Because of its central position, the Canaanite fortress would,
indeed, help to consolidate the hitherto precarious unity of
the twelve tribes, and to bring into subjection the neighbouring
Moabites, Ammonites and Edomites. This fulfilled the whole

[1] This very old psalm (23b, vv. 7-10) seems to tally perfectly with the transfer
of the ark as related in 2 Kings 6.
[2] Against the opinion of certain modern exegetes, we consider this psalm
to be very old and probably Davidic. Cf. "Ps. 47, v. 10a", in *Biblica*, 1957,
pp. 457-460, and Tournay, "Chronologie des Psaumes", in *R.B.*, July 1958,
p. 324, n. 2.

programme of the new monarchy, which consisted in the
definitive unity of the people of Israel, the domination of the
territory under the kingship of Yahweh and of his Anointed:

> The Lord said to my Lord (David): Sit thou at my right
> hand:
> until I make thy enemies thy footstool.
> The Lord will send forth the sceptre of thy power out of
> Sion:
> rule thou in the midst of thy enemies (Ps. 109. 1–2).[1]

The kingdom of God, therefore, appears at the beginning[2]
to identify itself with the realization of David's ambitions:
the setting up of a stable monarchy completing the divine work
undertaken on Sinai, namely the conquest of Canaan. From
the outset, nevertheless, the kingdom of Yahweh can be felt
to be something more than that. The hopes of Israel, founded
on the very indefiniteness of the divine promises, could never
be restricted to the narrow limits of some merely concrete
realization. No doubt when the psalmist speaks of the
"earth" (Ps. 46) he means the fatherland itself, just as the
"people" denote the tribes of Israel, and the "nations" those
neighbours who are reduced to dependence.[3] These terms,
however, all seem to be deliberately vague, as if they covered
some secret ambition. Was Israel even then dreaming of
universal dominion? Was it entirely without ulterior motives
that in defining the limits of its kingdom Israel used the
imperial terminology of Babylon: "And he (the king) shall
rule from sea to sea, and from the river unto the ends of the

---

[1] Although, here too, doubts have been expressed concerning the antiquity
of this psalm, we consider it one of the oldest and probably Davidic.

[2] The notion of Yahweh's kingship doubtless existed before the time of David
(cf. 1 Kings 8.7); but it cannot be proved to have existed long before this. It
certainly cannot be reduced, as some have tried to do, to the primitive image
of Yahweh as pastor of his flock. Here, as throughout the whole of the Ancient
Near East, the kingship of God implies possession of the ground itself, and,
therefore, a well-established and settled life.

[3] We translate by "people" the word 'ammîm, and by "nations" the word
gôyîm, terms which ultimately became synonymous, indicating, especially after the
Exile, all foreign peoples or nations.

earth" (Ps. 71. 8)? In a concrete sense, this can, of course, be interpreted: "From the Red Sea to the sea of the Palestines, and from the desert to the river (Jordan)" (Ex. 23. 31), but, in Babylon, the same expression meant: "From the Indian Ocean to the Mediterranean, from the Euphrates to the Nile", containing therefore the idea of dominion over the whole of the civilized world which was known at that time.

By its hope in the kingdom of God, Israel shows itself, from the earliest, to be more ambitious than would appear at first sight. Trusting in the promises of a faithful God who is more powerful than the world, the Israelites cannot confine their dreams within the prosaic limits of the present. Beyond the horizons which they can see, they suspect a more brilliant destiny which the hard shocks of their dramatic history will soon help to clarify.

From dream to heroic faith

The monarchic ideal on which the earliest hopes in the kingdom of God had been founded was not to stand the test of history. Immediately upon the death of Solomon, the ten northern tribes, which had always been reluctant to accept the authority of a king of Juda, resumed their political and religious autonomy. Thus ended David's cherished dream, the unity of Israel. The successors of David could never again assert their rights over the whole of the territory which Yahweh had given as a legacy to his people.[1] Such was the first failure of the politico-religious dream of Israel. No doubt the kings of Juda continued for some time yet to press forward their claims on the northern territories, treating their rivals in Samaria as rebels; finally they were obliged to give up and face facts. The very basis of the Davidic monarchy had collapsed, but hope in the kingdom of God remained intact. New, tragic historical circumstances gave a fresh reality to the anticipation of this reign; the time of trial even opened up unsuspected vistas to Israel's ancient dream.

[1] The idea of bringing about reunion between the two kingdoms persisted until the fall of Jerusalem. Thus Ezechias and especially Josias attempted to restore to Sion at least religious, if not political, unity.

Towards the middle of the eighth century, the Assyrian armies, advancing like a tidal wave, reached the gates first of Damascus then of Samaria, and laid siege to Jerusalem itself. The shouts of triumph accompanying the progress of the ark towards the sanctuary now turned to cries of distress. "May the Lord hear thee in the day of tribulation," cried out the priest of Jerusalem to the king, "May the name of the God of Jacob protect thee. May he send thee help from the sanctuary: and defend thee out of Sion" (Ps. 19. 2-3). The ark, the temple, the holy city now became symbols of the resistance of a whole nation the very life of which was at stake. In face of this deadly menace, the Israelites turned towards the King of glory, the Yahweh of the battles of yore, the Yahweh of armies whose holiness had been beheld by the prophet Isaias. During these tragic times, the God of victories remained the sole protector, the only fortress. His heralds would have no truck with the invader: "Yahweh alone" was their one and only policy. "Yahweh reigns", the acclamation which during the days of glory had beguiled the dreams of Israel, now became, in days of deep distress, the heroic expression of complete faith.

Thus when the hosts of Sennacherib came with insults on their lips to beleaguer Jerusalem, Ezechias took the letter from the Assyrian envoys and read it, then went up to the temple of Yahweh and spread it before the Lord (Is. 37. 14). It was Yahweh whom they were insulting, here was the proof. This magnificent gesture of king Ezechias received its reward in the great oracle of Isaias:

> The virgin the daughter of Sion hath despised thee,
> and laughed thee to scorn:
> the daughter of Jerusalem
> hath wagged the head after thee.
> Whom hast thou reproached,
> and whom has thou blasphemed,
> and against whom hast thou exalted thy voice,
> and lifted up thine eyes on high?
> Against the holy One of Israel (Is. 37. 22–3).

And soon shouts of joy followed the cries of lamentation. Defeated at Pelusium, the Assyrians loosened their grip and hastily fell back:

> With the joy of the whole earth
> is mount Sion founded,
> on the sides of the north, the city of the great king.
> In her houses shall God be known,
> when he shall protect her.
> For behold the kings of the earth assembled themselves:
> they gathered together.
> So they saw; and they wondered,
> they were troubled, they were moved. (Ps. 47. 2–6).

Yahweh the King is no longer the ancient master of the Palestinian tribes, he is the monarch who, from Mount Sion, now a holy mountain, inspires all the allied nations with awe. Even if the universe were to crumble and the world return to the chaos of the Flood, Jerusalem will not falter, for it is the city of the most High: "God is in the midst thereof, it shall not be moved" (Ps. 45. 6). "Therefore we will not fear, when the earth shall be troubled; and the mountains shall be removed into the heart of the sea. The waters roared and were troubled: the mountains were troubled with his strength" (Ps. 45. 3–4). At a time when the whole of the Fertile Crescent felt the on-slaught of the Assyrian invasion, when the Syrian gods were overcome and borne away in triumph to Nineve, King Yahweh, enthroned upon the cherubim of the ark in his inviolable city, listened unperturbed to the roar of the rising waves, for it is he, and he alone who is master of history: "The Lord hath reigned, let the people be angry: he that sitteth on the cherubims: let the earth be moved. The Lord is great in Sion, and high above all people" (Ps. 98. 1-2).

The Messianic hope

The dreams of glory conceived at the time of the early Davidic monarchy seemed destined to fade in the chaos and cruel horror of the Assyrian invasions. Under threat of extinction, the tiny kingdom of Juda could scarcely maintain its balance, even though it was sustained by unswerving faith in the kingship of its God in Jerusalem. But was Israel to submit henceforth to this needy existence, to an inglorious future, to this condition of semi-dependence in the midst of great empires? Was that resplendent epic conceived under the sign of the Covenant on Sinai to end like this? No indeed; the bleaker the existing situation appeared to be, the more intensely did Israel's dreams conjure up a new world of the brightest hues. Their inner vitality sapped by these many trials, the Israelites unexpectedly and almost savagely sought relief and relaxation in the joyful vision of peace and happiness stretching away on infinite horizons.

If the Assyrian armies were encamped in front of Jerusalem, it was not because the god of Ninive was stronger than the God of Juda; it was because Yahweh himself was striking his people, was washing away the iniquities that sullied them. Was not the essential task of royalty to ensure the prevalence of order and justice rather than to crush the enemy underfoot, or to strengthen control of territory, as had been the ideal of former kings? Such were the thoughts of the poet who composed the epithalamium in honour of Achab and Jezabel: "The sceptre of thy kingdom", he said to the King, "is a sceptre of uprightness" (Ps. 44. 7). And the people began to await the sovereign ideal which would herald the era of universal justice:

> Give to the king thy judgment, O God:
> and to the king's son thy justice:
> to judge thy people with justice,
> and thy poor with judgment.
> Let the mountains receive peace for the people:
> and the hills justice.
> He shall judge the poor of the people,
> and he shall save the children of the poor:
> and he shall humble the oppressor (Ps. 71. 1–4).

Such were the prayers that were uttered, perhaps each year, or at any rate whenever a new reign opened, with ever hopeful thoughts of the day when Yahweh would make manifest his divine kingship. Justice and equity (judgement), then, formed the support of the royal throne (Is. 9. 7), as they are the basis of the throne of Yahweh (Ps. 88. 15; 96. 2):

"The Lord hath reigned, let the people be angry. . . .
the king's honour loveth judgment.
Thou hast prepared directions:
thou hast done judgment and justice in Jacob.
Exalt ye the Lord our God:
and adore his footstool. . . .
for the Lord our God is holy (Ps. 98).

It seemed, however, as if Yahweh wished to delay this eagerly awaited moment. The horizons are still dark, because Israel is sinful and must be punished; but, after this period of affliction, there will appear the ideal king, Emmanuel, descended from the line of David; beyond the disasters of the present is discernible a new light. The world is, for the time, running with blood, but the holy God of Sion is already actively preparing a nation and a king worthy of his holy patronage. Then the whole of nature will bask in infinite joy and universal peace. The beasts, even, will no longer tear each other to pieces; no more blood will be shed on the ground, for, as in the first Creation (Gen. 1. 29-30), the animals will be content to eat the grass in the fields. Universal peace and harmony, such is the dream that comforts Israel in the dark hours of his history and makes him think of the coming time when everything shall obey the smile of a little child:

He (the new king) shall not judge according to the sight of the eyes,
nor reprove according to the hearing of the ears.
But he shall judge the poor with justice,
and shall reprove with equity for the meek of the earth.
And he shall strike the earth with the rod of his mouth,
and with the breath of his lips he shall slay the wicked.
And justice shall be the girdle of his loins:
and faith the girdle of his reins.

The wolf shall dwell with the lamb:
and the leopard shall lie down with the kid.
The calf and the lion and the sheep shall abide together,
and a little child shall lead them.
The calf and the bear shall feed:
their young ones shall rest together:
and the lion shall eat straw like the ox.
And the suckling child shall play on the hole of the asp:
and the weaned child shall thrust his hand
into the den of the basilisk.
They shall not hurt, nor shall they kill
in all my holy mountain:
for the earth is filled with the knowledge of the Lord,
as the covering waters of the sea (Is. 11. 3–9).

The darkest hours

The ideally just king, heralded thus by the prophets, did
not come at the expected hour to prevent faithless Israel from
succumbing beneath the blows of divine vengeance. Finally
Sion fell; the temple was destroyed and the *élite* dragged away
into exile. As a nation, Israel existed no longer, but the hope
of Israel did not die. Annihilated, Juda yet dreamed of the
imminent coming of Yahweh's kingdom:

In that day, saith the Lord
I will gather up her that halteth:
and her that I had cast out, I will gather up:
and her whom I had afflicted.
And I will make her that halted, a remnant:
and her that hath been afflicted, a mighty nation.
And the Lord will reign over them in mount Sion,
from this time now and for ever.
And thou, O cloudy tower of the flock,
of the daughter of Sion,
unto thee shall it come:
yea, the first power shall come,
the kingdom to the daughter of Jerusalem (Micheas 4. 6–8).

Already there is talk of extraordinary victories achieved by
a new conqueror: the power of Cyrus is beginning to shake

empires. The hearts of those in exile begin to throb with excitement; the hour has come at last, the glory of Yahweh is about to be made manifest; the captives will begin to make their way back in triumph; nature herself will be affected and deserts will turn to grass as the exiles return to their home. The kingdom of Yahweh will be a new and sensational Exodus: "How beautiful upon the mountains are the feet of him that bringeth good tidings, and that preacheth peace: of him that sheweth forth good, that preacheth salvation, that saith to Sion: Thy God shall reign!" (Is. 52. 7). Recalling the processions of old, caravans can already be seen departing: "You shall not go out in a tumult, neither shall you make haste by flight: for the Lord will go before you, and the God of Israel will gather you together" (Is. 52. 12).

Nothing of the sort, however, occurred; small groups of idealists did manage, with great difficulty, to get back to the land of their forefathers; there they led an existence which was usually precarious, for they were unwanted, as their brothers who had not accompanied them into exile had long since filled all available posts. This return was, therefore, a complete failure. Besides, Jerusalem was now merely an insignificant portion of the vast Persian empire, subject to the humiliating domination of the governor of Samaria. But God's people never give up; they continue to dream of a coming reversal of fate:

> Say ye among the Gentiles: The Lord hath reigned . . . .
> He will judge the people with justice.
> Let the heavens rejoice, and let the earth be glad,
> let the sea be moved, and the fulness thereof:
> the fields and all things that are in them shall be joyful.
> Then shall all the trees of the woods rejoice
> before the face of the Lord, because he cometh:
> because he cometh to judge the earth.
> He shall judge the world with justice,
> and the people with his truth (Ps. 95. 10–13).

The coming of God's kingdom is awaited more eagerly than

ever. For the time, no doubt, there can be no question of an earthly king, at least after the hopes founded on Zorobabel had come to nothing; furthermore, the sons of David were too deeply implicated in the sin of early Israel for anyone to think of them now. Similarly, the former carrying of the ark up to the temple is now but a distant memory, no longer of current interest. It is not Yahweh who is entering his sanctuary, but the God of heaven who, to the sound of the horn and shouts of greeting, in the midst of rejoicing nature, comes down to judge the universe:

> The Lord hath reigned, let the earth rejoice:
> let many islands be glad (Ps. 96. 1).
> Sing praise to the Lord on the harp,
> on the harp, and with the voice of a psalm:
> with long trumpets, and sound of cornet.
> Make a joyful noise before the Lord our king.
> Let the sea be moved and the fulness thereof:
> the world and they that dwell therein.
> The rivers shall clap their hands,
> the mountains shall rejoice together
> at the presence of the Lord:
> because he cometh to judge the earth.
> He shall judge the world with justice,
> and the people with equity (Ps. 97. 5–9).

Horizons have broadened out considerably since the time of the original conception of Yahweh's kingship. Formerly, King Yahweh was master of the land of Palestine, now he wields power over the whole of the known universe. At the time of Isaias, the city of the Great King awaited unflinchingly the attack of the combined enemies. Now, after a gigantic, decisive battle of Jerusalem, the disarmed nations will come and make their submission, doing homage to King Yahweh in his temple: "And all they that shall be left of all nations that came against Jerusalem, shall go up from year to year, to adore the King, the Lord of hosts, and to keep the feast of tabernacles" (Zach. 14. 16). "All the ends of the earth shall remember, and shall be converted to the Lord. And all the

kindreds of the Gentiles shall adore in his sight. For the
kingdom is the Lord's; and he shall have dominion over the
nations" (Ps. 21. 28-29).

Has there ever before been an example of such a small
nation harbouring such immense ambitions? Nor was it at
times of relative greatness that the Israelites allowed themselves
to be carried away by dreams of universal domination. On
the contrary, it was precisely when Israel had no share in the
political map of the world that it conceived the notion of
achieving a triumph without precedent in the history of
mankind. Therein lies perhaps the greatest miracle in the
whole Bible: the fact that, when hopes are at their lowest ebb,
God's people react in such a way that their very failure drives
them forward with tremendous impetus to even higher
ambitions.

It may seem wholly irrational that the psychological
resources of Israel should be most in evidence whenever
complete annihilation appeared imminent, yet this fact reveals
one of the profoundest lessons of the Bible: God scorns a show
of vainglorious pride, he holds in scant esteem the triumphs of
ephemeral power, and it is precisely because Israel no longer
counts for anything, no longer hopes to succeed by purely
human means, that it can confidently expect everything from
the hand of God:

> Let Israel rejoice in him that made him:
> and let the children of Sion be joyful in their king . . . .
> For the Lord is well pleased with his people:
> and he will exalt the meek unto salvation . . . .
> To execute vengeance upon the nations,
> chastisements among the people (Ps. 149. 2, 4, 7).

Failure or fulfilment of Israel's dream

There was one time, among the many others, when Israel
thought it was at last about to attain the object of its dreams.
Antiochus Epiphanes, one of the last successors of Alexander
who still held some prestige, had decided he would try to
hellenize the land of Juda and annihilate, by craft or by force,

the ancient Mosaic traditions. This time there was clearly a coalition of pagan nations against the people of God: surely the hour of God's kingdom was at hand! The apocalyptic writers were announcing the coming manifestation of divine glory in favour of the chosen people who were being persecuted: the Son of Man appearing in the clouds. But the Machabees, more practical, led an organized resistance and entered upon an epic struggle during which Israel lived through the most heroic hours of its history. The results of this war were in no way negligible: for the first time since the Exile, Juda regained political independence, and for a century the descendants of the Machabees ruled over a kingdom as great as David's. But since the time of David the ambitions of Israel had grown considerably vaster, and the State, such as it was, could not measure up to the imperialistic claims of God's people. Furthermore, the new dynasty, the Asmonean, soon showed signs of exhaustion and decadence, thus preparing the ground for the Romans. This, certainly, was not the kingdom of God.

The hopes of Israel, once again dashed to the ground, rebounded still higher. The expected king could not be a descendant of the Machabees, as the prophets had announced a Messias-King a son of David. With far more breath-taking perspectives in mind, the Israelites turned back to the ancient psalms and the prophecies concerning a Messias-King. The scribes, indeed, experienced some difficulty in reconciling the image of this king, son of David, with the divine figure, the Son of Man, as seen by Daniel in his vision. In this connexion, Jesus liked to embarrass those who sought to contradict him: "If Christ be the son of David, how then can he be called Lord?" The dreams of Israel, as they reached the last stages of their evolution, proliferated without much coherence. This agrees with a constant experience in our spiritual life, namely, that God alone has the power of fulfilling all at once the most contradictory desires of the human heart by providing, in his own good time, a solution known to him alone.

The Kingdom of God is at hand, cried John the Baptist one day, and crowds assembled from all sides to receive the

4

baptism of forgiveness. A man of humble origins, but sprung from an illustrious line of kings, began shortly afterwards to attract people's attention. At his hands, the sick were cured, the eyes of the blind and the ears of the deaf were opened, the dead were brought back to life. The hour was finally striking for all the sufferings of Israel: the poor were at last hearing the good news. But this man, endowed with such extraordinary faculties, seemed in no hurry to restore the kingdom of God: he even went away when there was talk of making him king; one word from him would have sufficed, however, to fire the crowds with immense enthusiasm; this son of David, marking his progress with one victory after another, could have imposed upon the world that peace and justice which had been announced by the prophets of old. This strange man did, indeed, demand that his disciples should abandon everything to follow him, but nothing could, in fact, be seen happening. This was because it is easier to recruit whole legions, to lead them into slaughter to the beating of drums, than to bring about a change of heart in the sons of Adam. Now God's action was designed to renew the whole man, and not merely to reform the political and social life of a nation. Jesus Christ, therefore, chose to devote himself to the training of a handful of disciples, rather than allow himself to be carried away by the superficial enthusiasm of the crowds and embark on grandiose adventures. The kingdom is like a tiny seed, the tiniest of all; once it is buried in the earth, it gives birth to a tall tree in which the birds of the air will seek shelter.

If the seed does not perish . . . By marching upon Rome, at the head of an army of fanatical followers, Jesus would not have transformed the world as completely as he did by dying on a cross. On Calvary, the Son of God bore the suffering and the wretchedness of a humanity steeped in sin, so that on the third day, history might witness the clear dawn of resurrection. Here was the fulfilment of every Mosaic revelation, from the conquest of Canaan to the baptism of John the Baptist; henceforth the kingdom of God was a reality; hearts which had grown tense with alternating hope and disappointment would finally dilate with joy in the alleluia of an eternal Pentecost, in the Amen of the Apocalypse.

In order to witness, however, the realization of its dreams, Israel had to resign itself to accept the ultimate and supreme disillusionment of its history: the death on the cross of its Messias-King. To only a small number of the elect was this privilege given; the majority could not overcome the final obstacle. After this, nothing could ever gratify to the full the wishes of these men who hoped for too much, for their dreams raised them far above any possibility the history of mankind could offer. When one has climbed too high, the only solution is to climb still higher. May this people, whose destiny henceforth holds no further significance, rediscover, through sad experience and after its first refusal, the one worthy object of its dreams!

II

FROM THE GOD OF HISTORY TO THE GOD OF THE UNIVERSE[1]

THE DYNAMIC vitality which has sustained Israel throughout the course of its dramatic history, has coloured its vision of the external world in an entirely new and original way. The chosen people, for example, has never appeared to be very impressed by the grandiose spectacle of a universe whose physical cause needed defining; the Israelites were busy living, and living with their God; what surrounded them merely obeyed that imperious voice upon which their fate depended. With other peoples, the sense of astonishment and powerlessness in face of the cosmos had aroused in the human heart an intuition of the divine, and it was because mankind found itself utterly helpless when confronted with the violent explosions of the forces of nature that it felt the need for many divinities and temples.

Alone with his destiny, man thus sought to tame, and to reduce to something like his own proportions, powers which far surpassed him and with which he had to reckon. But with the apparition of the burning bush a sudden change came about in the religious evolution of humanity. Someone had come forward with the simple words "Here I am!", and revealed his intention of liberating a handful of slaves in order to mould them into a race whose destiny was to be the envy of the whole world. No longer would mortals have to carve out for themselves their own future, groping blindly through a hostile world: there was Someone to take them in hand,

---

[1] This chapter appeared in *Liber Annuus IV (1953–1954) Studii Biblici Franciscani*, Jerusalem, 1954, under the title "Dieu de l'Univers et Dieu de l'Histoire".

who would make all things yield before him. There was no necessity to try and define the cosmic attributes of this God; it was sufficient that Israel should know him to be strong enough to lead them forward and to protect them against all enemies.

Feeling thus securely guided, the Israelites gradually came to be aware that the God who had freed them was absolute master of the universe, was, in fact, he who had created all things. This progress of biblical thought may upset our sense of logic, for we are accustomed to see things in a different light: we begin by affirming that God is Lord and Creator of the world before we analyse his work of salvation. It would be natural enough to assume that a people to whom was initially confided a revelation of the purest monotheism must normally arrive at an awareness of God's plan in history. Does not the idea of a God as master of the universe necessarily imply that of a God as master of history? There does not, however, exist any example of a monotheism which has been enriched in the course of time by the intuition of an assumption by God of responsibility for the destiny of mortal man. When such a notion is originally lacking, it never subsequently emerges in the development of theology, ethics and mysticism. Islam provides the best illustration of this truth.

It was only in the lengthy experience of its Election that Israel arrived at the theologically perfect formulation of a living monotheism. One would seek in vain to find any sort of dogmatic affirmation at the outset: everything began by a promise, a liberation, a covenant, a conquest. Only then did the Hebrews know that they belonged to a jealous, powerful God, and that, behind the natural phenomena which conditioned their everyday life, was a hidden hand, the hand of him who was guiding their destiny. All this might appear a little meagre to the rational demands of a philosopher, but it represents the germ of the purest form of monotheism that mankind has ever known.

Among the divine works, one was soon set apart and given increased importance with the passage of time: the creation of the material world. The idea of creation came late, however, in the evolution of biblical thought, and it was always treated by the inspired authors in the same context as the idea of the Covenant: they present it to us merely as the starting-point of the divine plan of salvation. The same may be said for early Christian literature, especially hymns and anaphoras. But, with the loss of the liturgical sense, and, no doubt, under the influence of philosophical controversies, the notion of creation has come to be given a predominant place and isolated from history; and history itself, relegated to the background, appears as if annexed to the work of the Demiurge, without forming an integral part of it. In the seventh century, the evolution was sufficiently advanced for Mohammed to present God to the Arabs as being essentially he who created the world.

It may perhaps be profitable to turn back the pages and return to the logic of the Bible, which is the logic of life itself. What humanity needs most of all to-day is not a metaphysical explanation, a statement from God giving full knowledge and satisfying the demands of reason; what humanity seeks is Someone who will condescend to guide its destiny and who will proclaim his sovereignty over all reality.

A. PROGRESSIVE DISCOVERY OF THE COSMIC POWER OF YAHWEH

In the elaboration of the monotheism of Israel, it is the Covenant which came first and not the formulation of the cosmic attributes of Yahweh. On this point, we must adjust our customary manner of seeing things, for we have the rather tiresome habit of attributing to the Ancients a logic we imagine to be universal. Many commentators, in fact, believe they can deduce the basic facts of biblical theology from a hypothetically initial formulation of the divine titles of "Creator" and of "God of heaven". In this way all would appear to be self-evident. The Creator is master of a universe that he can set to serve history, just as the God of heaven is in a favourable position to impose his omnipotent will through the roar of thunder or the flash of lightning. However logical this may appear, this reconstruction of revealed thought does not, in fact, explain anything at all. Antiquity was not lacking in creative or celestial gods, but it had no religion which could even remotely claim the purity of biblical monotheism. There is no reason to believe there was a doctrinal affirmation of this sort underlying the biblical revelation. It should, indeed, be realized that the idea of Yahweh's universal government only gradually asserted itself in the conscience of Israel, in proportion as its historical experience broadened; it should be realized that the progressive discovery of this notion in no way postulates the initial formulation of Yahweh's attributes as Creator and God of heaven.

The divine government of the universe

The idea of universal government by Yahweh is not, in the Bible, the result of doctrinal definition; it evolved in a gradual deepening of comprehension, closely linked, in its turn, with Israel's unfolding history. The notion of a universal Providence was not, indeed, completely unknown to ancient civilizations; it is magnificently celebrated, for example, in the hymn of Akhen-Aton. Yet our Psalm 103, in spite of its affinity with the famous Egyptian poem, is of relatively recent date. Biblical thought has here evolved in an original manner, following its own course, without any marked borrowing from outside religions.

The Old Testament did not seek to provide, from the outset, a general interpretation of cosmic realities. It simply stated that the God of Israel was a mighty God, who could, if necessary, make use of the material world in order to fulfil his plans, but it made no claim to explain facts of nature which did not directly concern the great drama itself. It is only an extension of this historical background that led on to the affirmation of belief in a Providence lovingly preparing from all eternity the well-being of each one of the elect (Rom. 8. 28). This generalization was the work of the few centuries immediately preceding the birth of Christ, and, even so, it was not until the preaching of the Gospel and the explosion of Jewish nationalist aspirations that it was seen to be universally applicable. Awareness therefore, of a collaboration by the forces of nature in the work of salvation did not derive from any *ab initio* doctrine; it is the fruit of experience, the consciousness of a divine purpose extending through time and space to set its seal ultimately upon the whole of history.

Proof that this realization of God's government over the whole cosmos results from a gradual extension of an originally limited experience, may be found in the different ways in which a series of identical facts are presented, as biblical thought developed. A typical example is the variety of descriptions of the Exodus given between the ninth and first centuries B.C. The oldest parts of the Pentateuch[1] suggest a direct, almost manual action on the part of Yahweh: he passes as the destroyer before the doors of the Egyptians (Ex. 12. 23), breaks the spokes of their chariot-wheels and overwhelms Pharaoh's troops in the sea (ib. 14. 25).

With the further developed Yahwistic and Elohistic narratives,[2] we witness a more or less concerted intervention of the forces of nature: the plagues of Egypt present us with the poisoning of the waters of the Nile, storms of hailstones, pestilence, darkness, invasions by frogs, flies and locusts. These phenomena may appear to be natural in origin, but they have the characteristic of being manifested in the Lord's appointed time: " To-morrow will the Lord do this thing in the land" (Ex. 9. 5; cf. v. 18, etc.); they strike only those lands, things and people he has designated: "And the Lord will make a

[1] While we admit these subdivisions are formal and often artificial in character, we feel we ought to take into account, if not the results achieved, at least the efforts made, by criticism. Some critics (e.g. Beer) have isolated from the J collection a more primitive layer, J[1]. Others have preferred, with Eissfeldt, to dissociate these latter elements from the Yahwistic tradition and constitute with them another unity called L. Cf. Otto Eissfeldt, *Hexateuch-Synopse*, Leipzig, 1922.

[2] After Ex. 3, the distinction between J and E seems to be most obscure, because we no longer have the major criterium of the difference in the divine appellations. We therefore adopt here with much reservation the traditional scheme. Cf. Rudolph, *Der "Elohist" von Exodus bis Josua* (Beiheft 68 zur *Zeitschrift für die alttestamentliche Wissenschaft*), Berlin, 1938.

wonderful difference between the possessions of Israel and the possessions of the Egyptians" (9. 4; cf. v. 26; 11. 7; etc.). This unprecedented manifestation of power forces Pharaoh to make this admission: "The Lord is just: I and my people are wicked" (9. 27), and makes him bow to the expression of a will stronger than his.   In all these texts, nature obeys the commands of Yahweh who intends to fulfil his plan of salvation; but these are precise and strictly limited occasions, and there is nothing to indicate that we should attribute to the action of the God of Israel all the calamities which may strike humanity at other times and in other places, for example, the famine which obliged Abraham to go down into Egypt (Gen. 12. 10), or which brought thither Jacob and his sons (ib. 43. 1).[1]

If we now move forward four or five centuries in time, we shall find ourselves in a world of vastly different ideas.   Israel is now aware of the originality of its destiny in a universe which has expanded considerably, and is henceforth under God's omnipotent sway.   Israel has now for all nations become the "witness of Yahweh", so God's gesture in coming to the rescue will have to be something spectacular.   We shall not, therefore, be surprised to see, in the priestly narrative, that the events of the Exodus have an element of magic about them.   There is a contest between Moses and the sorcerers of Pharaoh, who, after the third plague, have to admit defeat. It is no longer merely a question of compelling the Egyptians to liberate their slaves, but of astounding a foreign nation by a display of divine power of which Moses is the agent: "And the magicians said to Pharao: This is the finger of God" (Ex. 8. 19).   Moreover, Yahweh hardens the heart of the king in order to have the opportunity of working more and more extraordinary miracles: "Pharao will not hear you, that many signs may be done in the land of Egypt" (11. 9).   "And I will

[1] The Elohistic narrative, however, attributes to the divine will this great famine which spreads as far as Egypt: "God hath shewn to Pharaoh what he is about to do" (Gen. 41.25; cf. Ps. 104.16). The Elohistic tradition generally shows a more universalist tendency than J; it links the history of the chosen people more closely with that of the world; before the revelation of the divine name to Moses, Yahweh was the Elohim of the nations.

be glorified in Pharao, and in all his host, and in his chariots, and in his horsemen. And the Egyptians shall know that I am the Lord" (14. 17–18). In short, it seems here that the cosmic events occurring at the beginning of the history of Israel were directed less at liberating by force the Hebrew slaves than at offering to their oppressors a vindicatory demonstration of the might of Yahweh.

Such a varied presentation of facts is indicative of profound changes in the mentality of those who had reflected on the meaning of history. In the fifth century, the need is no longer felt to show how it was Yahweh, and he alone, who "with a strong hand and a stretched out arm" delivered Israel from slavery in Egypt. It is clearly established now that Yahweh is the Almighty; there remains only the need for apologetics *ad extra*: extraordinary events are necessary in order to justify the Jews in their belief that the master of the universe has assumed direct control of their history. Later, the Book of Wisdom will further stress this need, and will make a decisive effort to define and picture the miracle: "For every creature according to its kind was fashioned again as from the beginning, obeying thy commandments, that thy children might be kept without hurt" (Wisdom 19. 6; cf. 5. 18; 16. 19, 22–3, 25). The inspired writer, with his Greek conception of the order in the world, had already affirmed the doctrine of a universal divine Providence (*pronoia*) (Wisdom 1. 14; 14. 3; 15. 1); God's special favour shown towards his people necessarily, therefore, affected the normal course of things: "He will arm the creature for the revenge of his enemies" (5. 18; cf. v. 21; 16. 17-24).

Thus the presentation of the same set of facts enables us to perceive the gradual formulation of the doctrine of divine government of the universe for the fulfilment of history. Here, biblical thought most certainly did not have as its starting-point any sort of dogmatic definition. From the experience *in actu* of Yahweh's power working in its favour, Israel progressed to an awareness of the universal Providence of its God. The complete revelation, however, will come only when the work of salvation has been fully achieved: "We know that to them that love God, all things work together unto good" (Rom. 8. 28).

If the notion of Providence was not completely new to antiquity, it may be asked why Israel should have taken so long to discover what the pagan world had already dimly seen. The problem here is much the same as that which concerns transcendental retribution.[1] Such a delay enabled an old doctrine to be given an entirely new depth: history has placed an abyss between the monotheism of the Bible and the religious revolution of Amenophis IV. The Bible alone was able, at the end of a long and often painful experience, to give expression to this absolutely original notion that God wields his power over the world in order to fulfil a work of pure, gratuitous love.

The Sacred Books do not, therefore, present us from the very beginning with a religious explanation of all natural phenomena or with a theory on the government of the world. The thought of Israel did not derive from the need for man to explain those cosmic forces over which he has no control and which he must seek to appease. The Bible begins with a fact: God makes use of material elements in order to bring about salvation; the generalization of this experience will induce consciousness of a universal Providence.

Creation and Yahweh's cosmic power

Long and bitter experience finally enabled Israel to ascertain the absolute dominion of its God over the world. Having done so, would it not gradually, and in similar fashion, have inferred a fundamental fact: the creation by Yahweh of heaven and earth? For us to-day, every movement in nature has to be placed in relationship to laws established from the beginning. The Ancients, however, did not reason thus. Yahweh's cosmic power in no way postulates the affirmation of his creative act, for no connexion is seen

[1] On the familiar subject of retribution in the O.T., see M. A. Gelin, *Les Idées maîtresses de l'Ancien Testament*, Paris, 1948, pp. 54 ff.

between the occurrence of natural phenomena and the
original organization of the universe. And, in actual fact,
the cosmic power of Yahweh was not at first presented in the
context of his creative work. The pre-Exilic prophets make
no mention of Yahweh as creator,[1] whereas they constantly
refer to his mastery over nature. It may be noted, on the other
hand, that in the cosmogonic myths, it was far more a question
of God's kingship over the land than his power over the
totality of the cosmos. The idea of creation was then applied
strictly to fixed, stable realities, such as the sky, earth or
mountains; it was not concerned with the forces constantly at
work in the functioning of the universe.

It would serve little purpose to try and specify what the
Israelites considered as fixed once and for all, and what, in
their eyes, was always at the immediate disposal of the
divinity. It is, however, true that the Semites could well
distinguish between certain fleeting manifestations of divine
power and the persons and things affected by them: thus,
when Yahweh sent a great storm over the sea (Jonas 1. 4),
the wind is for him but an occasional instrument to act upon
the waves and to provoke their wrath. To sum up: mountains,
earth and skies, by their relative stability, suppose an initial
act of creation, whereas no need is felt to give precise definition
to the remote origins of the ordinary manifestations of life
in nature.

The Semitic mind does not appear to have had any concept
of a natural order, any idea of immutable laws controlling
from the very beginning the movement of the universe. Early
cosmologies and cosmogonies did not discern the inter-
dependence of elements and phenomena: the world was not

---

[1] As we shall see later, Jeremias seems to be the first prophet to argue from
the fact of creation. Many exegetes, in fact, have questioned the authenticity
of the doxologies of Amos 4.13; 5.8 ff.; 9.5 ff. Cf. F. Horst, "Die Doxologie im
Amosbuch", in *Zeitschr. f. d. alttestamentl. Wissensch.*, 37 (1929), pp. 45–54;
A. Vaccari, "Hymnus in Deum Creatorem", in *Verbum Domini*, 9 (1929), pp.
184–8. This last author sees it as an ancient poem composed at the time of the
epic struggles of Yahwism against Baalism. For E. Osty, *Amos, Osée*, Paris, 1953,
p. 16: "It is possible that the three doxologies are liturgical additions, inserted
for the requirements of public reading." See too P. G. Rinaldi, *I Profeti Minori, I*,
Turin, 1953, pp. 165 ff.

made like a perfectly wound up clock the working of which had been foreseen from all eternity. The forces of nature were distinct entities, with no physical bond between them, and God made use of each of them as the conductor of an orchestra calls upon the various instruments, as his inspiration and fancy dictate.

This conception finds its most magnificent expression in the poems comprising the Book of Job. The author pictures the Almighty as a scene-shifter, so to speak, constantly present off stage, introducing one after the other each of the characters in the drama. Night chases day, and, as soon as light re-appears, darkness leaves the stage and retires to the wings (Job 3. 4–9). The master arranges everything in its correct position: "Didst thou shew the dawning of the day its place?" (38. 12).[1] The sky possesses inner rooms, storehouses for snow (38. 22), or for hail, wind and rain (Ps. 134. 7). If these natural phenomena are to show themselves, their course is already indicated beforehand: a channel is carved out for the rain (Job 38. 25), the wind has its route (Eccl. 11. 5) and the light its path (Job 38. 24).

The divinity, then, exercises direct control over a universe made up of separate entities: "If he withhold the waters, all things shall be dried up: and if he send them out, they shall overturn the earth" (Job 12. 15); so that Yahweh can ask Job: "Canst thou send lightnings? And will they go, and will they return and say to thee: Here we are?" (ib. 38. 35). Everything thus bows before the orders of the Almighty: the stars, like his angels and saints, are his courtiers,[2] the thunder is his voice,[3] the wind his breath.

Of course, one has to take into account the personality of each author. Before the Book of Job was written, for example, Jeremias was already aware that Yahweh lays down laws (*huqqîm*) for the moon and the stars to follow (Jer. 31. 35–36);

[1] One also reads in Eccl.: "The sun riseth, and goeth down, and returneth to his place" (1.5); similarly in Ps. 103.19: "The sun knoweth his going down".

[2] Job 4.18; 5.1; 15.15; 38.7; 3 Kings 22.19; Zach. 14.5; Dan. 8.13; Ps. 103.4; etc.

[3] Job 37.4; Ex. 19.19; 20.18; 1 Kings 7.10; Amos 1.2; Jer. 25.30; Ps. 28.3.

elsewhere, in their daily life, men had certainly observed various simple rhythms, such as those of the seasons: "The kite (better: stork) in the air hath known her time : the turtle and the swallow and the stork (better: crane) have observed the time of their coming" (Jer. 8. 7). But it must be admitted that, taken as a whole, the Bible makes scant reference to natural order in the cosmos. With the approach of the Hellenistic era, however, more detailed observation of phenomena will be noted. Qoheleth, the Preacher, among others, notes that all things have their appointed time, and is the first of the sacred writers to remark sadly upon the apparently useless cycle of all the realities of this world. For his part, Ben Sira praises the impeccable order in creation: "The works of God are done in judgment from the beginning: and from the making of them he distinguished their parts . . . . They have not ceased from their works, nor shall any of them straiten his neighbour at any time" (Ecclus 16. 26–8; cf. 39. 37).

It can be seen that this approach comes relatively late in time, and only in the Book of Wisdom will genuinely philosophical considerations on the pre-established harmony of things be met with in the Bible.[1] It is here that we find ourselves confronted with a world in which permanent order exists, but which God can use or disrupt as he wishes in the furtherance of his purpose: "For every creature according to its kind was fashioned again as from the beginning, obeying thy commandments" (Wisdom 19. 6). "Snow and ice endured the force of fire, and melted not" (ib. 16. 22). "For while

---

[1] The author of the Book of Wisdom, in his attempt to put across popular apologetics, is also seeking to show himself well informed as to the views of his contemporary scientists and philosophers. The ancient wisdom of Solomon which consists in the composing of *māshāl* on plants and animals (3 Kings 4.32–3), is here raised to the level of a true encyclopaedic science: "For he hath given me the true knowledge of the things that are: to know the disposition of the whole world, and the virtues of the elements, the beginning, and ending, and midst of the times, the alterations of their courses, and the changes of seasons, the revolutions of the year, and the dispositions of the stars, the natures of living creatures, and rage of wild beasts, the force of winds, and reasonings of men, the diversities of plants, and the virtues of roots" (Wisdom 7.17–20).

the elements are changed in themselves, as in an instrument the sound of the quality is changed, yet all keep their sound" (ib. 19. 17). The Alexandrian author is clearly seeking to evoke a perturbation in the "cosmos", in the Greek sense of the word; he wants to show the working of a true miracle, for, in his conception, God, in creation, has "ordered all things in measure, and number, and weight" (ib. 11. 21). The insistence on this point seems quite new and completely out of keeping with the Semitic mentality prevailing throughout the rest of the Bible.

Since observed phenomena were not connected in people's minds with the initial organization of the cosmos, Yahweh's cosmic omnipotence could not have been deduced from his attribute of Creator. Given the relatively late emergence in the Bible of the theme of creation,[1] one might even be tempted to believe that the creation epic comes as the culmination of the previous acknowledgement of God's universal power over the universe. Thus, for the Second Isaias, the foundation of the earth and the stretching out of the heavens are the seal of his absolute sovereignty set by the master on his universe.

The celestial character of Yahweh[2]

Just as the divine government of the universe was not originally made to depend on the fact of creation, so the gradual discovery of Yahweh's universal dominion did not in any way imply a primitive affirmation of a story of creation

[1] The theme of creation must have been familiar long before appearing in inspired literature proper, and belonged no doubt to the the liturgy of the temple. Hence Melchisedech, in the fourteenth chapter of Genesis, pronounces the following benediction: "Blessed be Abram by the most high God, who created heaven and earth" (v. 19).

[2] We think it necessary to distinguish between the precise notion of "God of heaven", the only figure we here envisage, and the less clearly defined notion of "celestial divinity". Most of the Semitic divinities were of celestial type, which explains why in the primitive episode of the Tower of Babel, Yahweh "came down" to see the city and tower (Gen. 11.5,7), or, in the canticle of Deborah: "War from heaven was made . . . the stars remaining in their order and courses fought against Sisara" (Judges 5.20). There is an essential difference, not always sufficiently emphasized, between the notion of a supreme power over the universe, and that of a power which comes and goes and has its place with the rest of the celestial world.

by him.   Might not this affirmation, then, have been the logical
outcome of the celestial character of the God of the Bible?
Here again a negative reply has to be given.

Certainly, from the Exile onwards, the God of Israel
appeared to the pagans as the God of heaven, and the Jews
were not reluctant to present him in this light (Jonas 1. 9).
Hence the Achaemenidae, who did not disguise their sympathy
for the celestial divinities, gave some consideration to the
religion of Yahweh: "Thus saith Cyrus king of the Persians:
The Lord the God of heaven hath given to me all the kingdoms
of the earth, and he hath charged me to build him a house
in Jerusalem, which is in Judea" (1 Esd. 1. 2; cf. 6. 3–12).

This celestial character of Yahweh appears to be too clearly
affirmed by this time for its origin to be attributed to Ezechiel,
as certain exegetes of the school of Wellhausen have attempted
to do.[1]   Besides, the notion is certainly pre-Exilic, since it
is found in some royal psalms (2. 4; 19. 7; 143. 5), as well as in
passages from the Pentateuch and historical books also dating
from before the Exile (Gen. 24. 3, 7; 28. 12; 3 Kings 22. 19).
The papyri of Elephantine, which, it is thought, reflect the
religious conceptions of Israel before the reform of Josias,[2]
frequently refer to "Yaho, God of heaven".[3]   May one therefore conclude from this evidence that the title "is a specifically
Israelitic term going back to earliest times, even before the
revelation on Sinai, and merely conveys in one word two
ideas which are seen on every page of the Old Testament:
that Yahweh, having created heaven and earth, is thus their
God, and that heaven is his abode"?[4]   In spite of the author-
ities invoked,[5] this view appears to us to be superficial and
based on mere assumption.   It cannot be confirmed by any truly
ancient evidence, for chapter 24 of Genesis, which is continually

[1] B. Stade, *Biblische Theologie des Alten Testaments*, 1905, p. 291.

[2] A. Vincent, *La Religion des Judéo-Araméens d'Éléphantine*, Paris, 1937, pp.
377 ff.; but see also Kraeling, Emil G., *The Brooklyn Museum Aramaic Papyri*,
New Haven, 1953, pp. 41 ff.

[3] A. Vincent, *op. cit.*, pp. 100 ff.

[4] *Ibid.*, p. 104.

[5] Especially Ewald, Kautzsch, Sellin, quoted by G. Beer, *Exodus* (Handb.
z. A.T., 1. Reihe, 3), Tübingen, 1939, p. 30.

being quoted in support of this assertion, belongs to the most recent part of the Yahwistic collection. [1]

Nevertheless, this silence on the part of the most ancient texts does remain difficult to interpret. In order to establish whether the celestial character of Yahweh is a primitive notion, therefore, we should approach the question from a different angle. In the mind of the Ancients, the idea, God of heaven, signified something totally different from what we find in the Bible. It cannot, therefore, have derived as it stands from current conceptions. Between the two interpretations of this same divine attribute, a long evolution of religious thought must be assumed, since the biblical notion of the God of heaven implies an already mature consciousness of a divine purpose working through the universe and through history. To be more precise, it suggests the well-established power of Yahweh, in close connexion with the setting up of the monarchy and the foundation of the temple.

If it is desired to link biblical monotheism closely with the initial definition "Yahweh is a God in heaven", then this celestial establishment of power, it may quite naturally be thought, implies the government of the world and of history. But it is precisely this sort of reasoning which is far from primitive. This is, for example, how Mircea Eliade interprets the significance of heaven in the general history of religions: "The sky shows itself as it really is: infinite, transcendent. The vault of heaven is, more than anything else, 'something quite apart' from the tiny thing that is man and his span of life. The symbolism of its transcendence derives from the simple realization of its infinite height. 'Most High' becomes quite naturally an attribute of the divinity. The regions above man's reach, the starry places, are invested with

---

[1] It is no longer believed to-day that the document J can be the work of a single author. We have here a tradition built up over the course of several centuries. As far as our text is concerned, the most acceptable opinion seems to be that of G. von Rad, *Das erste Buch Mose* (Das A. T. Deutsch, 3), Göttingen, 1952, pp. 217–223. Here, the author states clearly: "This unequivocally universalist epithet is quite unparalleled in the stories of the patriarchs, and is one of the signs of the relatively late origin to be attributed to this one" (p. 218).

the divine majesty of the transcendent, of absolute reality, of everlastingness."[1] The author concludes his chapter on the celestial gods with this remark: "We can discern in the 'history' of Supreme Beings and sky gods one phenomenon which is extremely significant in the religious history of mankind: these divine figures tend to disappear from the cult. Nowhere do they play a leading part, but have become remote and been replaced by other religious forces: by ancestor worship, worship of the spirits and gods of nature, spirits of fertility, Great Goddesses and so forth. To sum up very briefly, one may say that 'history' has effectively pushed in to the background the divine 'forms' of a celestial nature (as with Supreme Beings) or corrupted them (as storm gods or fecundators), but that 'history', which is simply man's ever-fresh experimentation and interpretation of the sacred—has not been able to do away with the direct and abiding revelation that the sky is something sacred; it is a revelation neither impersonal, nor temporal, and it is quite outside history."[2]

This last idea brings us back to our examination of the discovery of history in Israel. Here we have generalities which naturally admit of some exceptions; but this common tendency is nevertheless most revealing, and it runs exactly counter to the orientation of biblical thought. Instead of evoking "something totally different" and having no possible relationship with material existence, the canopy of heaven, in the Bible, is a starting-point for effective action; it does, indeed, guarantee the divine freedom of action. Mention of the God of heaven is usually made with the sole purpose of emphasizing his intervention on earth: "Be thou exalted, O God, above the heavens, and thy glory above all the earth" (Ps. 56. 6; cf. 112. 5, etc.). "The Lord he is God in heaven above, and in the earth beneath, and there is no other" (Deut. 4. 39; cf. v. 36). One could go on giving quotations indefinitely. From his abode, Yahweh listens and watches: "Look from thy sanctuary, and thy high habitation

[1] *Patterns in Comparative Religion,* London, 1958, pp. 38 ff.
[2] Eliade, *Patterns,* pp. 109, 111.

of heaven, and bless thy people Israel, and the land which thou hast given us" (Deut. 26. 15). He controls all human affairs: "For what part should God from above have in me, and what inheritance the Almighty from on high?" (Job 31. 2) with supreme liberty: "Our God is in heaven: he hath done all things whatsoever he would" (Ps. 113. 11; 134. 6; cf. Jonas 1. 14). The word "height" in the Bible generally evokes a first-class strategic position, an impregnable, secure fortress; so it will not be surprising to find the psalmist referring to heaven thus: "Thou hast founded a bulwark because of thy foes" (Ps. 8. 3).[1] If Yahweh, in fact, "sitteth upon the globe of the earth, and the inhabitants thereof are as locusts" (Is. 40. 22), this is because he thus possesses an unrivalled observation post: "The Lord hath looked from heaven: he hath beheld all the sons of men. From his habitation which he hath prepared, he hath looked upon all that dwell on the earth";[2] this conception becomes at times boldly anthropomorphic: "The Lord hath looked down from heaven upon the children of men, to see if there be any that understand and seek God" (Ps. 13. 2). From up there he is intimidated by no one: "He that dwelleth in heaven shall laugh at them: and the Lord shall deride them" (Ps. 2. 4; cf. 58. 9), for he is the sovereign judge of all mortals: "The Lord hath prepared his throne in heaven: and his kingdom shall rule over all" (Ps. 102. 19; cf. 9. 8). Since the world is built from down below and stretches upwards,[3] it follows that his gaze can penetrate the very roots of the universe (Job 26. 5–6): "Hell and destruction are before the Lord: how much more the hearts of the children of men!" (Prov. 15. 11). So when one is in the depths of the abyss (Ps. 129. 1), one can always cry out to heaven: "Put forth thy hand from on high, take me out, and deliver me from many waters" (Ps. 143. 7; cf. 17. 17); for God, from his lofty habitation, knows how to render justice, and how to set upright again those whom he loves:

[1] (Translator's note: Revised Standard Version).

[2] Ps. 32.13 ff.; cf. 10.5; 101.20; 112.5–6; 137.6; Lam. 3.50; etc.

[3] The expression "heaven and hell" is used to evoke the totality of the universe; cf. Is. 7.11; 14.13 ff; Ps. 138.8; Job 11.8; etc.

"Raising up the needy from the earth, and lifting up the poor out of the dunghill" (Ps. 112. 7). "The praise of him is above heaven and earth: and he hath exalted the horn of his people" (Ps. 148. 14); whereas he can bring low the mountain-dwellers (Is. 26. 5). His throne is set so high that no one can escape him: "Though they go down even to hell, thence shall my hand bring them out: and though they climb up to heaven, thence will I bring them down" (Amos 9. 2).

In inspired literature, therefore, the skies never suggest the idea of "something totally different" or "inaccessible", in the abstract sense of standing outside what is contemporary or historical. We have given numerous examples in order to stress the originality of the Bible in this respect. The concept "God of heaven" was not of itself capable of inspiring a similar intuition of the historical omnipotence of Yahweh, since the symbolism of heaven was not originally pointed in this direction. For this divine title to acquire the new, vital significance with which the Bible invests it, the notion of history had beforehand to permeate the whole psychology of Israel. In other words, the fixing of Yahweh in heaven presupposes rather than precedes the consciousness of a divine will imposing itself upon the world.

It also appears possible to specify with a certain degree of accuracy the date at which this divine title must have appeared in Israel. The celestial character of Yahweh evokes the idea of a sedentary power, which implies that the chosen people were by now well-established, and no longer nomadic. Besides, the royal psalms, especially Psalm 2, seem to be the first inspired texts to refer to the God of heaven; for them the firmament represents the throne on which Yahweh is seated (see again 3 Kings 22. 19). No doubt the idea arises from the notion of Yahweh's kingship which in turn implies perhaps the establishment of the Davidic dynasty.[1] This is all, of course,

---

[1] In his study of Ps. 109, E. Podechard, *Études de Critique et d'Histoire religieuse*, Lyons, 1948, p. 21, shows that Yahweh became the supreme God, assimilated to 'El 'Elyōn, at the time of David's installation in Jerusalem: "If one bears in mind the fact that Yahweh was not by origin a Canaanitish God, that he had come from Sinai and that he possessed Canaan by right of conquest, then, (contd. opposite)

pure theory, but the fairly constant parallel drawn by the Bible between heaven and earth appears to substantiate this hypothesis. In any case, there are no grounds for assuming that the definition of Yahweh as "God of heaven" goes back to the origins of Mosaic religion.

Biblical monotheism is not, therefore, a sort of fixed, millennial monolith, made up of notions transplanted in their entirety from the surrounding world of religious beliefs, ideas of a Providence, of a Creator and of a God of heaven. It owes nothing to an initial formulation of a divine kingship exercised over the universe. It is an original, living synthesis, gradually built up in the development of an historical experience.

B. AWARENESS TO HISTORY AND THE FORMATION OF BIBLICAL MONOTHEISM

Biblical monotheism is essentially an historical monotheism. It was not the outcome of mere observation of external nature, it is the result of an experience, namely, that the forces of nature serve to further a plan of salvation.

The Bible quite obviously did not attain, at the first attempt, the expression of that pure form of monotheism which it affirms from the beginning of the seventh century[1] and to which the Second Isaias will give the perfect and final formulation.[2] We can discern in the ancient texts the echo of a vaguer conception. At first, Yahweh appears as a God comparable to the gods of the neighbouring peoples; he reigns in Israel just as the other divinities rule their respective lands: "Are not those things which thy god Chamos possesseth, due to thee by right?" Jephte asks the Moabites, "But what the Lord our God hath obtained by conquest, shall be our

for the majority of people and according to the ideas of the time, he could become master of the land only when Sion had been taken, when he had been permanently installed in the most famous high place of the region, on the throne, one might say, of the God whom Melchisedech had served; only when he had been substituted for or identified with this latter God, and only when a magnificent and lasting temple had housed him." On the full implications of this same psalm, see also R.-J. Tournay, "Psaume CX", in *Vivre et Penser*, IIIᵉ Série, 1943–1944 (=*R.B.*, LII), pp. 220–237.

[1] Jer. 2.11; 10.7; 3 Kings 8.60; 4 Kings 19.18 ff.; Deut. 4. 35.
[2] See especially: Is. 41.29; 43.10; 44.8; 45.5 ff.,14, 21; 46.9.

possession" (Judges 11. 24). Later, David complains to Saul that, in denying him the inheritance of Yahweh, he has sent him to serve strange gods (1 Kings 26. 19). Finally, we read in the Book of Kings that Israel had to abandon the siege of Kir-Harasheth because of the anger of the national god to which the King of Moab had just sacrificed his own son.[1] Thus Yahweh appears at first to have been regarded as the only God worshipped in Israel before asserting himself as the sole master of all creation.

This transition from simple monolatry to strict monotheism is, nevertheless, a fact unique in history. In order to explain it, one has to admit that Yahweh must have possessed originally some particular quality which enabled him at a later date to eclipse all his rival gods, and, in point of fact, the slow evolution of the religion of Israel is not due to the regular, mechanical contribution which the thought of successive generations made to it, divorced from all organic connexion with a starting-point or fidelity to an original impulse. We cannot, for example, agree with the assumptions of Wellhausen's school, according to which prophetism represents a revolution, completely breaking with all previous tradition. There are certain evolutionist explanations which do not explain anything at all, and Wellhausen himself is forced to admit this: "Why Israel's history, which began much in the same way as that of the Moabites, should have led in such an utterly different direction, is a fact that cannot in the last analysis be satisfactorily explained."[2] The only example that enables us to understand the coherent elaboration of biblical monotheism and the internal unity of its development is the image of the growth of living organisms: historical experience brought with it a widening and deepening of an initial revelation which contained in essence the potentiality of its subsequent development. However far back one goes in time,[3] one always finds the notion that a God is guiding

[1] 4 Kings 3.27. This interpretation has nevertheless been challenged. Cf. R. De Vaux, *Les Livres des Rois*, Paris, 1949, p. 133, note b.

[2] *Israelitische und Jüdische Geschichte*, p. 38.

[3] Inspired literature does not, of course, enable us to go back to the actual origin of Mosaic religion. Besides, one can only grasp the full significance of a biological evolution when the living organism has reached a certain stage of development.

the destiny of men through material realities. This constant belief is made up of two complementary ideas: that of history itself, and that of the "other world" or of transcendency. Yahweh, the God of the "other world", defies any attempt either to pin-point his cosmic power or to fix a definite localization. After first being the God "who cometh", he later takes his place in heaven in order to control everything from "above".

The impossibility of specializing Yahweh's cosmic power

Yahweh has been represented as a god of the hills (3 Kings 20. 23), or shown riding the clouds, like the Phoenician Baal of Ras Shamra, or[1] even given the precise features of the gods of tempests, with thunder as his voice and flashes of lightning as his arrows.[2] Yet the God of Israel steadfastly refuses to reveal the exact nature of his might. Whereas primitive peoples invented images in an attempt to render the force of their gods more tangible, Yahwism, on the contrary, instinctively resisted any attempt to convey a picture of the divinity. Yahweh, for example, breaks right away from the "calf of Samaria" (Osee 8. 5; 10. 5–6; 13. 2), which the prophets will call "the sin of Samaria" or "the sin of Jeroboam"; Osee will go so far as to claim that Yahweh could never have been the object of such a cult, and Bethel (the house of God) is called by the prophet Bethaven (the house of vanity).[3] Yahweh does indeed assure the prosperity of the land of Israel, but he has nevertheless no intention of being confused with the god of tempests and fertility traditionally represented as a bull; he is not a cosmic power whose goodwill has to be coaxed, but a God of salvation whose might eludes the control and the grasp of mortals.

The significance of divine names in antiquity is well known: the name expresses the reality of the person or thing named.

---

[1] Ps. 17.11; 67.5; Deut. 33.26; Is. 19.1; 66.15; Nahum 1.3; Hab. 3.8.
[2] Ps. 17.15; 76.18; Hab. 3.9,11; Zach. 9.14.
[3] Osee 4.15; 5.8; 10.5. On the question of images in the cult of Yahweh, see especially the article "Idole" in the *Dict. de la Bible* by Vigoureux, Suppl. IV, col. 170 ff.

Now, in the Exodus narratives, the meaning of Yahweh's name was not conveyed to his people. The message of salvation was all they were supposed to be interested in. "Thus shalt thou say to the children of Israel: The Lord God of your fathers, the God of Abraham, the God of Isaac, and the God of Jacob, hath sent me to you" (Ex. 3. 15). "I am the Lord who will bring you out from the work-prison of the Egyptians, etc." (6. 6). Even his revelation to Moses (3. 14) comes almost in parenthesis, the main stress of the message falling on the mission which was being confided.[1] Whether one takes it in an affirmative sense: "It is I, I am", or, on the contrary, as a refusal to reply: "I am who I am, and it is no concern of yours", the interpretation of the divine name emphasizes that Yahweh is a God of salvation, but does not give any details of his cosmic power. Hence, the prohibition of images which occurs in the decalogue (Ex. 20. 4; Deut. 5. 8), and which will frequently recur, is very much in keeping with early Yahwism.

Defined as the God of salvation, and refusing to be further specified, Yahweh nevertheless claims to bring the forces of the universe into play. Indeed, the earliest version of the Exodus simply read: "And the Lord delivered Israel on that day out of the hands of the Egyptians. And they saw . . . the mighty hand that the Lord had used against them" (Ex. 14. 30–1). Later Yahwistic tradition attempted to give more specific details about this hand of Yahweh; thus are evoked for us the series of disasters that struck the land of the Pharaohs, the burning east wind Yahweh raised to bring the locusts (10. 13), the strong wind which blew from the west and cleared them (v. 19), the fierce sirocco that blew all night by which the Lord turned the sea into dry land (14. 21), the wind that brought a flight of quails over the sea towards the desert (Num. 11. 31). If, then, Yahweh's historical action comes first, it does, nevertheless, require the participation of cosmic realities.

[1] "The meaning is made known only to the founder of the religion, and even then, simply in a parenthesis; the main emphasis is laid on the message of liberation." W. Eichrodt, *Theologie des Alten Testaments,* Berlin, 1948, Part 1, p. 86.

Atmospheric phenomena, in particular, are very early looked on as weapons in the hand of the God of Israel: the storm in the canticle of Deborah (Judges 5. 4–5, 20), the hailstones sent during the battle of Gabaon (Josue 10. 11), the thunder striking terror into the Philistine camp (1 Kings 7. 10), or the earthquake which spreads a "divine terror" (1 Kings 14. 15). The Eliseus cycle, in the Book of Kings, makes several allusions to the celestial chariotry of Yahweh, corresponding to the chariots and horsemen of earthly armies: fiery horses and a chariot of fire bear Elias off in a storm (4 Kings 2. 11), whilst Yahweh "opened the eyes" of the servant of Eliseus for him to see the whole mountainside beset with flaming horses and chariots round his master (4 Kings 6. 17). We also read, further on: "The Lord had made them hear, in the camp of Syria, the noise of chariots, and of horses, and of a very great army" (4 Kings 7. 6).[1]

The expression *Yahweh Sebā'ôth*[2] leads us to believe that Israel perceived at an early date this participation of the forces of nature in the combats of Yahweh: "It seems to me that the expression Yahweh Seba'ôt was invented during the heroic period of conquest and was originally applied to Yahweh in his rôle of fighter with and for his people. But it does not follow from this that his *Seba'ôt* are exclusively or even mainly the armies of Israel, for Yahweh possesses other troops: the stars, the celestial powers, 'the heavenly host', and natural phenomena. Most probably, the expression was, from the very beginning, invested with these various meanings, and was used to imply the full extent of the power that Yahweh placed at the disposal of his people in battle: thus is sanctioned the new meaning the prophets will bring to it."[3] Here again, history comes first, involving in the progress of time the phenomena of nature.

---

[1] Cf. also the expression used for the prophets Elias and Eliseus: "My father, my father, the chariot of Israel, and the driver thereof" (4 Kings 2.12; 13.14).

[2] Opinions differ as to the original meaning to be ascribed to this expression. See, on this point, W. Eichrodt, *op. cit.*, I, p. 89; E. Dhorme, *La Religion des Hébreux nomades,* Brussels, 1937, pp. 360–362; A. Vincent, *op. cit.*, pp. 60–91; B. N. Wambacq, "Épithète divine 'Yahvé Seba'ôt' ", in *Étude philologique et exégétique,* and the review by R. De Vaux, in *R.B.*, LV (1948), p. 587.

[3] De Vaux, *loc. cit.*

The Bible and the localization of Yahweh

We have said that the God of salvation makes the forces of nature work for him, without our being justified in pinpointing any specific cosmic power as his and attaching him exclusively to it. Similarly, he resists, in the Bible, any attempt at particular localization. The sequence proposed by the school of Wellhausen is well known: Yahweh was first of all the God of Sinai, later became installed in the high places of Palestine, and finally with Ezechiel, went up to take his place in heaven. Apart from this last feature, the presentation as a whole may be taken as substantially accurate; but there still remains the explanation of how and why these changes of abode should have taken place. On this point, too, the originality of the religion of Israel will have to be explained.

First of all, we see an effort made to substitute Yahweh for the Baals in the sanctuaries of Canaan; the Yahwistic and Elohistic accounts of the patriarchal epic bear witness to this first stage. Later, the Deuteronomic reform of Josias (4 Kings 23) centralizes all worship in Jerusalem, until Jeremias announces the fall and destruction of the temple itself (Jer. 7. 12–14). This process of delocalization[1] is clear evidence of the Bible's resistance to any idea of definitely anchoring the God of Israel to a particular place.

As for the mountain of Horeb, though northern traditions do, indeed, readily call it "God's mountain" (*Har Elōhîm*; Ex. 3. 1; 3 Kings 19. 8), there is not really any question of any stable residence by Yahweh there. In the accounts of the Exodus which appear to be of Yahwistic tradition, the references are to the descent of God upon Sinai (Ex. 19. 11, 18, 20; 34. 5). Moreover, there is no indication that fervent Israelites felt the necessity of making for the mountain in the desert in order to pray there to their national God. In this connexion, the case of Elias is unique, and merits some consideration. His journey is a pilgrimage to the fountain-head; he wanted to proclaim his fidelity to this religion of Moses which the *Benê-Yisrā'ēl* who had settled in the land of the baals

---

[1] On this point see A. Gelin, *Les Idées maîtresses de l' A. T.*, pp. 18 ff.

were in the act of betraying. Besides, Sinai here appears as the privileged place of divine manifestations rather than the permanent habitation of the divinity. In fact, in this impressive extract from the Book of Kings, it is merely a question of Yahweh's "passing by": "Go forth, and stand upon the mount before the Lord: and behold the Lord passeth, and a great and strong wind before the Lord overthrowing the mountains, and breaking the rocks in pieces: the Lord is not in the wind. And after the wind an earthquake: the Lord is not in the earthquake. And after the earthquake a fire: the Lord is not in the fire. And after the fire a whistling of a gentle air. And when Elias heard it, he covered his face with his mantle" (3 Kings 19. 11–13). Thus the author has substituted for the storm which was one of the earliest and most classical manifestations of the God of history, the more homely contact of a light breeze, for Yahweh will not be restricted to any particular mode of theophany. But the text further suggests that, if there do exist chosen places where the God of Israel appears in order to make known his will to men, he does no more than merely pass by as a breath of wind.

The Bible, therefore, most frequently presents Sinai and the sacred hills of Palestine as centres where Yahweh appears, but only in passing: he merely touches them with the soles of his feet. Any materialization or prolonged localization of the divine presence is thus modified, in the inspired texts, by this intuition of an arrival from "somewhere else".

A power capable of acting anywhere

Neither specialized, nor localized, the power of Yahweh is therefore enabled to act anywhere; and it is this sense of effectiveness in history that will make it possible for progress to be made in the Bible's reflexion on God. To come to the help of his people, Yahweh, it was thought at first, has to move physically, and he will signal his arrival by a breath of wind or a storm-cloud; then, as it becomes more and more settled, Israel will see its God, in heaven, directing all from above, with no longer any need to change position. One intuition remains common to both conceptions: Yahweh is a power of salvation capable of operating anywhere. So, the same idea will be found, expressed in differing forms, depending on the stage of civilization attained and on historical conditions.

To take the most ancient texts: Yahweh arrives at the height of battle. He comes from Sinai (Deut. 33. 2) to lead the armies of Israel, or simply, in a less precise way, he emerges from the south: "O Lord, when thou wentest out of Seir, and passedst by the regions of Edom" (Judges 5. 4). Even more than the wish to remain faithful to the memory of the desert, this image expresses the mobility of God in his act of salvation: he can always be present where and when he desires. Like a tired traveller, Yahweh appears suddenly to Gedeon (Judges 6. 11), he goes to meet Moses (Ex. 4. 24) and Josue (Josue 5. 13), or stands in Balaam's path (Num. 22. 22–35);[1] finally, he comes down to see the tower which men were building in the land of Sennaar (Gen. 11. 5). The ancient Hebrews had, therefore, this first intuition that at any moment and no matter where, their God could intervene in their history.

The most familiar atmospheric phenomena announced quite naturally this coming of the God of salvation: the wind, for example: "And when thou shalt hear the sound of one going in the tops of the pear trees, then shalt thou join battle: for then will the Lord go out before thy face to strike the army of the Philistines" (2 Kings 5. 24); "They heard the voice of the Lord God walking in paradise at the afternoon air" (Gen. 3. 8; cf. v. 10). But the arrival of the God of Israel is especially marked by an image which became famous in inspired literature, that of the storm-cloud, lowering and fiery:[2] "He that is mounted upon the heaven is thy helper. By his magnificence the clouds run hither and thither" (Deut. 33. 26).

This great biblical theme was, indeed, at first linked with

---

[1] Cf. Num. 23.3, 15; Gen. 7.16; 28.13; Ex. 12.23; 14.25a and 27b.

[2] The image appears to have been borrowed from Phoenician literature. On "Baal, rider of the clouds", see especially the text of the legend of Danel, 44, quoted by R. Dussaud, *Les Découvertes de Ras Schamra (Ugarit) et l'Ancien Testament*, Paris, 1937, p. 90, note 1.

the intervention of Yahweh in battle; such, at least, is the sense the Yawistic tradition gives it. In Exodus 14. 20, for example, the cloud corresponds to the Angel of Yahweh in the Elohistic text,[1] so that, further on, one can read: "And now the morning watch was come, and behold the Lord, looking upon the Egyptian army through the pillar of fire and of the cloud, slew their host" (v. 24). This storm-cloud seems, therefore, to be the seat of divine might, but, as in Judges 5. 4, and Deut. 33. 2, it represents this power in so far as it is mobile, coming from somewhere else, and able to function in any place; Yahweh will exercise this power in coming down to speak with Moses on Sinai: "Lo, now will I come to thee in the darkness of a cloud" (Ex. 19. 9), or to guide the troop of fugitives: "And the Lord went before them to shew the way by day in a pillar of a cloud, and by night in a pillar of fire that he might be the guide of their journey at both times" (ib. 13. 21). In short, the cloud is, in this primitive period, a concrete manifestation of the "coming" of the God of salvation.[2]

Thus one finds, at first, the notion of direct intervention by Yahweh, then this divine mobility in action receives concrete form in the wind or the ride of the scudding clouds; finally, the God of Israel will be able to direct all things from above, without need to move from his position. The Elohistic tradition, taken as a whole, brings us to this final stage. The God who walks through Eden on the evening breeze is replaced by the God of Jacob's vision (Gen. 28. 12–17), who calls to Agar or Abraham from heaven (Gen. 21. 17; 22. 15). In this way, the Elohistic texts show evidence of a purer conception of God's transcendence: but, for all this, they never lose sight of the significance of divine intervention in history. There is no need to refer again to the "historical" implications of the

[1] Verses 19b and 20b (J) of chapter 14 correspond respectively to vv. 19a and 20a (E).

[2] These images and expressions will, indeed, be repeated later on (Hab. 3.6; Ps. 67.8; 103.3 ff.; Is. 19.1; cf. also Deut. 1.29 ff.; Ps. 77.14; 104.39), but the original sense will not be retained. They will be poetic metaphors; Yahweh will not be considered as actually present behind the cloud, but will control everything from a higher level.

celestial character of Yahweh: if the seat of God's power is in heaven, it is so that he may the better govern all from above. Whenever he wishes to make his effective power most keenly felt,[1] all he has to do is to lower the level of the clouds: "He bowed the heavens, and came down: and darkness was under his feet" (Ps. 17. 10; cf. 143. 5).

A similar type of development is discernible in the reflexions of the Sages. Without specifying the location of his abode, the ancient parables of Solomon began by affirming that Yahweh could see everything: "The eyes of the Lord in every place behold the good and the evil" (Prov. 15. 3). He steadies and guides men's steps (16. 9; 20. 24), and weighs men's hearts. Later, after the exile, this divine power and omniscience have their source in the celestial heights, from where the eyes of Yahweh can scan the whole earth (Zach. 4. 10).

The intuition of a power which can be exercised no matter where, is a constant notion in the Bible, and an essential one, underlying the elaboration of its monotheism. This intuition explains in particular why, contrary to what we know of the gods of heaven in the pagan pantheons, Yahweh's dwelling in heaven has as its corollary an action which is efficacious, sovereign, and beyond the control of man.

From power which is beyond limitation to power which is universal

The power of Yahweh, which is not specialized or particularly localized, which always seems to emerge from somewhere beyond and to intervene anywhere, contained in essence, from the beginning, the possibility of total universalization. This transition from the non-limited to the infinite properly so called once again presupposes the historical experience of Israel. We have already noted that the mobile activity of Yahweh corresponded to the occupation of Canaan, whilst his establishment—his "sitting"—in heaven followed the definitive, stable installation of the tribes; and this explains more particularly why Elohistic tradition, which had its roots in the northern kingdom, where a sedentary mode of life was adopted

[1] Ex. 33.9; Num. 11.25; 12.5.

earlier, should have been the first to refer to the God of heaven.

But it should be noted that the celestial character of Yahweh does not imply, at the beginning, the notion of absolutely universal domination. Deut. 33. 28 will speak, for example, of the sky of the land of Jacob; thus Yahweh's sky will at first be the sky of Palestine, beneath which the chosen people lives out its destiny, and, more especially, the sky above Jerusalem. From above, we read, seated in his habitation (Is. 18. 4), Yahweh guides the progress of history, whistling up the flies from the Nile and the bees from the land of Assyria (Is. 7. 18). Besides, this localization is not restrictive; for Yahweh is no more attached to the land and sky of Canaan than he is tied to his people (Amos 9. 7). He can be perceived above Sion simply because that is where the centre of his field of action appears to be.

Before the Exile, in fact, the Bible pays scarcely any attention to what goes on beyond the confines of the promised land,[1] feeling no need to suppose that Yahweh's power might be wielded there also. Certainly, Yahweh has no equal in the whole world: "In truth, I know there is no other God in all the earth, but only in Israel" (4 Kings 5. 15); but this does not prevent Naaman, the Syrian, from taking away with him part of the soil of Israel in order to enjoy the protection of the God of Eliseus (ib. v. 17).[2] Besides, the main object of Elias's prophetism was to persuade Israel that in its territory the Syrian baals had no business at all: "O Lord God of Abraham, and Isaac, and Israel, shew this day that thou art the God of Israel" (3 Kings 18. 36). Yahweh is sole master here; but, beyond the frontier, his zone of influence ceases: "So I will cast you forth out of this land, into a land which you know not, nor your fathers: and there you shall serve strange gods day and night, which shall not give you any rest" (Jer. 16. 13). The same idea will be found in the Deuteronomic discourses,

---

[1] In order to realize to what extent geographical and historical horizons broadened after the exile, one may compare, for example, the accounts of J and P concerning primitive humanity, especially the two genealogies in Gen. 10.

[2] Before the Exile, all foreign territory was considered impure: Josue 22.19; Amos 7.17; Osee 9.3 ff.

which, however, lay more stress on the futility of these foreign divinities: "And there you shall serve gods, that were framed with men's hands" (Deut. 4. 28; cf. 28. 36).

With the Exile and the dispersion of the Jews throughout the world, the necessity of making Yahweh intervene wherever his elect were to be found, gave this celestial fixation of the God of Israel the sense of a dominion over the whole of the visible universe. Henceforth, from high up in the heavens, God brings his providential action to bear on every part of the inhabited earth. Jeremias had already promised the exiles that where they were, God would hear their prayers and supplications (Jer. 29. 12–13), but it is with Ezechiel that the decisive step is taken. The Jews remaining in Israel still thought they were the only ones who could benefit from the protection of the national God: "Get ye far from the Lord," they say to the exiles, "the Land is given in possession to us" (Ez. 11. 15). The prophet, on the contrary, can see the divine chariot departing from Jerusalem, while he conveys this message of consolation to the captives: "I will be to them a little sanctuary in the countries whither they are come" (11. 16).

The priestly accounts of the Exodus will generalize Ezechiel's view: from heaven, God can descend at any point of the globe, so that his glory may rest there; thus, at each stage of the journey through the desert, the cloud spreads out over the ark: "If at any time the cloud removed from the tabernacle, the children of Israel went forward by their troops: if it hung over, they remained in the same place. For the cloud of the Lord hung over the tabernacle by day, and a fire by night" (Ex. 40. 34–36; Num. 9. 15–18).[1] Just as the fixed temple in Jerusalem corresponded to the sky of Palestine, here the mobile sanctuary evokes a celestial throne which has its jurisdiction over the whole world. This universalization of the idea of heaven results from the realization that Yahweh must everywhere

[1] The text of Num. 10.29–32 (J[1] or L) suggests that it was Hobab who directed the march through the desert: in verse 33 (E), it is the ark, whilst the rôle of guide is attributed to the cloud in verse 34 (P). For the priestly account, naturally enough, the mobile sanctuary occupies the central place in the Hebrews' life in the desert: this sanctuary is the ark *and* the cloud of the divine presence.

watch over and govern the inhabited earth, wherever his elect are dispersed.

Yahweh above the entire universe

The initial perception of the victorious intervention of a power coming from the "other world" remained clear throughout the centuries and led to the definitive formulation of biblical monotheism: by following the rhythm of the chosen people's historical experience, the might of Yahweh finally came to extend as far as the limit of all creation. This idea of "above and beyond" is not merely the starting-point, it is found at the conclusion of all Israel's thought, for the Scriptures, not satisfied with placing God in heaven, have finally asserted that he is above all things, including the heavens and the heavens that are above the heavens: "Is it then to be thought that God should indeed dwell upon earth? for if heaven, and the heavens of heavens cannot contain thee, how much less this house which I have built?" (3 Kings 8. 27).

The Book of Job, in particular, lays great stress on this idea of "above": God's universal domination here leaves a unique impression of dizzy perpendicularity: "Dost not thou think that God is higher than heaven, and is elevated above the height of the stars?" (Job 22. 12). From up there, of course, he guides the stars in their courses: "Shalt thou be able to join together the shining stars the Pleiades, or canst thou stop the turning about of Arcturus? Canst thou bring forth the day star in its time, and make the evening star to rise upon the children of the earth?" (Job 38. 31–32). The Almighty summons day after night (3. 4), sends out lightnings to do his errand (38. 35), pours out the water-skins of heaven (38. 37), wraps the sea in dark mists (38. 9), finally to swoop down upon man from his great height: "I that was formerly so wealthy, am all on a sudden broken to pieces: he hath taken me by my neck, he hath broken me" (Job 16. 13).

This intuition of lordly exaltation and loftiness magnificently

6

expresses the idea of God's absolute transcendence, a major theme of the poem:

> Peradventure thou wilt comprehend the steps of God,
> and wilt find out the Almighty perfectly?
> He is higher than heaven, and what wilt thou do?
> He is deeper than hell, and how wilt thou know?
> The measure of him is longer than the earth,
> and broader than the sea.
> If he shall overturn all things,
> or press them together,
> who shall contradict him? (Job 11. 7–10).

God thus goes beyond the universe in every dimension; and mortal man has no refuge left where he can hide from him; he must admit himself conquered and disarmed, with no alternative but to fall on his face in dust and ashes.

The Second Isaias also evokes for us a divine power of salvation acting from above the skies: "Is my hand shortened and become little, that I cannot redeem? . . . I will clothe the heavens with darkness and will make sackcloth their covering" (Is. 50. 2–3). But the prophet generally prefers to make us aware of the idea of divine transcendence in relation to the world by opposing time to eternity, indicating the fragility of the universe in comparison with the unswerving constancy of God's plan of salvation:

> Lift up your eyes to heaven,
> and look down to the earth beneath:
> for the heavens shall vanish like smoke,
> and the earth shall be worn away like a garment,
> and the inhabitants thereof shall perish in like manner:
> but my salvation shall be for ever;
> and my justice shall not fail (Is. 51. 6; cf. Ps. 101. 27).

If the heavens are most frequently represented in the Bible as a *firmamentum*, as the solid and eternal throne of Yahweh, here the God of Israel no longer has the need of such a buttress. He is satisfied with a delicate fabric which he can fold and unfold at will: "He that stretched out the heavens as nothing, and spreadeth them out as a tent to dwell in" (Is. 40. 22; cf. Ps. 103. 2).

The apocalyptic writings will later treat at far greater length the theme of a generalized cosmic upheaval; Is. 34. 4, for example, shows the heavens rolled up like a scroll, and their army reduced to dust. But the essential had already been said: God transcends the universe in every spatial and temporal dimension; he is the absolute "above". The road may have appeared long and tedious, but who will regret the early faltering stammers of Israel, once attained heights never suspected by any other religion of antiquity? It was not an isolated effort of human reflexion, at a certain moment in time, which obtained for us this definitive formulation of monotheism; it was an experience of several centuries' duration, which began very humbly the day the God of Israel spoke to humanity in a voice from "beyond" summoning the universe to the service of history.

C. Creation, The First Chapter in History

With growing awareness of a transcendent purpose, of a history, the thought of Israel asserted itself in the spotless purity of a monotheism which compelled recognition throughout the world. Here, therefore, history proved to be first, with the notion of a Creator coming later. This last notion, in fact, is not superadded, but becomes an integral part of this history, of which the Hebrews were first aware on Sinai and of which it forms the opening chapter. This fact is easy to illustrate: it will be sufficient to study in turn those texts recalling the creation of the world.

Our analysis will take into account the emergence of this theme in the different kinds of writing contained in the Bible. Although the psalms are not always easy to date with indisputable accuracy, the witness of the ancient civilizations suggests that the liturgy was the basis whereon was elaborated Yahweh's creative epic. Jeremias (33. 25–26) is, in fact, the first prophet to allude directly to it,[1] whereas certain of the psalms analysed here must go back earlier in the royal period. The Second Isaias will, furthermore, be the only one to interpolate systematically in the presentation of his prophetic message this initial act of the God of Israel. The author of Prov. 1–9 introduces the theme into the world of sapiential reflexion, to be followed shortly after by the Book of Job, whilst legist literature will also fall into line with Ben Sira. Finally, there remain the two accounts, Yahwistic and priestly, in Genesis; we will say nothing of the first here, for it seems less centred on the origin of the universe itself than on man's sin and its cosmic repercussions.[2] As for the second, we shall study it in the context of Jewish reflexion on the Torah although by so doing we upset our chronological scheme. We have, therefore, the following plan: the evocation in the prayer of Israel of Yahweh's act of creation, its recollection in the consolatory poems of the Second Isaias, its relations to Wisdom and the Law.

The place of the creation in the prayer of Israel

Whatever the situation Israel is confronted with, each new feature in the national or individual drama is woven into the texture of a history in the full sense of the word. The various

[1] In Is. 11.6–9, an allusion to the Creation can already be found, but it is rather different in manner. It concerns a new creation that will mark the coming of the reign of Emmanuel. The notion of a re-creation, paradoxically enough, seems to have preceded the strictly historical presentation of Yahweh's initial creative act. If the theme of the Creation has, in fact, developed out of the liturgy, it must have originally possessed the cyclical character which is ascribed to it elsewhere in the Ancient Near East. If this theory is true, the impulse provided by the fact of revelation tended to transform the original cyclical presentation into a linear perspective of the development of the world and of history.

[2] "We come to the same conclusion as Werser when he observes that the Yahwist does not expound a true cosmogony, but that, from the creation of man and the world, he chooses to relate only what may serve as a background to the history of paradise and the fall" (P. Humbert, "Mythe de Création et Mythe paradisiaque dans le second chapitre de la Genèse", in Rev. d'Hist. et de Philos. relig., 16 (1936), pp. 459 ff.). Nevertheless, we already find in this text a strongly marked historical perspective, in as far as the organization of the known world is concerned. Nature is made for the service of man; if things do not proceed normally, this is the fault of sin, and paradise brings with it a hope of divine grace and the Messianic restoration.

liturgical reminiscences of Yahweh's initial work are the result of this ever living and real sense of history: the "sacred legend", a setting for the future as well as the present, forms but a part of the great whole which is God's general plan for the universe.

Nevertheless, this integration of the event in a history was not perceived in the earliest stages of Mosaic religion. The oldest songs of the Bible[1] scarcely go beyond the immediate contours of the divine exploit which they are recounting: they are content to describe it and to evoke it lyrically: "Let us sing to the Lord, for he is gloriously magnified: the horse and his rider he hath thrown into the sea" (Ex. 15. 21). We should not be surprised, therefore, to find no account of the creation in the most ancient hymns, such as the canticle of Deborah, Psalms 23b;[2] 28; 46; there is apparently no inkling of anything more than the recent event in which the might of the national God has been manifested. When disappointments or catastrophes are the subject, the poet likewise merely depicts the actual, heart-rending situation, together with all appropriate cries, gestures and rites, obviously hoping to elicit thereby a reply from the divinity (cf. Judges 20. 23–28; Josue 7. 6–15; 2 Par. 20. 1–17). The early prophets also expressed themselves in this way, giving brief oracles in rhythmical, suggestive language apparently designed to forecast what the future held in store.

But, from the prophet Osee onwards, recollections of sacred history permeate all forms of the religious thought and life of Israel. In the throes of national disasters, the memory of the original creative exploit of Yahweh is evoked and his "fidelity" is called to witness. On the day of victory, on the other hand, the latest exploit of Yahweh's might is celebrated by including it in the series of great feats performed by him, presented according to a conventional pattern and magnified with loving affection.

*   *   *

[1] Cf. A. Causse, *Les plus vieux chants de la Bible*, Paris, 1926.

[2] It is generally accepted that Ps. 23 (=Hebrew, 24) is composite in nature: see Podechard, *Le Psautier. Traduction littérale et explication historique*, Lyons, 1949, pp. 112 ff.

Let us begin, then, with the lamentations.[1] During tragic moments of its destiny, if it wishes to touch the heart of its God, Israel knows no better argument than the recalling to memory of his promises, and the recollection of his constant love; his "fidelity" is called on, for the divine behaviour all through the days gone by of history is alone able to open up some prospect of hope in the gloom of the present. Quite naturally, the initial work of Yahweh is placed at the head of this evocation of the past: "O Lord God, behold thou hast made heaven and earth by thy great power and thy stretched out arm: no word shall be hard to thee . . . Who hast set signs and wonders in the land of Egypt even until this day, and in Israel, and amongst men . . ." (prayer of Jer. 32. 17–25). In prayer, creation is thus bound up with history; the one is evoked by the other: "Thou alone art the God of all the kingdoms of the earth: thou hast made heaven and earth" (prayer of Ezechias, Is. 37. 16–20); and the argument from "fidelity" will involve references to the very first divine action in time: "If I have not set my covenant between day and night, and laws to heaven and earth: surely I will cast off the seed of Jacob, and of David my servant, so as not to take any of his seed to be rulers of the seed of Abraham, Isaac and Jacob" (Jer. 33. 25–26).

The creation itself is not, indeed, referred to in all the collective lamentations. There is nothing stereotyped about Yahweh's great epic, and history is always presented in it with a great deal of freedom. Generally speaking, among all his acts, only those are chosen which seem to be in closest relationship with the relevant situation. Nevertheless, with the Exodus and the foundation of the temple of Jerusalem, the forming of the earth and the heavens is one of the most frequently adopted themes. It is never, however, treated for its own sake; it forms an integral part of the classical

[1] It has been established by H. Gunkel, *Einleitung in die Psalmen. Die Gattungen der religiösen Lyrik Israels*, Göttingen, 1933, that the collective lamentations belong to a well defined literary type. In their number may be included Psalms 43, 59, 73, 78, 79, 88b, 89. We here place alongside them a certain number of prayers inserted in the prophetic and historical books.

list of the great achievements of the God of Israel.

Closely linked with the evocation of the "sacred legend", the creative epic will be adapted in its method of presentation to the exigencies of the moment. Notwithstanding its theological indigence, when military disasters and political collapse are upon them, it is to the primitive myth of a primeval combat that the Israelites will turn:[1] "Thou by thy strength didst make the sea firm: thou didst crush the heads of the dragons in the waters. Thou hast broken the heads of the dragon: thou hast given him to be meat for the people of the Ethiopians" (Ps. 73. 13–14). Similarly, Ps. 43 will say: "Thou hast crushed us as thou didst the dragon" (v. 20).[2] Too great an emphasis should not be placed on this image, which supposes an anterior element already existing at the time of creation and serving as a target for the might of Yahweh; there is here a similarity with the idea of the redemption, in which one is left with the impression that God wishes to restore something to someone. Just as the term "redeem" is used to describe Yahweh's simply rescuing Israel from a desperate situation, in the same way and just as improperly, his act of creation is depicted from a martial angle when the need is felt to evoke the irresistible omnipotence of Yahweh, the "gibbôr"[3] of antiquity.

[1] The *Enûma Elish* provides the classic example of this myth. See Dhorme, *Choix de textes religieux assyro-babyloniens*, Paris, 1907.—More recently, R. Labat, *Le poème babylonien de la Création*, Paris, 1939.—A. Heidel, *The Babylonian Genesis, the Story of the Creation*, Chicago, 1942.—The latest discovered fragments, translated by E. A. Speiser, are included in J. B. Pritchard, *Ancient Near Eastern Texts*, Princeton, 1950, pp. 60 ff. A brief analysis will be found in E. Dhorme, *Les Religions de Babylonie et d'Assyrie* (Coll. "Mana", 1, 2. Paris, 1949), pp. 303-308.

In Phoenicia this myth is expressed by the struggle between Baal and Yam. See, on this point, Dussaud, *Les Découvertes de Ras Schamra (Ugarit) et l'A. T.*, p. 78; and, by the same author, *Les Religions des Hittites et des Hourrites, des Phéniciens et des Syriens* (Coll. "Mana"), pp. 573-579. The texts will be found in the following work, the classic edition: G. H. Gordon, *Ugaritic Handbook* (Analecta Orientalia, No. 25), Rome, 1947; there is a good English translation in *Ugaritic Literature*, Rome, 1949, by the same author.

[2] We have adopted here the exegesis by Podechard, *Le Psautier*, p. 78. The translation of the psalter in the "Bible de Jérusalem" (Tournay-Schwab, *Les Psaumes*, Paris, 1950) seeks, on the contrary, to eliminate all allusion to the primeval combat or to give it a straight historical interpretation: see, for example, Ps. 73.15 ff.

[3] (Translator's note: "powerful warrior").

Besides, once the old cosmogonic myth has been well and truly forgotten, the cosmic work of the Creator will still, when occasion demands, be given an appearance of violent struggle: "O Lord God of our fathers, thou art God in heaven, and rulest over all the kingdoms and nations. In thy hand is strength and power; and no one can resist thee" (2 Par. 20. 6). Similarly, we read in Judith's prayer: "O God of the heavens, creator of the waters, and Lord of the whole creation . . . Lift up thy arm as from the beginning" (Judith 9. 17 and 11), the watery realm always suggesting to the Semitic mind a power hostile to the divine organization of the cosmos.

In the collective lamentations, creation is thus always presented in close liaison with history. As the first of Yahweh's great works, it lends support to the argument of divine fidelity. Not only is it brought in here by the "sacred legend", in which it forms the first link, but, in the very nature of its evocation, it is well adapted to the needs of the moment.

*   *   *

In the hymns, as in the collective lamentations, the reference back to the creation is always made in connexion with a definite, concrete situation. Such a reference, furthermore, may be developed to a greater or lesser degree; a simple mention, such as "who made heaven and earth" will suffice, for example, to give greater force to a blessing in the name of Yahweh (Ps. 113. 23 [=115. 15]; 133. 3) or will help to strengthen the confidence of the just (Ps. 120. 2; 123. 8; 145. 6). Certain psalms, however, show at greater length this bond which exists between the initial act of Yahweh and his intervention in history:

For the word of the Lord is right,
and all his works are done with faithfulness.
He loveth mercy and judgment;
the earth is full of the mercy of the Lord.
By the word of the Lord the heavens were established;
and all the power of them by the spirit of his mouth . . .

For he spoke and they were made:
he commanded and they were created.
The Lord bringeth to nought the counsels of nations (Ps.
32. 4–10).

The "word" (dābār) here reveals the unity of the divine
purpose, it is a creative word which is "right" (yāshār) and
invites all "right" or just men to praise God (v. 1); whilst
the verse: "And all his works are done with faithfulness",
is intended to sum up the cosmic and historical action of God,
considered as a whole.

Linked with the entirety of God's government in time,
creation may be placed at the head of a chronologically
arranged series of Yahweh's exploits as in Ps. 135. Here, in
fact, are found enumerated all the manifestations of the
divine mercy (hèsèd), with this refrain: "Praise the Lord,
for he is good: for his mercy endureth for ever." Reasons for
offering thanks to God are listed in chronological order: the
creation of heaven (135. 5), of earth (v. 6), of the great celestial
luminaries (7–9); then the crossing of the Red Sea (10–15),
the sojourn in the wilderness (v. 16), the defeat of the
Amorrhite kings (17–20), finally the occupation of the land
of Canaan (21–22). At this point, the "sacred legend" usually
stops, but our psalm continues its outline of history by evoking
the various attacks which the Israelites had to withstand
afterwards, and the list ends with a reference to God's ever-
present solicitude: "Who giveth food to all flesh: for his
mercy endureth for ever" (v. 25).

The hymns of the psalter do not, therefore, recall the
creation as if it were an isolated act, valid in its own right
but no more than this; its mention, coming in the general
account of Yahweh's great achievements, always has an
element of contemporary interest in it, a particular significance
for the present and the future. Was it always thus in ancient
Israel? Mowinckel, followed by such eminent exegetes as
Volz and Hans Schmidt, claimed to find traces, especially
in the psalms of the Kingdom, of a liturgy of Yahweh's

enthronement, corresponding in every way with the enthronement of Marduk during the Babylonian festivities of the
Akitu.[1] Paul Humbert[2] even thought that our Ps. 103 was
an exact replica of the *Enûma Eliš* recited in Babylon at the
New Year ceremonies. In any case, he thinks, there existed a
biblical account of the creation linked with the proclamation
of Yahweh's kingship. It is difficult to know how much can
be accepted of this hypothesis, which is rather fascinating than
solidly established. In spite of likely parallels, an essential
difference must always be pointed out between the recurrent
revivals of the creative myth in Babylon and the actual
purport of the biblical hymns; the actions and the destiny of
man appear to have a completely different significance. If we
follow the interpretation suggested by Mircea Eliade, in *The
Myth of the Eternal Return*, the great events of life—the annual
renewal of plant-life, the establishment of a monarchy, the
foundation of a temple—constitute everywhere except in Israel
a replica, the resumption of an archetype, of an identical
primitive act, that of creation. In the Bible, on the contrary,
after the prehistoric stage of our texts' history the creation
appears as the first of a series of facts, each of which has a
particular importance in itself: the cycle of the myths has
become an historical line.

This view, of course, can claim to be valid only for the
psalter as we have it to-day. It may be assumed that a number
of texts have passed through a "pre-biblical" stage. It is
precisely this transformation which they underwent on being
incorporated in the Bible that provides a valuable guide as
to the way revelation itself came to be understood. Thus, at

[1] The most precise details concerning the New Year procession can be found
in the texts of Uruk and Babylon, translated and annotated by F. Thureau-
Dangin, *Rituels Accadiens,* Paris, 1921, pp. 86 ff. and 127 ff. See also the brief
reconstruction by Dhorme in "Mana", *op. cit.,* p. 243. Reference should also
be made to Labat, *Le caractère religieux de la Royauté assyro-babylonienne*, Paris,
1939, p. 95. On the O. T. and Israelite royalty, see the work by J. De Fraine,
L'aspect religieux de la royauté israélite (Analecta Biblica, 3), Rome, 1954, especially
pp. 285 ff. and 309 ff; in this book will be found a very pertinent, if not always
convincing, criticism of the Scandinavian school.

[2] Humbert, "La relation de Gen. I et du psaume 104, avec la liturgie du
Nouvel An israélite", in *Rev. d'Hist. et de Philos. relig.,* 15 (1935), pp. 1–27.

the beginning, many fragments may have sung the epic of creation without the slightest reference to the drama of salvation; but it is significant that Holy Scripture has not reproduced them as such, preferring instead to incorporate them with other hymns, so as to place them in an historical setting. The first two verses of Ps. 23, for example: "The earth is the Lord's and the fulness thereof: the world and all they that dwell therein. For he hath founded it upon the seas; and hath prepared it upon the rivers" (Ps. 23. 1–2), may have formed a separate hymn;[1] but in the psalter they serve to introduce certain precepts for intending worshippers: "Who shall ascend into the mountain of the Lord: or who shall stand in his holy place? The innocent in hands, and clean of heart, etc." (Ps. 23. 3–6). Similarly, Ps. 88a (6–19) forms a prelude to the great lamentation which follows (v. 20–50), just as the famous canticle, *Caeli enarrant gloriam Dei* (Ps. 18. 1–7), which some consider to be an adaptation of a pagan poem to the sun,[2] becomes the magnificent preface to a legist psalm: "The law of the Lord is unspotted" (v. 8–15).

The place of the creation in the Second Isaias

The creation is not a theme of pre-Exilic prophetism. Jeremias is the first prophet to allude to the initial work of God, and this occurs in a prayer (32. 17). Is it merely a liking for liturgical hymnology which has led the Second Isaias to bring our theme to the forefront? In any case, the study of the link existing between creation and history is here all the more interesting because there are not a few references to the forming of the world; we shall thus, with each quotation, have the opportunity of confirming that a mention of the creation is not included for its poetic value or in order to give

[1] Such is at least the opinion of Duhm, Gunkel, Stärk, Kittel: see Podechard, *Le Psautier*, p. 113.

[2] Podechard, *op. cit.*, pp. 93 ff. Nor do we think that the phrase of the psalm: "Caeli enarrant gloriam Dei", alludes to the creation. It refers, in our opinion, to the enthusiastic acclamation by the universe at the appearance of the sun, symbol of law.

greater theological precision, but that it is always justified by a definite relationship with the vocation of Israel at that particular time.

*   *   *

The salvation in which the exiled Israelites placed their hopes has been decided by God from the very outset: "Who hath wrought and done these things, calling the generations from the beginning? I the Lord, I am the first and the last" (Is. 41. 4).[1] The appearance on the scene of Cyrus, therefore, so full of promise for the victims of the might of Babylon, is no mere accident of history; it has not been provoked by the spells of magicians or predicted by soothsayers; it belongs to a plan conceived *ab initio* by God:

> I am the Lord, that make all things,
> that alone stretch out the heavens,
> that establish the earth, and there is none with me . . .
> Who say to Cyrus: Thou art my shepherd (44. 24–28).
> I made the earth:
> and I created man upon it:
> my hand stretched forth the heavens:
> and I have commanded all their host.
> I have raised him (Cyrus) up to justice
> and I will direct all his ways (45. 12–13).

After the epic of the Achaemenidae, when the "servant of Yahweh" will occupy the foremost place in the pattern of salvation to come,[2] his vocation will also appear rooted in the origins of time: "Thus saith the Lord God that created the heavens and stretched them out: that established the earth and the things that spring out of it . . . I, the Lord, have called thee in justice, and taken thee by the hand, and preserved thee" (42. 5–6).

*   *   *

Since there is a continuity between creative and historical

---

[1] Cf. Is. 44.6; Apoc 1.8,17; 21.6; 22.13.

[2] We think that these hymns of the servant were probably written by the anonymous prophet of the second part of the Book of Isaias. Cf. our book *Sous la Main de Dieu*. I: Le Prophétisme et l'élection d'Israël, ch. VII, Le Second Isaïe.

action, God's initial work can be used as a sign and a lesson
for the present:

> For thus saith the Lord that created the heavens,
> God himself that formed the earth, and made it,
> the very maker thereof:
> he did not create it in vain;
> he formed it to be inhabited:
> I am the Lord, and there is no other.
> I have not spoken in secret,
> in a dark place of the earth:
> I have not said to the seed of Jacob:
> Seek me in vain (45. 18–19);

it results from the same divine desire for light and order.
And, in the Second Isaias, as in the psalms, the creation is not
evoked by means of hackneyed expressions, but is always
presented in a manner adapted to the conclusion that is
intended to be drawn.

If, for example, there is need to show that the wicked shall
be torn up when they have scarcely taken root, the prophet
will evoke the only stability possible, that which derives
its origin from the Creator: "Have you not understood the
foundations of the earth?" (40. 21). Is Israel afraid? Does it
feel it is being crushed to death by an unjust world? Let it
take heart! The universe, in the hands of its God, weighs
no more than the vain agitation of mortals; Yahweh is the
master of history in the same way as the architect of the
universe has complete control over his work:

> Who hath measured the waters in the hollow of his hand,
> and weighed the heavens with his palm?
> Who hath poised with three fingers the bulk of the earth,
> and weighed the mountains in scales,
> and the hills in a balance? . . .
> Behold the Gentiles are as a drop of a bucket,
> and are counted as the smallest grain of a balance (40. 12–15).

And when the exiles seem to grow faint, as fatigue draws

upon them, the story of God's wondrous works takes on a martial rhythm:

> The Lord is the everlasting God,
> who hath created the ends of the earth:
> he shall not faint, nor labour,
> neither is there any searching out of his wisdom.
> It is he that giveth strength to the weary,
> and increaseth force and might to them that are not (40. 28–29).

The old myth of the primeval combat then reappears with all the ruggedness of Psalms 73 and 88:

> Arise, arise, put on strength,
> O thou arm of the Lord,
> arise as in the days of old,
> in the ancient generations.
> Hast not thou struck the proud one,
> and wounded the dragon?
> Hast not thou dried up the sea,
> the water of the mighty deep? (51. 9–10).

The mention of the creative act, therefore, passing from the plane of liturgical practice to that of prophetic preaching, retains throughout the stamp of applied appropriateness which it possessed in the prayer of Israel; prefacing the drama of redemption, it serves to foster confidence in the coming salvation, clearly indicating the essential attributes of the God of history.

The creation and the great problems of humanity

When we come to the wisdom literature, we no longer find a concrete situation, as in the liturgical prayers or the poems of the Second Isaias, but we find problems and questions concerning existence in general. The initial act of Yahweh is here recalled in order that standards of human behaviour may be woven into the vaster pattern of the cosmos. It is after the Exile that accounts of the creation will fill the pages of sapiential literature; they will not be made a pretext for mere poetic digressions: since the human drama is now an integral part of the cosmic organization, every difficulty put before the wise writers will find its solution in the original, unchanging purpose of God for the universe.

*   *   *

Although the fear of God is frequently enough mentioned in the collections of maxims which form most of the Book of Proverbs,[1] it is difficult to see in what way these very matter-of-fact sayings can be linked with the religion of the Covenant. Apart from a monotheism which they presuppose at all times, we have here a production largely similar to that of other sages in the Ancient Near East. But the biblical proverbs are preceded by a preface which gives an entirely fresh orientation to the whole: the first nine chapters of the work form a magnificent approach, investing with a religious significance the ancient collections and bringing them immediately into the general economy of biblical revelation. Antique wisdom, teacher of "prudence", of "learned thoughts" and of "counsel and equity" (Prov. 8. 12–14), is henceforth elevated to the highest dignity: "Because the Lord giveth wisdom: and out of his mouth cometh prudence and knowledge" (2. 6); now initiated into the secrets of God's government of the universe, it will no longer be content to guide the destiny of mortals who trust in its efficacy, it will assume responsibility for the whole of the created order: "The Lord by wisdom hath founded the earth, hath established the heavens by prudence. By his wisdom the depths have broken out, and the clouds grow thick with dew" (3. 19–20).

What does this presence of _hokhmāh_ at the creation mean? It is simply a matter of bridging the gap between the present destiny of mankind and the initial putting in order of the cosmos. Wisdom, now elevated so close to God, never loses

[1] These lines were written before the completion of our volume _Sous la Main de Dieu_. II: La Sagesse et le Destin des Élus. We have not, however, considered it necessary to modify our text, although, on certain points, our interpretation of the Books of Proverbs and Job has gone quite a long way in the interval.

sight of its essential mission, which is to direct the actions of men: "She is a tree of life to them that lay hold on her: and he that shall retain her is blessed" (3. 18).   Whatever profit Christian meditation on the Trinity may derive from verses 22–31 of the eighth chapter of Proverbs, we certainly run the risk of distorting their meaning if we read them out of context. This chapter must be taken as a whole.   Wisdom, in the guise of a prophet, first takes up her stand at the crossroads to summon all men; then she calls to mind the blessings her action brings; to justify her propaganda and provoke a final commitment, she recalls her influence at the very origin of the divine work:

> The Lord possessed me in the beginning of his ways,
> before he made any thing from the beginning.
> I was set up from eternity,
> and of old before the earth was made.
> The depths were not as yet, and I was already conceived:
> neither had the fountains of waters as yet sprung out . . .
> When he prepared the heavens, I was present:
> when with a certain law and compass he enclosed the
>   depths . . .
> I was with him forming all things:
> and was delighted every day,
> playing before him at all times;
> playing in the world:
> and my delights were to be with the children of men (8. 22–31).

We must not speak here of eternity in the modern sense of the word; for *hokhmāh* it is simply a matter of priority in relation to the cosmos.   Wisdom preceded it, for she had to be present when the world emerged.   We should not be too beguiled by this charming picture of a little girl playing beside the Creator: this image merely aims at showing that everything which materialized at the beginning of the world had to undergo the influence of Wisdom.   Certain exegetes, it is true, have recourse to various and learned philological arguments in order to try and discover here the idea of a divine hypostasis of Wisdom, an adumbration of the revealed doctrine of the Trinity.[1] Our text can certainly make no such claim. To discuss in this manner the implications of thus personifying *hokhmāh* amounts to a consideration of side issues and a neglect of the direct and obvious significance of this passage in its immediate context.

By reducing the question once again to humbler proportions, we are in no way detracting from the theological value of our text. The relation it establishes between the standard of life for mortals and the very foundation of the universe, is a fact which has, perhaps, no equivalent in the whole history of religions. In any case, with Prov. 1–9, biblical thought makes an essential, definitive step forward: it will no longer be possible to raise any great human problem, such as the mystery of suffering, the promulgation of the law by God, or the fact of Jesus Christ, without referring back to the initial setting in order of the cosmos.

*   *   *

The two references to the creation in the Book of Proverbs are intended to establish a link between the principles which should guide the lives of men and nothing less than the organization of the universe. But the principles themselves reposed on pretty rudimentary notions, more especially the idea of temporal retribution or God's immanent justice. They were soon to come up against the simple, if hard, facts of experience; the righteous are no more frequently rewarded on this earth than the wicked are punished. The Book of Job frankly takes up this matter and arrives at the conclusion that the problem must be placed somewhere beyond these over-simplified categories, and that its solution must remain God's secret, as is the creation of the world itself. As in Prov. 8, Wisdom is present at the creation: "[He] made a weight for the winds, and weighed the waters by measure. When he gave a law for the rain, and a way for the sounding storms. Then he saw

[1] A. Robert, "Les attaches littéraires bibliques de Prov. I–IX", in *R.B.*, **43** (1934), pp. 42–68; 172–204; 374–84; 44 (1935), 344–65; 502–25.

it, and declared, and prepared, and searched it" (Job 28.
25–27), with the difference, however, that Wisdom must elude
the grasp of human intellect: man cannot know the way of it
(28. 13), for God alone knows it (ib. v. 23).[1] The idea we
analysed above has now become deeper and more extensive:
it is a question of mystery rather than wisdom; but this
mystery, the least fathomable of all those upon which the wise
writers will have to reflect, will always have to be included in
the initial mystery of the work of the Creator.

In the Book of Job, the theme of the creation is treated with
lavish virtuosity; it often, therefore, gives the impression of
being merely a dramatic setting chosen in order to allow the
poet to bring freely into play all the resources of his art. The
modern reader, in fact, is especially interested in the human
aspect of the drama; but this amounts, in my opinion, to restrict-
ing the scope of the work: this drama, while remaining human,
raises the question of the organization of the cosmos. The
cosmological argument is, indeed, brought into the debate
and developed by each of the disputants, by Job, his friends,
Eliu and God; it is not always clear what contribution it
makes to the discussion, since it would seem to have equal
validity for the support of contradictory theses. Nevertheless,
in each case, the evocation of Yahweh's act of creation has
varying significance; it loses none of its value in thus passing
from one side to another; far from remaining on the fringe of
the subject, it reaches to the very heart of the problem: the
mystery of the human order and of justice is bound up with
that of the harmony of the world.

The friends of Job, in fact, take up the question at the point
where Prov. 8 had left it: the order in the universe guarantees
the immanent justice of God as it had been defined by "the

---

[1] For the authenticity of this chapter 28 of the Book of Job see P. Larcher,
Le Livre de Job, Paris, 1950, pp. 11 ff. "The poem on Wisdom (28) seems to many
critics to be a heterogeneous element in the literary structure of the whole."
We agree with the author's conclusion: this poem, "the work of the same author,
or at least of one belonging to the same *milieu* and having similar preoccupations,"
shares the essential significance of the work: "It aims at discouraging any attempt
to penetrate the divine mysteries."

Fathers". Thus Eliphaz will discover in the divine work an invitation for Job to do penance: "Wherefore I will pray to the Lord . . . Who doth great things and unsearchable and wonderful things without number . . . Blessed is the man whom God correcteth: refuse not therefore the chastising of the Lord" (Job 5. 8–17). Because of his mastery over nature, the Creator can reveal himself to be more exacting than man imagines: "Can man be justified compared with God, or he that is born of a woman appear clean? . . . He stretched out the north over the empty space, and hangeth the earth upon nothing . . . By his power the seas are suddenly gathered together, and his wisdom has struck the proud one" (25. 4; 26. 5–13).[1] In brief, man has but to bow his head and admit that he is a sinner in the sight of the author of all things who imposes his will upon mortals because he is the "Almighty". Without identifying herself with the Creator, Wisdom, proselytizing in public, availed herself of the same argument: the fact of being at the root of all creation confers a right to the obedience of mankind. Here, therefore, we do not go beyond the horizon of Proverbs.

Job does not in any way challenge this last argument: "Indeed I know it is so, and that man cannot be justified compared with God . . . He . . . alone spreadeth out the heavens, and walketh upon the waves of the sea" (Job 9. 2–10), but he wants to go further than his friends, whose wise memories will vanish into dust and blustering contentions prove to be things of clay (13. 12). The prosperity of the wicked, like the suffering of the just, is a fact which must be faced squarely: "I will teach you by the hand of God, what the Almighty hath, and I will not conceal it" (27. 11). And since Eliphaz and his colleagues fail to come to grips with the question, the "holy man" boldly asks God to provide a solution. Yahweh then "answered Job out of a whirlwind" (38. 1): "Where wast thou when I laid the foundations of the earth?" (v. 4). In the mouth of the Almighty, questions succeed one another with great irony:

Didst thou since thy birth command the morning? . . .

[1] We follow here the reconstruction of the text proposed by Larcher, *op. cit.*

Hast thou entered into the depths of the sea? . . .

Hast thou considered the breadth of the earth? . . .

Hast thou entered into the storehouses of the snow? . . .

Shalt thou be able to join together the shining stars, the
Pleiades? . . .

Canst thou lift up thy voice to the clouds,

that an abundance of waters may cover thee? (v. 12–34).

And in the magnificent chapters which conclude the poem
(38–41), the Almighty summarizes his cosmic work from the
very beginning, for he has no other reply to give; mortal man
does not know the ultimate nature of things, he must remain
in ignorance of the reason for his suffering no less than of the
secret of creation itself: "Therefore I reprehend myself, and
do penance in dust and ashes" (42. 6). Here, the evocation
of the origin of the world assumes quite a different significance
from the one Job's friends give it. It no longer serves to give
support to the traditional thesis of temporal retribution; it
emphasizes the "mystery" of divine action.

The unity which had been ratified in Prov. 8 between the
destiny of mankind and the origin of the universe, loses its
identity, with the Book of Job, in the impenetrable secret of
God: "Man cannot find out the work which God hath made
from the beginning to the end" (Eccl. 3. 11). "As thou
knowest not what is the way of the spirit, nor how the bones
are joined together in the womb of her that is with child: so
thou knowest not the works of God, who is the maker of all"
(ib. 11. 5). This disillusioned conclusion of Ecclesiastes is
therefore comparable with that of our great poems on the
suffering of the righteous.

In the thought of the sages, the first setting in order of the
world appears as the starting-point of history in the wider
sense of the word: Wisdom and the secrecy which presided
over the birth of the world envelop the destiny of mortal men.

The initial organization of the world and the Torah

When the Exile made priestly groups seek to take stock of all
the riches of the past, they went back to the origin of the world

in order to sketch out the general picture of God's divine plan; the first word which called the universe into existence opens the series of words addressed by Elohim to his people. In the last few centuries before the birth of Christ, Jewish devotion to the judgements of God led to the cult of the Torah. Arising thus in priestly circles, the legist current spreads through the whole of biblical thought; Wisdom becomes so impregnated with Judaism that it merges with the Law of sacred history. In any case, the proof of God's government of Israel will continue to be the reference back to the initial act of creation.

*　　*　　*

The first chapter of Genesis is, theologically speaking, the most developed account the Bible gives of the creation. Yet here too, the divine purpose of salvation is no less closely linked with the initial cosmic work. "This position given to the history of creation at the very beginning of the Bible has often led to the wrong idea of considering the doctrine of the creation a central fact of O.T. belief. That is a complete misconception. The witness of the creation has no more value in itself in Genesis than in the Deutero-Isaias . . . In the Yahwistic as well as in the priestly account, what counts fundamentally is faith in salvation and vocation. This faith is sustained by the fact that the Yahweh of the Covenant made with Abraham and renewed on Sinai, is also the master of the world."[1] Indeed as it comes in our Sacred Books, this famous text is inseparable from the drama of salvation which it announces. It certainly does not seem to have been written at one and the same time. If the fact that it was written up after the Exile is now generally accepted, there is, nevertheless, at present a growing tendency to believe that this account presupposes long centuries of meditation upon more ancient data. Should the origin be sought in the liturgy, as

[1] G. von Rad, *Das erste Buch Mose*, p. 34. See also the work by the same author: "Das theologische Problem des alttestamentlichen Schöpfungsglaubens", in *Werden und Wesen* (Beiheft 66 zur *Z.A.W.*, 1936), pp. 138 ff.

is the view of Mowinckel and his school, or on the contrary should it be taken to be the elaboration of official teaching made known in the form of public recitation?[1] The question is unimportant, as far as we are concerned; in its present state the text has no particular value taken in itself alone, but it does serve as an introduction to history, by relating the first of God's commands.

The mere placing of the priestly account of the creation at the beginning of the Bible would be sufficient evidence to warrant the supposition that it is meant as an introduction to the drama of salvation. But there is more to it than this: in its very purport, it is bound up with history as P sees it. In the latter, God's plan develops in successive, irreversible stages, from Adam to the flood, from Noe to Abraham, to finish with the time of Israel's election. From one period to the next, the sin of mankind can be seen increasing in prevalence, at the same time as God confirms his plan of salvation and strengthens his covenant with the chosen portion of humanity. Our account, then, is situated exactly at the beginning of this linear perspective and forms, as it were, the first link in the chain. The episode is not finally rounded off, for whereas the work of the first six days ends with a reference to the coming of evening and of morning, no such mention occurs after the seventh day. On the other hand, the initial work is not to be done afresh; it points the way up a pyramid, the summit of which is man, and it concludes with the Creator resting, his work achieved.

The first chapter of Genesis, worked up into a "history", leading up to the coming drama of salvation, is also linked with the election of Israel by a whole series of common themes which have been clearly indicated in Dom Thierry Maertens' study.[2] We certainly have no intention of reopening the subject. The author places particular emphasis, in this presentation of the initial work of God, on the way in which it prepared

---

[1] A. Van der Voort, "Gn. 1, 1 à 11, 4a et le Psaume CIV, in *R.B.*, 58 (1951), pp. 221–347.

[2] Thierry Maertens, *Les Sept Jours (Gn. 1)*, Bruges, 1951.

the liturgical developments of priestly legislation.[1] All we need note is that the divine words, commands and orders are at the centre of P's preoccupations:"Thus the priestly account presents a development of history, seen in the light of the divine orders and prescriptions, those orders which establish and assure the salvation of God's people."[2] Now, while it retains traces of a more primitive conception of the work of creation (God "made" the firmament, the luminaries, the beasts of the earth, man himself), our text stresses, in the organization of the universe, the efficacy of the divine "word"; 'āmar is the word used here, "God said", a solemn expression of God's authority which will be found in the decrees of the law, and which "prophetic literature will in its turn use with particular insistence". So it is possible to conclude: "We consequently find here a stock formula, inaugurating with due solemnity and giving authority to the articles of the law as avenging decrees of divine Justice. Now it is precisely this expression which introduces, in the account of the creation, the different phases of God's action (verses 3, 6, 9, 11, 14, 20, 24, 26, 28, 29). The God of Sinai who organizes the life of his people and spreads through it the leaven of his Word, who, by the words of the prophets, later jealously avenges the breaking of this Law, this God is also the God of the creation."[3]

The later sapiential writers and the psalmists who write on the subject of the law will continue to uphold this view. For them, too, what comes "out of the mouth of the most High" (Ecclus 24. 5) unites the universe and history. They will thus identify the Torah with little Wisdom playing near

---

[1] Certain parallels may appear to be a little strained. The remarks on the sabbath, however, seem to us more decisive and important (pp. 64 ff.). In spite of ancient sources, the sabbath is here referred to the creation, not to the sojourn in the desert or the departure from Egypt: "The arranger had made us too familiar with his practice of transposing the realities of the election on to the cosmic plane, for us to be surprised that an institution intended to commemorate Yahweh's combat against the Red Sea and Egypt, should now become the feast of the creation, first fruits of the liberation of all men" (ib., p. 64).

[2] Von Rad, op. cit., p. 19.

[3] Maertens, op. cit., p. 34.

the Creator in the Book of Proverbs (Ecclus 1. 2–10; 24), and with the creative word of the first chapter of Genesis:

> For ever, O Lord, thy word standeth firm in heaven:
> thy truth unto all generations.
> Thou hast founded the earth, and it continueth.
> By thy ordinance the day goeth on:
> for all things serve thee.
> Unless thy law had been my meditation . . . (Ps. 118. 89–92).

Thus, wherever the fact of the creation is evoked in the Bible, it is always placed in relation with one aspect or other of the drama of salvation. It is not as if there were the creation on one side and the redemption on the other; one and the same purpose animates the universe and with it, history, which takes root *ab initio*: "Who hath wrought and done these things, calling the generations from the beginning?" (Is. 41. 4). "In the beginning was the Word . . . All things were made by him: and without him was made nothing that was made. In him was life: and the life was the life of men" (John 1. 1–4).

However, all that Israel was conscious of in the first instance, was its election, and the idea of creation was merely an extension of it into the most remote past. The God of the universe was first of all the God of history.

III

THE UNIVERSE AS A WITNESS TO HISTORY

THE GOD whom the Bible presented to the world as the master of the universe was first of all known as the God of history, the God who came to ensure that justice was done to the sons of Abraham, enslaved in Egypt; and the Hebrews were to have to dwell under his all-powerful and tender care for a long time before being in a position to define his theoretical power over the world. It was not the beauty and magnificence of the universe which awakened in the soul of Israel a sense of the divine, and it was not through the contemplation of nature that the chosen people came to an idea of the supreme greatness which characterized the master in whose hands their destiny lay. This they discovered in the irresistible might which brought them out of the land of Egypt and led them into Canaan; and it is in this epic story, handed down from generation to generation, that their descendants learnt to know their God.

This is not to say that, in the Bible, the universe is shown as entirely devoid of religious meaning; on the contrary, it too bears witness to God; but it does so in a new and original manner. The inspired writers do not scan the universe for proof of a first cause; nor do they, like the ancients, envisage it as the scene of "hierophanies" or manifestations of the "sacred". To them it simply provides a sign of Yahweh's loving solicitude for his people; it testifies to the presence of a friend rather than to the existence of a monarch. And it owes its greatness only and solely to its being able to co-operate in the fulfilment of the divine purpose of salvation.

The external world, therefore, will indeed be called upon to reveal the presence of God, but of a God who intervenes on behalf of his elect. Furthermore, it will enable them to have foreknowledge of what God has in store for them. For in the very organization of the universe can be found manifested the final triumph of the elect and the broad outline of their destiny. If he is attentive enough, man can discover in the universe the essential themes of his drama, and can recognize in the movement of the cosmos, the movement of his own history, the pattern of his own destiny.

This is no mere romantic day-dream, in fact it is just the opposite. For instead of seeking in nature, as did the poets of the nineteenth century, a mute confidant of frustrated hopes and ideals, the children of God find in nature reason for renewed optimism and trust in the future. The Bible depicts nature, not as a maternal refuge for those who have abandoned the fight with history, but as a comrade in arms or an audience ever willing to applaud enthusiastically the great conquerors of the world. Whereas we suspect that the romantics looked for some secret harmony existing between the bitter disappointments of the sons of Adam and the universe to which they confided their frustration, the Bible reveals an uninterrupted harmony which extends from the primitive impulse of the creation to the final triumph of the saints.

A.   THE THEOPHANIES OF THE GOD OF HISTORY[1]

The biblical theophanies announce the advent of a God who has come to save mankind and will brook neither check nor restraint. If Yahweh showed himself to be only a cosmic force, man might well nourish the hope of harnessing in some way the power of God so as to enlist his support; but here he is face to face with something superior to every other existing force, something which is capable of disrupting the very order of creation; man has therefore no alternative but to bow before this omnipotent power. Thus the biblical theophanies

[1] Article published in *Bible et Vie chrétienne*, No. 3, 1952, under the title: "Orage et Nuée, signes de la présence de Dieu dans l'histoire".

reveal the holiness of the God of the Covenant, while the mission of nature is to denote the active presence of God and yet hide the mystery from the indiscreet gaze of the sons of Adam.

The crashing din of the storm and the holiness of Yahweh

Without any doubt, the most famous biblical theophany is the one which, in the Book of Exodus, accompanies the promulgation of the law: "And now the third day was come, and the morning appeared: and behold thunders began to be heard, and lightning to flash, and a very thick cloud to cover the mount. And the noise of the trumpet sounded exceedingly loud, and the people that was in the camp, feared. And when Moses had brought them forth to meet God from the place of the camp, they stood at the bottom of the mount. And all mount Sinai was on a smoke: because the Lord was come down upon it in fire, and the smoke arose from it as out of a furnace. And all the mount was terrible. And the sound of the trumpet grew by degrees louder and louder, and was drawn out to a greater length: Moses spoke, and God answered him" (Ex. 19. 16–19). "And all the people saw the voices and the flames, and the sound of the trumpet, and the mount smoking: and being terrified and struck with fear, they stood afar off" (ib. 20. 18).

What meaning can be attributed to all this noise? The second passage just quoted might appear to indicate that such a manifestation of force was intended to give this stiff-necked people a scare which should develop into the experience of a truly religious awe of the Almighty. If this is true, then the theophany of Sinai is the first revelation of the terrible God of the Old Testament whose myth has not yet been finally exploded by modern exegesis. It must be admitted, however, that the reason for the fear experienced by the Israelites was not the exceptional violence of the storm over the desert mountain; we have here, undoubtedly, an example of the instinctive recoil of all primitive peoples before manifestations of the "sacred".[1] If we take any other revelation of God in the Old Testament, we find, though perhaps less vividly expressed, this same fear of death; for example, Moses hides his face before the burning bush (Ex. 3. 6), and Elias covers his head with his mantle (3 Kings 19. 13), for it is an oft-repeated truth that none can see God and not die.[2] In fact, when the theophany of Sinai is evoked in Deuteronomy, it is precisely this notion which is given prominence: ª[Ask if] it hath been known at any time, that a people should hear the voice of God speaking out of the midst of fire, as thou hast heard, and lived" (4. 32–33).

If it is with fear that any manifestation of God is received, it should not be forgotten that such manifestations were the prelude to the communication of a message of salvation; the theophany of the desert prepares the conquest of the promised land. Rather than frighten his people by appearing in a raging storm, it was Yahweh's desire to inspire confidence and courage; would the best way of rousing the energy of the Hebrews before their attack upon the land of Canaan have been to terrify them by noisy atmospheric disturbances? It is the irresistible power of God which Israel here recognized, and the thunder and lightning, the earthquake and, later, the whirlwinds and the hailstorms, already appear to them as the weapons which *Yahweh Sebā'ôth* will use to destroy his foes:

> O Lord, when thou wentest out of Seir,
> and passedst by the regions of Edom,
> the earth trembled, and the heavens dropped water.
> The mountains melted before the face of the Lord,
> and Sinai before the face of the Lord the God of Israel (Judges 5. 4–5).

Thus from the oldest battle songs to the royal hymns of the time of Ezechias or Josias (Ps. 17 and 143), all the biblical theophanies serve to proclaim the arrival, in the fullness of

[1] It is what Rudolf Otto calls the "numinous" in a work which has now become standard: *Das Heilige,* Stuttgart-Gotha, 1917. English translation, *The Idea of the Holy,* Oxford, 1928, translated by John W. Harvey.

[2] Judges 6.23; 13.22; Ex. 33.20; Is. 6.5.

his power, of the God of salvation: "Thou wentest forth for
the salvation of thy people: for salvation with thy Christ".[1]

In the din of the storm, therefore, Yahweh makes it clear
that he has come to bring salvation; but, at the same time, he
reveals one of his essential attributes, one which the prophet
Isaias will particularly stress: he is the "Holy One", which
means that for everyone he remains the one who is in every
way different, over whom no one can exercise any control,
and before whom everything, even the whims of his friends,
must yield. He replies to Job "out of a whirlwind" (Job 38. 1;
40. 1), he comes "in a tempest and a whirlwind" (Nahum
1. 3) to let it be known that it is useless to try and resist him.
His intervention, therefore, excites an enthusiasm which is
mingled with fear: "And, behold, a fire, coming forth from
the Lord, devoured the holocaust, and the fat that was upon
the altar: which when the multitude saw, they praised the
Lord, falling on their faces" (Lev. 9. 24), for Israel can foresee
the exacting demands of him who hastens to the aid of his
people. The divine message is rich in promise for them, but
also full of menace.

So the chosen people seem very small in their own eyes
when brought before this God who imposes his will upon the
world in order to save it: "The lofty eyes of man are humbled,
and the haughtiness of men shall be made to stoop: and the
Lord alone shall be exalted in that day" (Is. 2. 11). In this
roaring of the whirlwind, they had, perhaps, their earliest
intuition of what was to be the drama of their existence,
namely, it was a Holy God who had assumed control of their
destiny and was going to lead them forward.

An intervention that moves heaven and earth

The raging of the storm evokes the idea of Yahweh's sanctity
because it announces the coming of a God who is stronger
than the world, before whom everything trembles and whom
nothing can resist successfully. The God of Israel, therefore,
does not appear like one of those forces of nature in which

[1] Hab. 3.13; cf. Ps. 45.7; 75.9.

the peoples of old saw a manifestation of the sacred, rocks and hills and the ever-renewing cycle of plant-life, for example.[1] One cannot imagine that he was at first envisaged as a sort of fire spirit,[2] or even a mere storm divinity like the Syrian god Hadad. Psalm 28 may have been inspired by old Canaanite hymns to this latter god,[3] but a single sentence in the conclusion is enough to bring us back to the strictly historical perspective of Mosaic religion: "The Lord will give strength to his people". This is not, perhaps, a great deal, but with it the evocation of the storm assumes a new significance; it is no longer a question of the force of the tempest alone, but of the help brought by a God who is mightier than the universe and overthrows everything in his path:

> The voice of the Lord is upon the waters. . .
> The voice of the Lord breaketh the cedars:
> yea, the Lord shall break the cedars of Libanus,
> and shall reduce them to pieces:
> as a calf of Libanus,
> and as the beloved son of unicorns . . .
> The voice of the Lord shaketh the desert.

Thunder, especially, offers a most expressive image of this irresistible power of Yahweh. Before the commotion occurs, Someone speaks: "At his voice he giveth a multitude of waters in the heavens" (Jer. 10. 13; cf. 51. 16). "Canst thou lift up thy voice to the clouds, that an abundance of waters may cover thee?" (Job 38. 34). Like a lion about to emerge from the jungle, Yahweh roars;[4] before riding on the storm-wind of the south, he sounds the trumpet (Zach. 9. 14), he raises his voice at the head of his army (Joel 2. 11). People flee before this ominous warning of judgement (Is. 33. 3) and the earth sinks into a deep, liturgical silence (Ps. 75. 9), as it awaits

[1] On the subject of these hierophanies, see Eliade, *Patterns in Comparative Religion*, London, 1958, ch. 1: "The Structure and Morphology of the Sacred".
[2] See Eichrodt, *Theologie des Alten Testaments*, Berlin, 1948–50, vol. 2, p. 2.
[3] See De Vaux's critique of Fr Castellino's thesis, in *R.B.*, 1946, p. 158. It may be noted, however, that in the same review Fr Tournay puts forward a point of view which we find difficult to accept.
[4] Amos 1.2; 3.8; Jer. 25.30; Joel 3.16.

universal destruction: "He uttered his voice, the earth
trembled" (Ps. 45. 7).

Announcing Yahweh's entry upon the scene, the thunder
peals out with a voice as imperious as it is awe-inspiring
(Is. 30. 30). The atmospheric phenomena which ensue are
sufficient to prove that nothing can resist his might. For the
storm appears to challenge the very stability of the universe
itself; and we may note, in this connexion, that the ancients
seem to have been unable to define its effects with any precision, and that, quite spontaneously, all known cataclysms
were included, such as earthquakes, volcanic eruptions, tidal
waves, etc.:

> Lord, bow down thy heavens and descend:
> touch the mountains, and they shall smoke.
> Send forth lightning, and thou shalt scatter them! (Ps.
>   143. 5-6; cf. 103. 32).
> The earth shook and trembled:
> the foundations of the mountains were troubled and were
>   moved . . .
> And the Lord thundered from heaven,
> and the Highest gave his voice . . .
> And he sent forth his arrows, and he scattered them.
> Then the fountains of waters appeared,
> and the foundations of the world were discovered:
> at thy rebuke, O Lord,
> at the blast of the spirit of thy wrath (Ps. 17. 8–16).
> The Lord's ways are in a tempest, and a whirlwind:
> and clouds are the dust of his feet.
> He rebuketh the sea and drieth it up
> and bringeth all the rivers to be a desert.
> Basan languisheth and Carmel:
> and the flower of Libanus fadeth away.
> The mountains tremble at him (Nahum 1. 3–5).

Certainly one should not try and discover in these images
any precise evocation of specific cosmic disturbances; the idea
alone is what counts: a God who upsets all that lies in his
path is on his way. Besides, the theophanies tend less and less

to act as a setting for the particular, localized facts of Israelite history, and more and more as a prelude to the great phases in the divine plan, the creation, the Exodus, even the crossing of the Jordan:

> The waters saw thee, O God,
> the waters saw thee: and they were afraid,
> and the depths were troubled.
> Great was the noise of the waters:
> the clouds sent out a sound.
> For thy arrows pass:
> the voice of thy thunder in a wheel.
> Thy lightnings enlightened the world:
> the earth shook and trembled.
> Thy way is in the sea,
> and thy paths in many waters:
> and thy footsteps shall not be known.
> Thou hast conducted thy people like sheep,
> by the hand of Moses and Aaron (Ps. 76. 17–21).[1]

The storm which here precedes the actual Exodus (according to v. 20, it would seem at first to have been a question of the Creation) thus appears as the usual, almost necessary sign of any important intervention of God in history: everything is pushed aside in order to let him pass, nothing can withstand his presence.

In order to demonstrate conclusively the absolute, universal power of this God who comes to the assistance of Israel, the discussion would have to be given an even wider basis of reference: to the terrestial upheavals caused by the great storm would have to be added the fall of the stars, immortalized as gods by the Babylonians. It is true that earlier writers had mentioned the stars which, in the tempest, fought on behalf of Israel,[2] but the ancients, on the whole, saw in the starry vault the very mark of stability, and, to express the concept

[1] Cf. Ps. 113.3–4.

[2] Judges 5.20. In fact "certain stars were thought by the Babylonians, and are still thought by the Arabs, to bring rain". Lods, A., *Israël, des origines au milieu du VIII*[e] *siècle*, Paris, 1949.

of eternal duration, the formula: "As long as the heaven hangeth over the earth" (Deut. 11. 21) was employed, a formula which will be found in the royal psalms and which was customary in court language.[1] It is precisely this stability which is challenged, after the Exile, in the books written in apocalyptic vein, when the well-known phenomenon of the stars darkening[2] will assume the proportions of a catastrophic collapse of the heavens.[3] Thus, in face of the devastating invasion of locusts, "the earth hath trembled, the heavens are moved", while "the sun and moon are darkened, and the stars have withdrawn their shining" (Joel 2. 10). So the primitive tempest of biblical theophanies becomes an explosion of generalized cosmic upheavals: "Yet one little while, and I will move the heaven and the earth, and the sea, and the dry land. And I will move all nations: and the desired of all nations shall come" (Aggeus 2. 7–8). "I will move both heaven and earth. And I will overthrow the throne of kingdoms, and will destroy the strength of the kingdom of the Gentiles" (ib. 2. 22–3).

As can be seen by this last example, the cosmic perturbation is on the same scale of greatness as the divine intervention: the whole universe is implicated because the judgement will be exercised against all the nations of the earth. It may also be noted that, in apocalyptic eschatology, these accumulated earthquakes form, as it were, a sum-total of all past theophanies, in exactly the same way as the final intervention by Yahweh recapitulates the whole historic exploit of the God of Israel. Thus, in Ezechiel's poem on Gog, king of Magog, all the scourges and cataclysms which marked the stages in the destiny of the people of the Covenant are gathered together in a single, comprehensive experience: "The fishes of the sea, and the birds of the air, and the beasts of the field, and every creeping thing that creepeth upon the ground, and all men that are upon the face of the earth, shall be moved

---

[1] Ps. 71.5; 88.38; cf. this promise made by an Egyptian god: "I grant thee years unto eternity, as long as the heavens shall subsist, such shall be thy name", text quoted by Podechard, *Le Psautier*, p. 311.

[2] Hab. 3.11; Is. 13.10; Ez. 32.7; Joel 3.15 (=4.15); Job 9.7.

[3] Is. 13.13; 34.4.

8

at my presence: and the mountains shall be thrown down, and the hedges shall fall, and every wall shall fall to the ground. And I will call in the sword against him in all my mountains . . . And I will judge him with pestilence and with blood and with violent rain and vast hailstones: I will rain fire and brimstone upon him" (Ez. 38. 20–3). And, it is perfectly true, the invasion by Gog and the final combat which is prophesied form a general review of the whole history of Israel, the final struggle against the assembled nations representing a synthesis of all the wars that God's people had had to endure; here is the culmination of all that had been announced by the prophets in the course of the preceding centuries: "Thou then art he, of whom I have spoken in the days of old, by my servants the prophets of Israel, who prophesied in the days of those times that I would bring thee upon them" (ib. 38. 17).[1]

There is the key to these universal cosmic catastrophes which all apocalypses depict in so solemn and fearful a manner: they are essentially the final manifestation of the God who formerly came in thunder and tempest, and whose supreme intervention now involves the whole of creation:

> For the flood-gates from on high are opened,
> and the foundations of the earth shall be shaken.
> With breaking shall the earth be broken,
> with crushing shall the earth be crushed,
> with trembling shall the earth be moved.
> With shaking shall the earth be shaken as a drunken man,
> and shall be removed as the tent of one night (Is. 24. 18–20).

This is but the description of an enormously magnified storm, which conveys, on a much vaster scale, the same notion as the primitive theophanies: when he intervenes in history, God asserts himself to be stronger than the world, by laying waste all that lies in his path.

[1] This would appear to be a reference to the oracles of Sophonias and Jeremias concerning the coming invasion of Israel from the North.

The universe, its revealing and concealing of God

God shows himself to mankind by demonstrating his superiority over the universe, and marks his intervention by making all things flee before him:

> The sea saw and fled:
> Jordan was turned back.
> The mountains skipped like rams,
> and the hills like the lambs of the flock . . .
> At the presence of the Lord the earth was moved,
> at the presence of the God of Jacob (Ps. 113. 3–7).

Nature thus reveals the presence of God just as a herd of animals may, by their behaviour, indicate the approach of the huntsman. Even though one may not actually see who comes to disturb the normal order of things, his presence is impossible to deny. Thus the universe makes the all-powerful action of the master keenly felt, without, however, allowing his countenance to be seen. In the earliest texts, for example, Yahweh arrives from the south, hidden behind the clouds which bear him along. Later, when he is firmly established in heaven, he comes down, still without revealing himself, by lowering beneath him the thick ceiling of clouds:

> He bowed the heavens, and came down:
> and darkness was under his feet.
> And he ascended upon the cherubim, and he flew:
> he flew upon the wings of the winds.
> And he made darkness his covert,
> his pavilion round about him (Ps. 17. 10–12).

It is the clouds which both reveal and screen the presence of the God of heaven; if they are lowered earthwards, this indicates that the Almighty is drawing close, ensuring, however, that he is still covered. We may note that this cloud theme, while it retains throughout the Bible its general significance, may appear in a different light according to different theological points of view. In the Yahwistic tradition of the

Pentateuch, Yahweh makes use of the clouds to fly to the assistance of his elect; in the Elohistic tradition, in which heaven is shown to be his fixed abode, he descends in a cloud in order to enter upon a dialogue with them: "And when he was gone into the tabernacle of the covenant, the pillar of the cloud came down, and stood at the door and he spoke with Moses" (Ex. 33. 9). "And the Lord came down in a cloud, and spoke to him" (Num. 11. 25). "The Lord came down in a pillar of the cloud, and stood in the entry of the tabernacle, calling to Aaron and Mary" (ib. 12. 5). For the authors of the priestly account of the Exodus, the cloud was no longer to figure in the dialogue between man and the God of heaven, its new role would be to provide the means whereby God's glory could rest on the ark; instead of standing at the entrance of the tent where the "meeting" would take place, it would remain above and cover it: "The cloud covered the tabernacle of the testimony, and the glory of the Lord filled it" (Ex. 40. 32). "For the cloud of the Lord hung over the tabernacle by day, and a fire by night, in the sight of all the children of Israel throughout all their mansions" (ib. v. 36).

In this last example can be seen how light and darkness together accompany the manifestation of the God of Israel: "And when Moses was gone up, a cloud covered the mount. And the glory of the Lord dwelt upon Sinai, covering it with a cloud six days: and the seventh day he called him out of the midst of the cloud. And the sight of the glory of the Lord was like a burning fire upon the top of the mount, in the eyes of the children of Israel" (Ex. 24. 15–17). But light and darkness both have the same significance: a presence is made manifest but must remain hidden. In fact, a centre of light may well illuminate without allowing itself to be watched by the naked eye, and, in the vision of Ezechiel, it is a fire which marks the spot occupied by Yahweh (Ez. 1. 27). Psalm 103, taking as its starting-point a similar intuition, shows how God is clothed with light as a garment, an idea which is echoed in the psalm of Habacuc: "His brightness shall be as the light: horns are in his hands: there is his strength hid" (Hab. 3. 4).

The cloud is not alone, of course, in making us aware of the active presence of this God who insists on remaining concealed. A psalmist attributes these words, for example, to Yahweh: "I heard thee in the secret place of tempest" (Ps. 80. 8). Generally speaking, the whole universe both reveals and screens from view the master of history; for Yahweh is everywhere manifested as he who sees without being seen: "If to the left hand, what shall I do? I shall not take hold on him: if I turn myself to the right hand, I shall not see him. But he knoweth my way" (Job 23. 9–10). So when he hurries to the assistance of his friends, he remains the "holy one", the "different" one, over whom no one can ever gain the advantage. The universe enables him to approach his elect, but places between him and them an impassable barrier; it enables him to share extensively in the intimate life of mortals, yet maintains an infinite distance between them.

B. THE CREATION, A PRELUDE TO THE MYSTERY OF SALVATION[1]

The inspired writers never evoked the creation for its own sake, independently of the Covenant which Yahweh had concluded with his people. The first page of Genesis, which always comes to mind when the creation is mentioned, does not in fact claim to do more than suggest the great themes on which rests the whole history of Israel: the progress towards the light, the search for a refuge which the storms of the proud and raging sea will no longer smite. This is the first image with which the Bible opens, and it will be the last, when darkness and chaos will have at last given way to the mountain of peace where night is unknown (Apoc. 22. 5), to the new land which will have no ocean to threaten its stability (id. 21. 1).

Are the Christians of to-day truly aware that their faith implies this definite vision of the universe which encompasses them? Do they fully realize that the God of the Bible is quite other than a remote, indifferent agent who merely gave

[1] Article published in *La Vie spirituelle*, April, 1958.

things their initial flick into existence? That he is, on the other hand, the master who, with the same gesture, in the pursuance of a single plan and the fulfilment of a single word, guides at one and the same time the universe and the course of history? He who will spread, for example, the light of Easter morning over the whole of creation, just as he had at the beginning brought the first ray of light out over the darkness of the abyss? Thus universe and history are seen to have the same starting-point, and to be converging towards the same end: the whole work is opened with the same alpha, and is closed with the same omega. Man, therefore, by contemplating the gradual organization of the cosmos, can have some inkling of what is to be his own destiny, and the various aspects of the great act of creation will appear to him as the splendid prelude to the history of his salvation.

Light and creation

Everything begins in darkness and everything ends in light. The transition from darkness to light initiates the work of the Creator before characterizing that of the Redeemer.

God said "Be light made. And light was made." There we have the first word, the first act of the Creator.[1] For a long time now, astonishment has been felt that the Bible should show light as appearing before the creation of the stars. The sacred writer, however, is no more ignorant of the source that gives the light of day (Gen. 1. 15), than are his contemporaries (see, for example, Jer. 31. 35). It is not, therefore, an inaccuracy on his part, either in the scientific order[2] or in the realm of everyday observation of natural phenomena. It was therefore quite deliberately that he showed light as appearing first, since he did not envisage it as really forming part of the series of created things; it is first, because, with its emergence, the whole is invested with meaning; all that God undertakes will be enveloped in light. This is how it is presented to us in

[1] The first verse: "In the beginning God created heaven, and earth" does not describe a single, first act of the Creator, but sums up the whole of the work that follows.

[2] Concordists will not, in fact, fail to remark that modern science teaches that the radiation of light precedes the formation of the stars.

Psalm 103, which is commonly assumed to be a poetic development of the first chapter of Genesis: "Thou hast put on
praise and beauty: and art clothed with light as with a garment.
Who stretchest out the heaven like a pavilion"(1–2).

The Book of Job will reveal the deep significance of this
general superiority of light over all created things. God
himself explains how there is in light a suggestion of the justice
which the Almighty will one day cause to reign undisputed
over the world:

> Didst thou since thy birth command the morning,
> and shew the dawning of the day its place?
> And didst thou hold the extremities of the earth shaking
> them?
> And hast thou shaken the ungodly out of it? . . .
> From the wicked their light shall be taken away:
> and the high arm shall be broken" (Job 38. 12–15).

Just like Wisdom, or the Word itself, light evokes an
orientation of the whole creative purpose, and only quite
secondarily a particular phenomenon; its appearance on the
very threshold of creation gives an indication of the significance
of the divine work in its entirety.

We use the term "orientation", because light and darkness
do not, in fact, represent two realities which may be placed
on the same plane: the transition from one to another is an
irreversible stage forward, a promotion to a new state. God
does, indeed, give a name both to the day and to the night;
but, whereas day receives a name which ratifies its "election"
—it alone is said to be good—God imposes upon night a
name which registers the first divine victory over the rule of
darkness, a victory which each morning will recall, until night
shall at last, in a new heaven and a new earth, give way
completely to a dawn which knows no setting.

In the curse which he utters against the day of his birth,
Job clearly and strikingly sets forth this scale of values; he
goes to the extent of wishing to thrust back into darkness the

ray of light whose brilliance has proved to be so cruelly
disappointing to him:

> Let that day be turned into darkness . . .
> and let not the light shine upon it.
> Let darkness, and the shadow of death cover it . . .
> Let a darksome whirlwind seize upon that night . . .
> Let the stars be darkened with the mist thereof:
> let it expect light and not see it,
> nor the rising of the dawning of the day (Job 3. 4–9).

Light and the destiny of man

With the "darkness–light" antithesis, there is a rapid
transition from the plane of cosmic realities to that of historical
events. "The darkness–light dichotomy will become a constant in the history of the chosen people: the major phases of
salvation, those in which God most impressively and solemnly
intervenes, are all represented as a passing from darkness
into light: whether it be the going up out of Egypt under the
protection of the cloud, which is dark for some and luminous
for others, or the return from exile, or, again, the coming of
the Messias or the setting up of the final, eschatological
kingdom, all these stages on the road to salvation are presented
as a more and more effective deliverance from darkness and a
more and more active organization of light."[1]

This darkness–light dichotomy is, indeed, more often than
not represented in the Bible as symbolizing the opposition
between the contraries, anguish and happiness: "I expected
good things, and evils are come upon me: I waited for light,
and darkness broke out" (Job 30. 26). "I form the light, and
create darkness, I make peace, and create evil" (Is. 45. 7).
From Amos onwards, the prospect of approaching darkness,
a portent of misfortunes to come, constantly obscures the
horizon for God's people: "Shall not the day of the Lord be
darkness, and not light: and obscurity, and no brightness in
it?"[2] "And it shall come to pass in that day, saith the Lord

[1] Maertens, *Les Sept Jours (Gn. 1)*, Bruges, 1951, p. 16.
[2] Amos 5.20; cf. Soph. 1.15-17; Joel 2.2; Jer. 13.16, etc.

God, that the sun shall go down at mid-day, and I will make the earth dark in the day of light: and I will turn your feasts into mourning."[1] Darkness leads, naturally enough, to the idea of sorrow, disease and all the difficulties lying in man's path (Eccl. 5. 16). But, in the Bible, it evokes more precisely a black tunnel, dread (in the strongest sense of the word), the ruin of all hope, a blankness for the future; it is the deep night when the lamp has been quenched (Prov. 20. 20). "Sit thou silent and get thee into darkness" (Is. 47. 5). "They have laid me in the lower pit: in the dark places, and in the shadow of death . . . and my acquaintance is nothing but darkness" (Ps. 87. 7, 19 Hebrew). Finally, darkness is equated with death: "Before I go, and return no more, to a land that is dark and covered with the mist of death: a land of misery and darkness, where the shadow of death, and no order, but everlasting horror dwelleth" (Job 10. 21–22).

But, with light, hope is reborn: "Arise, be enlightened, O Jerusalem: for thy light is come" (Is. 60. 1). And the mere sight of a burning lamp is sufficient to evoke the idea of a long line of descendants;[2] if it were to be extinguished, then with it would disappear the cries of joy and songs of mirth, the voices of bride and bridegroom and the sound of the mill turning (Jer. 25. 10). For, in Israel, as on the banks of the Nile in the times of the Pharaohs, light brings with it the chance of life: "Because thou hast delivered my soul from death, my feet from falling: that I may please in the sight of God, in the light of the living" (Ps. 55. 13). "For with thee is the fountain of life: and in thy light we shall see light" (Ps. 35. 10).[3]

We should, however, note that, in general, the sacred writers are not particularly interested in the brightness of light as such; what strikes them above all is its sudden apparition in the depths of night, its emergence from the darkness: "To

[1] Amos 8.9–10; cf. Micheas 3.6; Is. 5.30; 8.20–22; 13.10; Ez. 30.18; 32.7; Joel 2.31(=3.4); 3.15(=4.15); etc.

[2] For the "lamp of David", see 3 Kings 11.36; 15.4; 4 Kings 8.19; Ps. 131.17.

[3] For the comparison between light and life, see especially Job 3.20; 18.18; 33.28; 38.15. For the fountain of life, cf. Ecclus 21.16 (=21.13); Jer. 2.13. Note that the apocalypse of the Book of Isaias speaks of "the dew of the light" when referring to the resurrection (26.19).

the righteous a light is risen up in darkness" (Ps. 111. 4).
"Because his soul hath laboured, he shall see and be filled"
(Is. 53. 11). "Thy light shall rise up in darkness, and thy
darkness shall be as the noon-day" (Is. 58. 10; cf. Job 11. 17).
The Bible is especially aware of the anguished wait of nature
for the first gleams of dawn; here, more than anywhere else,
the impression remains that, to be saved, one has only to hold
out until early dawn: "The burden of Duma calleth to me
out of Seir: Watchman, what of the night? Watchman, what
of the night?" (Is. 21. 11). "My soul looks towards the Lord,
more eagerly than the watchmen look for the morning" (Ps.
129, 5–6).[1] In the evening, terror reigned at the sight of
countless armies besieging the town; with the coming of dawn,
everything has gone, like a dream that vanishes with the
night (Is. 17. 14; 29. 7). For Yahweh will help his city "in
the morning early" (Ps. 45. 6), at the hour when, normally,
he bestows liberally his graces[2] and when, in exchange, man
utters his joyful thanksgiving.[3]

The explanation of such a yearning for light should not be
sought in comparisons with the romantic destiny of a Byron
or in dreams of the enchanting colours of the East.[4] What
interests the people of God is simply the opportunity to march
forward, and for this it is necessary to see clearly. No doubt, like
all Orientals, the sons of Abraham are not insensitive to anything that shines, and Yahweh makes himself manifest to them
in brilliance as well as in noise: "His glory covered the heavens:
and the earth is full of his praise. His brightness shall be as the
light: horns are in his hands" (Hab. 3. 3–4). But, generally
speaking, the biblical theme of light remains closely associated
with the obsession of a march which has to be accomplished:
here light serves essentially to show the way (Prov. 4. 18; Job 29.
3; Ps. 42. 3). To gain convincing proof of this, one has merely
to take at random a few examples from the Book of Isaias alone:

---

[1] (Translator's note: Hebrew version).
[2] Is. 8.20; 33.2; Lam. 3.23; Ps. 16.15; 29.6; 89.6,14; 142.8.
[3] Ps. 5.4; 56.9; 91.3; 107.3.
[4] See the article in *Bible et Vie Chrétienne* entitled: "Poésie et sens de la nature dans la Bible" (No. 11, 1955, pp. 25–32, and *infra*, chap. V, A, p. 147).

Let us walk in the light of the Lord (2. 5).
The people that walked in darkness
have seen a great light (9. 2).
And I will lead the blind into the way which they know not:
and in the paths which they were ignorant of I will make
them walk:
I will make darkness light before them,
and crooked things straight (42. 16).
We looked for light, and behold darkness:
brightness, and we have walked in the dark.
We have groped for the wall,
and like the blind we have groped as if we had no eyes.
We have stumbled at noonday as in darkness (59. 9–10).[1]

The anguish of heart and mind provoked by the darkness arises
from the fear of stumbling, of losing balance, of falling without
the possibility of rising again, a fear which is echoed, for
example, in so many psalms:

The way of the wicked is darksome:
they know not where they fall (Prov. 4. 19).
Give ye glory to the Lord your God,
before it be dark,
and before your feet stumble
upon the dark mountains (Jer. 13. 16).

"Walk whilst you have the light", the Lord will say later
(John 12. 35); for if the Creator brought the world out of its
profound darkness, it was precisely so that one day humanity
might clearly see its way towards eternity: "Thou (Jerusalem)
shalt shine with a glorious light: and all the ends of the earth
shall worship thee. Nations from afar shall come to thee . . .
and shall adore the Lord in thee" (Tobias 13. 13–14).

Earth and water in the work of creation

Just as he causes light to emerge from darkness, God seeks,
all through his work, to establish solid ground which will
resist the assaults of the raging oceans. What he creates will,

[1] See also, for example, Deut. 28.29; Job 5.14; Soph. 1.17; Lam. 3.2; 4.14.

therefore, possess substance as well as luminosity, and he will bring everything from chaos to peace in the same way as he brings everything from darkness to daylight.

The restless, aimless ferment of the sea, like darkness itself, represents an initial state of non-organization which might be taken as an image of total nothingness:[1] "The earth was wasteland and desert, and darkness was upon the face of the deep, and the breath of God beat upon the surface of the waters" (Gen. 1. 2).[2] But, after making a solid vault arise in between the two masses of water, God said: "Let the waters that are under the heaven, be gathered together into one place: and let the dry land appear. And it was so done. And God called the dry land, Earth; and the gathering together of the waters, he called Seas" (ib. 9–10). This apparition of dry ground constitutes the first victory of God over the proud might of the oceans. From now on, these will be held fast with bolt and bar, doubly secured; since breaking forth from the womb, they had never ceased to be aggressive and impetuous (Job 38. 8) and now they are limited by frontiers of sand (Jer. 5. 22). Their waves remain, a menace to the newly formed mainland, as the story of the flood will soon clearly demonstrate, and they will continue to hold a threat over the work of the Creator until a new earth is created, where the sea is no more (Apoc. 21. 1). Meanwhile, God will keep incessant watch: "Am I a sea, or a whale, that thou hast enclosed me in a prison?" (Job 7. 12).

[1] As it stands, this might give the impression that there was something pre-existent to the act of the Creator. But, in prefacing his whole description with the statement: "In the beginning God created heaven, and earth", the writer presumably wished to forestall such an interpretation. Furthermore, other inspired writers (see Ps. 103, for example) clearly state that the abyss and the monsters that live there were, in fact, created by God.

[2] We adopt here the translation and exegesis of Dom Maertens (*op. cit.*, p. 22): "The interpreters who consider God's breath over the primeval waters to have exercised a vivifying action have yet to prove their point. We have not seen convincing proof of this, and we prefer to see, in the divine *rûah* or breath of v. 2, the storm which, sweeping the surface of the waters, heightens the sombre colours of the author's picture. Besides, the parallel development of Hebraic style requires that to the words 'darkness was upon the face of the deep' should correspond a similar descriptive member: 'the breath of God beat upon the surface of the waters'; the darkness is balanced by the storm."

In the same way as darkness and light are not two realities to be placed on a similar footing, so there is a scale of values to observe when referring to sea and land. The transition from one to another denotes that a decisive stage has been passed; as in the emergence of light, the apparition of the dry land represents a step up. It is not without a certain degree of solemnity that the Creator issues the command: "Let the dry land appear." As Dom Maertens observes: "One may wonder whether the author has not used the jussive in his narration in order to mark in some way the solemnity of the divine audiences: as if the dry land were to present itself before the countenance of God to obtain his blessings and graces, just as the pilgrims will in the temple of Jerusalem."[1]

All the peoples of Antiquity, from Egypt to Sumer, had undoubtedly seen in water the most primitive of the elements, the one on which the world had been built. The essential originality of the Bible, in this matter, was to give this perfectly normal representation a deep significance which had hitherto never been suspected. Transcending the ancient cosmogonies, it had discovered the true significance of creation: the universe is not destined, any more than history, to be the prey of disorderly agitation; chaos must of necessity give way to peace.

Firm foundations for the history of mankind

Yahweh, who founded the earth upon the waters, also willed to give his holy city, Sion, equally solid foundations, so that it might become a sort of Noah's ark, capable of withstanding the most terrible floods: "The Lord hath founded Sion, and the poor of his people shall hope in him" (Is. 14. 32). This holy mountain, facing the north wind (Ps. 47. 3), will stand firm against all storms, for God dwells within (Ps. 45. 6), and has built there his indestructible sanctuary: "And there he built his sanctuary, immovable as heaven or earth, his own unchanging handiwork" (Ps. 77. 69).[2] Gathered together in this city, around this temple, Israel will have nothing to

[1] *Les Sept Jours*, p. 40.   [2] (Translator's Note: Knox version).

fear for the future; it is as if it had itself become a foundation of Yahweh, "the house of the Lord".[1] And, whereas the "daughters of Moab" are like young birds flying from a nest (Is. 16. 2), Israel, on the other hand, is like "an undisturbed dwelling-place . . . tent securely fixed, its pegs immoveable" (Is. 33. 20).[2] The assaults of history will never, therefore, prevail against Israel, always provided it builds on the rock of Yahweh; but if it sought protection elsewhere, it would very soon totter and topple over (Ps. 59. 4), as if it had drunk too heady a wine (Jer. 25. 27).

The existence of individuals, like the life of nations (see Ez. 30. 4), presupposes solid foundations which ensure that it shall continue: "My generation is at an end, and it is rolled away from me, as a shepherd's tent" (Is. 38. 12), groaned Ezechias on his sick-bed; a psalmist can beseech Yahweh to destroy his enemies and not build them up again (Ps. 27. 5), whilst Isaias can promise a certain royal official that he shall be securely fixed "as a peg in a sure place" (Is. 22. 23). For every worthy Israelite, the true house is the family whose fertility guarantees the duration of the name; for David, a lineage which Yahweh guarantees shall always rule in his holy city (2 Kings 7. 11). As Yahweh had built the world with wisdom (Pr. 8. 22–31), so it is with wisdom that kings shall build the State, and through wisdom (for example, the judicious choice of a wife) that the just shall build themselves a house (Pr. 9. 1; 14. 1).

In any case, no life is possible in the eddy of winds or waves; whether collective or individual, existence has need of an anchor, and all beings seek permanent installation: "And I will appoint a place for my people Israel, and I will plant them, and they shall dwell therein, and shall be disturbed no more" (2 Kings 7. 10). The fugitive who has neither fatherland nor home, like a bird without its nest, is considered to have been cursed.[3] The history of humanity must, therefore,

---

[1] Osee 8.1; 9.15; Jer. 12.7; Zach. 9.8.
[2] (Translator's note: Knox version).
[3] Gen. 4.14; 4 Kings 21.8; Ps. 58.12; 108.10.

have as solid a foundation as that which was originally secured for the earth; thus Israel rises from the waters of the Red Sea and goes up towards the sanctuary which its God, with his own hands, has prepared for it (Ex. 15).

The threat of the deep

The frenzied assault of the waves constantly tests the solidity of the continents; races and individuals alike have to face the storms of history, storms which threaten to drag into the deep, not only their present existence, but all chances of survival. Speaking of Tyre on its rock, it seems perfectly natural that Yahweh should speak of bringing wave upon wave from the sea to overthrow her towers (Ez. 26. 3). But, in fact, nothing and no one can be proof against a triumphant upsurging of the deep sea, unless protected, like Jerusalem, by the presence of the Almighty: "Therefore we will not fear, when the earth shall be troubled; and the mountains shall be removed into the heart of the sea. Their waters roared and were troubled: the mountains were troubled with his strength" (Ps. 45, 3–4).

A sea which has burst its dikes—that is what the armies are like which, since the beginning of history, have never ceased to make their assaults on ancient empires, consigning famous cities to oblivion: "I will cause many nations to come up to thee, as the waves of the sea rise up" (Ez. 26. 3). Roaring like the sea, the barbarians hurl themselves in attack upon Babylon (Jer. 50. 42); and it is this sinister rumbling which Jerusalem was to hear on the day when the invincible armies of Assur were unleashed upon her territory: "Wo to the multitude of many people, like the multitude of the roaring sea: and the tumult of crowds, like the noise of many waters" (Is. 17. 12). For, in order to escape from the coalition of Samaria and Damascus, Achaz, king of Jerusalem, neglecting the protection of his God (the peaceful waters of Siloe) had been rash enough to appeal for help to the king of Assyria (the immense River Euphrates). Like the sorcerer's apprentice, he was to open flood-gates of gigantic proportions which neither he nor his successors could ever again control: "Therefore behold the Lord will bring upon them the waters of the river, strong and many, the king of the Assyrians, and all his glory: and he shall come up over all his channels, and shall overthrow all his banks" (Is. 8. 7).

The same threat of a triumphant sea hovers as much over the destiny of individuals as over that of nations. If he wishes to depict the misfortunes of Job, his friend will speak of an unexpected flood which has overwhelmed all (Job 22. 11); likewise, the forsaken psalmist will lament: "Thy wrath hath come upon me: and thy terrors have troubled me. They have come round about me like water all the day: they have compassed me about together" (Ps. 87. 17–18).[1] Here, equilibrium is no longer possible; the house is swept away and the ground crumbles; like the prophet floundering in the filth of his dungeon, one has lost balance (Jer. 38. 6). How then can one continue the march forward? Why, the Lord undertakes to raise up those poor servants of his who have sunk deep in the mire, to set them with his own hand on dry ground: "He brought me out of the pit of misery and the mire of dregs. And he set my feet upon a rock, and directed my steps" (Ps. 39. 3).[2]

To leave thus the shifting waters of the deep in order to walk steadily on solid ground, is equivalent to following in the direction of the great creative work, or, as we should say to-day, in the direction of history. On the other hand, it would be an act of despair, a renunciation of the impulse, of the dynamism that God has implanted in his whole work, if one were to let oneself be carried away, if one were to melt, like the mountains which dissolve away beneath the feet of the Almighty, "as wax before the fire, and as waters that run down a steep place" (Micheas 1. 4). Spilt water that runs away without any hope of its ever returning, is a symbol of

---

[1] Cf. Ps. 17.17; 31.6; 41.8; 68.2; 123.4; 129.1; 143.7; Lam. 3.54; Jonas 2.6.
[2] Similar images will be found in Ps. 17.34; 26.6; 41.10; 60.3.

what has disappeared for ever: "We all die, and like waters that return no more, we fall down into the earth" (2 Kings 14. 14). "I am poured out like water; and all my bones are scattered. My heart is become like wax melting in the midst of my bowels" (Ps. 21. 15).[1] To this is opposed the stout heart (Ps. 56. 8), in which can be seen man's determination to share in the upward movement of the universe and of history.

Towards the peace of the mountain

When the flood rises, everyone, of course, thinks of reaching a safe height, for from there the mounting waters can be watched without immediate danger. In the Bible, Yahweh alone must be considered to be this rock of safety which the swollen waters can never cover (Ps. 31. 6). His holy mountain will, in fact, resist all assaults. Just as it broke the attack of Sennacherib's invincible troops, so will it one day bring crashing down the pride of a world which has had the audacity to unite against Israel and its God (Ez. 38–39; Zach. 14).

Built on rock (Is. 33. 16), this fortress will hold firm even when all has collapsed around it. Therefore, all the faithful of Yahweh go up towards it as to the only refuge which cannot be touched by the swirling tide of history, and they never cease to dream of establishing their permanent dwelling on it (Ps. 14. 1; 23. 3; etc.). This fact, we may note, is peculiar to the religion of Israel; for the sacred mountains of Antiquity remained the exclusive dwelling-place of the gods, and there was never any question of man's setting foot there. But the hill of Sion seems, on the contrary, to have been built especially to accommodate those who had placed their trust in the God of Israel and to provide a safe welcome to those who had survived the great floods. The chosen people, dispersed among the Gentiles, will keep their eyes constantly turned in this direction, hoping eventually to be gathered there for ever, and to regain there strength and life itself: "In that day, saith the Lord, I will gather up her that halteth: and her that I had cast out, I will gather up: and her whom I had afflicted.

[1] For the image of the melting heart, cf. Josue 2.11; 5.1; 7.5; 14.8; Deut. 1.28.

And I will make her that halted, a remnant, and her that hath been afflicted, a mighty nation: and the Lord will reign over them in mount Sion" (Micheas 4. 6–7).

After so many shocks and setbacks, Israel will obtain on Sion that well-deserved rest, so long promised (see Psalm 94. 11), and so long awaited. On this summit, Israel's adventure will reach its conclusion, an end to all anguish, failure and humiliation. This people, a victim of sufferings and calamities to a greater degree, so it seemed, than all other races put together, had surely the undisputed right to conceive, before the rest of mankind, a vast plan for universal disarmament. For it is on Israel's mountain that swords shall be fashioned into ploughshares, and spears into sickles (Micheas 4. 3); it is here that the great bonfire of peace shall be lit and shall, for seven years, burn up all the weapons of war that have ever been made (Ez. 39. 9).

Nor is it the tortured destiny of Israel alone that will thus reach its fulfilment in the peace of mount Sion; the whole world will come and seek upon this hill a worthy conclusion to its history. For, from all the corners of the universe, people shall look towards this holy place where evil no longer exists, where not even one single animal dares eat the flesh of another (Is. 11. 9); and every nation shall set out towards its light: "And in the last days the mountain of the house of the Lord shall be prepared on the top of mountains, and it shall be exalted above the hills, and all nations shall flow unto it" (Is. 2. 2).

The reader will, no doubt, have felt that, behind this vision of a cosmos and a history on the march forward, lies something more than a mere poetic flight of fancy. Although it is built up on the inadequate material which is all the ancients had at their disposal when they observed natural phenomena, this panoramic view of the divine work, in which the compelling force of the universe and the religious destiny of men are so simply yet so strongly merged, reaches a depth of intuition which the most modern cosmologies can never question;

one may find the cosmogonies of Babylon or Egypt irritating or merely amusing, but no one would think of smiling or protesting when faced with the Bible's assertion that God draws everything together, out of darkness into light and from the storm-racked surge of the sea to the peace of the mountain.

Christian tradition in no way sought to abandon such vistas. If one reads the prologue to the gospel of St John, the opening salutations of the captivity Epistles, or the first anaphoras and hymns of the primitive Church, it is impossible to avoid the conclusion that there exists but one divine plan, which reaches its fullness in the light and peace of the resurrection. As St Justin pointed out,[1] the Church has always desired to unite in the one eucharist the creation of the world and the redemption of mankind.

Associated thus closely with the mystery of salvation, the universe assumes a direction and a significance; it is not condemned, as was the belief among the civilizations of Antiquity, to the ever recurrent crises of an eternal cycle. For, in revealing to the world a voice which is not of the world, the Bible has fired with the same impulse both the universe and man who lives in it, in order to urge them forward together towards a light and a peace which they will find only at some point beyond.

Here will be recognized the major themes of the Paschal liturgy; we shall not have wasted our time if these few pages help to give us something on which to meditate in the course of this Easter night. Shall we admit to something more ambitious than this? Might not one dream that, in an age of artificial satellites, above all at a time when life is beginning to reveal a few of the secrets of its history, Christians should be learning to hear in nature, as in a sort of grand Wagnerian prelude, the principal themes of the coming of God's kingdom, and that they should keep Christ and his Church constantly before them in their vision of the world? For nature should not be for them merely the clock that presupposes the hand of

[1] *Dialogue with Trypho*, XLI, I.

the clock-maker, it should rather be the garden which everywhere reveals the parables of the Kingdom.

"All things were created by him and in him: and he is before all, and by him all things consist" (Col. 1. 16–17).

IV

THE UNIVERSE, A GIFT FROM THE GOD OF HISTORY

A SENSE of what history really is, gives us a new vision of the universe, which henceforth shows itself to be a sign of Yahweh's loving concern for his elect and announces their final triumph. But man was not created just to look at the world; he has to assume responsibility for it: "The heaven of heaven is the Lord's: but the earth he has given to the children of man" (Ps. 113. 24) (=115. 16). For Adam, essential man, image of the Jesus Christ who is to come, is not only the crown of the work of creation in the first chapter of Genesis; his mission is to lead creation forward by the hand so as to offer it up in homage to the Creator, since God has decided to "re-establish all things in Christ, that are in heaven and on earth, in him" (Eph. 1. 10).

The sedentary peoples of Antiquity were all, indeed, of the belief that the earth they occupied and whose fruits they ate, were a gift from the divinity; for them, the true owner of the land was the national god whose lieutenant, priest, son and general administrator was their prince. Only the Bible differs. There is no question of God's being a mere property owner yielding up his rights over his land in exchange for a rent in the form of regular sacrifices and oblations in his temple; the Bible will speak of the God of history entrusting to his elect the fruit of their common conquest, made together after the solemn swearing of a Covenant.

Yahweh is not to be confused with the principal divinity of any country, nor with a land's deified vital forces. He is, as we have seen, a God from the beyond, who proves himself to be stronger than anything in existence, by overturning all that lies in his way. When he reaches Canaan with the Hebrews, Yahweh will no doubt expect to be considered as the only master of life upon the territory, thus supplanting all rustic fertility baals: "Are there any among the graven things of the Gentiles that can send rain? Or can the heavens give showers?" (Jer. 14. 22), but the prophets had to react violently against the way in which attempts were made to equate Yahweh with an agrarian divinity, a baal like the others, a *mèlèk* (land-owning king). Thanks to them, Yahweh never became a god dying and coming to life again, regularly bringing showers at each rainy season, but only if he was encouraged by ritual practices of a more or less licentious nature; he always remained the God who came to seek out the Hebrews in their bondage in Egypt, welded them into a people in the desert so that they might be given their own territory. At all times he will insist on being able to say to Israel: "I am the Lord thy God from the land of Egypt" (Osee 12. 9; 13. 4; 11. 1). The gift of a fatherland is a great act of history, inspired by freely-given, gratuitous love.

Entirely dependent upon the Covenant, the possession of the land of Canaan involves Israel more and more deeply in the transcendent purpose of the God who had chosen this people. This possession becomes for Israel a mission, for it has meaning, and meets a precise, exacting requirement of the divine plan. Yahweh surrenders none of his rights over the world when he confides to man responsibility for it; on the contrary, it is through man, a creature freely obeying him, that he intends to render all things subservient to himself. Is it not, in fact, in Christ Jesus that "it hath well-pleased the Father that all fulness should dwell: and through him to reconcile all things unto himself, making peace through the blood of his cross, both as to the things on earth and the things that are in heaven" (Col. 1. 19–20)?

Great spiritual values are attached to this gift of the soil which is so closely linked with a vocation. Far from coarsening the soul of Israel by giving it the desire for material possessions, this gift awakens a feeling of obligation to the God who has deigned to call it his people: "For all are yours. And you are Christ's. And Christ is God's" (1 Cor. 3. 22–23). However paradoxical it may appear, possession of the promised land gradually prepared the Jews to accept in their hearts the poverty of the Gospel: "Seek ye therefore first the kingdom of God and his justice: and all these things shall be added unto you" (Mat. 6. 33).

A. Man's Calling to be Ruler of the World[1]

The story has often been told of the Bedouin, who, rather than allow himself to be over-awed by the latest inventions of modern technological science, exclaimed on gazing up to the starry skies: "What is all that in comparison to the work of Allah?" There has never been any lack of preachers to include in their repertoire this edifying anecdote which draws such a vivid contrast between the pure and proud faith of the worshipper of Allah and the monstrous pride of an atheistic civilization. Perhaps we may be permitted to treat this story with less enthusiasm. For this method of confronting the work of God directly with that of man seems to us most unfortunate. Is there really any need to give people the impression that any new scientific triumph represents a further blow to divine omnipotence? At this rate, they might soon come to accept this nonsensical Marxist view: "The more man ascribes to God, the less he retains for himself."

Of course God and man do not contend thus for possession of the world. Their respective powers over the universe are not in competition with one another. The wise Ben Sira, for example, after recommending to the sick man the customary prayers and sacrifices, feels no embarrassment in advising him: "Then give place to the physician. For the Lord created him" (Ecclus 38. 11–12). And, indeed, never in the Bible does the Creator appear so great as when he entrusts his creation to the sons of Adam, putting all things under their dominion

[1] Article published in *Cahiers du clergé rural,* December, 1958.

(Psalm 8). Could he have asserted his sovereign power over the world in any better way than by giving responsibility for exerting it to someone of his own, free choice? "The heaven of heaven is the Lord's: but the earth he has given to the children of man" (Ps. 113. 24) (=115. 16). All the glory of this human action upon the cosmos thus belongs ultimately to God, and it provides his elect with yet a further opportunity of being at one with the crowds of Galilee in glorifying the Almighty who has given such power to men (Mat. 9. 8).

We may go further and say this: the world will not really belong to God until man has fully taken possession of it in his name; never, for example, was the land of Canaan considered to belong to Yahweh before its conquest by the Hebrews, and it is only with the gesture of God the Son handing over the vanquished cosmos to God the Father that the last page of history will have been written: "And when all things shall be subdued unto him, then the Son also himself shall be subject unto him that put all things under him, that God may be all in all" (1 Cor. 15. 28).

The cult of unspoilt nature

Rather than open their eyes wide to these far-reaching and stimulating vistas, however, certain people, reacting strongly against a kind of Promethean cult of science, prefer to put forward the desert and the spiritual qualities it would appear to represent. It is even claimed that Islam can provide the West with enough evidence of the virtues of the desert to put our corrupt, materialist society to shame. Encouraged by fashionable theories, eminent exegetes have, for their part, given themselves up to expounding *con amore* "the nomadic ideal of the prophets". To remove any uncertainty on the subject, let us state quite clearly that the Bible in no way canonizes the desert, and never sought to make it an ideal. In Holy Scripture, God manifests his glory, not by spreading out the splendour of uncultivated, unspoilt nature, but by making fruitful the work of men: "Let all the people give

praise to thee; the earth hath yielded her fruit" (Ps. 66. 6–7).
"Look upon thy servants and upon their works: and direct
their children . . . direct thou the works of our hands over
us" (Ps. 89. 16–17).

In any case, it may be noted, in the hypothesis which we
are contending, that the Bible would not have been first in
claiming that God can be found where man is absent. The
religions of Antiquity, taken as a whole, taught that a certain
number of elemental forces untouched by man were "sacred".
Now, it is precisely here that the religion of Israel refused to
recognize any manifestation whatever of the divinity. It
cannot be denied that the liturgy did retain some traces of
current conceptions in this matter, as, for example, when
Moses, according to the Code of the Covenant, is told: "And
if thou make an altar of stone unto me, thou shalt not build it of
hewn stones" (Ex. 20. 25), or when Deuteronomy demands a
sacrificial heifer that has never borne the yoke (21. 3–4).
In a similiar context might be mentioned the "new" cart
to be used to transport the ark (2 Kings 6. 3), the purifying
virtues attributed to "living" water (Lev. 14. 5, 52; 15. 13;
etc.), or even to ground that has never been ploughed or sown
(Deut. 21. 4). These examples should be taken as representing
mere relics of a past mentality. The primitive significance
of such ritual practices had early been forgotten, and more
often than not pains had been taken to substitute another
meaning for it. Let us just take the offering of first-fruits to
illustrate our point. Here is the explanation suggested by an
historian of comparative religion: " 'Primitive' man lived in
constant terror of finding that the forces around him, which
he found so useful, were worn out. The anxiety became
sharper still when the disintegration of the 'forces' appeared
to be the result of some interference on the part of man: the
gathering of the first fruits, the harvest, and so on. In this
case sacrifices known as 'the first fruits' were offered to
reconcile man with the forces at work in them and obtain
permission for him to use them without danger."[1] Totally

[1] Eliade, *Patterns in Comparative Religion*, p. 346.

different is the sense attributed to the same act by Deuteronomy; here, the one who brings the first fruits says: "The
Syrian pursued my father . . . and the Egyptians afflicted
us . . . and we cried to the Lord God of our fathers: who heard
us . . . and brought us out of Egypt . . . and brought us into
this place, and gave us this land flowing with milk and honey.
And therefore now I offer the first-fruits of the land which
the Lord hath given me" (26. 5–10). On the one side, the
divine power of vegetation which has been profaned by the
sickle has to be placated, and on the other, Yahweh's gracious
kindness in giving Israel the land of Canaan is recognized.

In any case, how could one suspect anything sacrilegious
in man's treatment of the world, since he is only fulfilling the
mission entrusted to him by God?

> God of my fathers, and Lord of mercy,
> who hast made all things with thy word,
> and by thy wisdom hast appointed man,
> that he should have dominion over the creature that was made
> by thee,
> that he should order the world according to equity and
> justice,
> and execute justice with an upright heart (Wisdom 9. 1–3).

Without man, the universe would, of course, remain incom-
plete; we are told in Genesis that at first no woodland shrub
had grown nor wild plant yet sprung up, because "the Lord
God had not rained upon the earth; and there was not a man
to till the earth" (2. 5). This explains why, a few verses
further on, the same author tells us how God formed man
and placed him in the garden of Eden "to dress it, and to
keep it" (v. 15). The first account of the creation, known as
the priestly account, develops the same idea, but with greater
breadth, introducing infinitely vaster cosmic perspectives.
Here, the creation of man is shown to be the crowning
achievement of the whole cosmic work; hitherto, all was
"good"; when created man was placed in command of the
universe, all was "very good" (Gen. 1. 31). So God pauses
a moment as if to reflect: "Let us make man to our image and

likeness: and let him have dominion over the fishes of the sea,
and the fowls of the air, and the beasts, and the whole earth,
and every creeping creature that moveth upon the earth"
(Gen. 1. 26).

Man's authority over the world, it is true, is not the only
aspect of this divine resemblance alluded to in our text;
but, as Ben Sira saw, it is an essential element: "God created
man of the earth, and made him after his own image . . . and
clothed him with strength according to himself . . . He put
the fear of him upon all flesh, and he had dominion over
beasts and fowls" (Ecclus 17. 1–4). Adam, indeed, never
appears nearer to God than when he is invested with this
royal power over creation: "Thou hast made him a little less
than the angels: thou hast crowned him with glory and honour,
and hast set him over the works of thy hands" (Ps. 8. 6–7).
This text has rightly been given a Messianic interpretation
in the Epistle to the Hebrews (2. 2 ff.), for it is not, at least
in the beginning, a question of man in general, but of the
ideal man, the man *par excellence,* i.e., the king. Whichever
way we look at it, the absolute and definitive master of the
cosmos will not be man of the atomic age but the resurrected
Christ.

The biblical spirituality of the desert

It may be objected that, whatever importance is attached
to the above passages, they represent but isolated features.
Before coming to any conclusion, might it not be advisable to
examine certain texts in which a totally different orientation
of thought is evident? It is true that only occasionally does
one come across passages extolling the work of man, as in
this poem in the Book of Job which evokes work in a mine:

> He hath stretched forth his hand to the flint:
> he hath overturned mountains from the roots.
> In the rocks he hath cut out rivers:
> and his eye hath seen every precious thing.
> The depths also of rivers he hath searched:
> and hidden things he hath brought forth to light (Job 28. 9–11).

Prophet and sage alike are far more often inclined to brand with infamy the insolence and ingratitude of pampered, sleek man, his heart blocked up with the fat of self-indulgence:[1] "According to their pastures they were filled, and were made full: and they lifted up their heart, and have forgotten me" (Osee 13. 6). So the only result of Israel's establishment in the land of Canaan was for it to forget God's goodness and to turn to apostasy. That being so, would it not be right to see in the desert the necessary condition for total fidelity?

> I will allure her
> and lead her into the wilderness:
> and I will speak to her heart (Osee 2. 14).
> I have remembered thee, pitying thy youth
> and the love of thy espousals,
> when thou followedst me in the desert
> in a land that is not sown (Jer. 2. 2).
> The people that were left and escaped from the sword
> found grace in the desert (Jer. 31. 2).

We should realize, however, that in all these passages the prophets are talking of an adventure which has failed and has to be recommenced. They talk of going back to the desert in order to be able to start again from scratch on a new conquest of the promised land: "And I will give her vine-dressers out of the same place, and the valley of Achor for an opening of hope" (Osee 2. 15). Here, as everywhere else in the Bible, the desert is not therefore an end to the journey, an ideal objective, it is a starting-point, a zero point on the scale; for the gift of God presupposes, at the outset, that man has absolutely nothing left.[2] Throughout the whole of inspired literature this plan for the history of Israel will be faithfully followed: "It is I that brought you up out of the land of Egypt, and I led you forty years through the wilderness, that you might possess the land of the Amorrhite" (Amos 2. 10).

---

[1] Jer. 5.28; Job 15.27; Deut. 32.15; Ps. 16.10; 72.7; 118.70.

[2] Cf. our article: "Le Don de la terre et sa richesse spirituelle. III: Le pressentiment de la pauvreté évangélique", in La Vie spirituelle, June 1957. See below, section B of this chapter, p. 131.

It is inconceivable that the adventure of the Covenant should end in the desert; death here would, indeed, be the final failure: "So I lifted up my hand over them in the desert, not to bring them into the land which I had given them" (Ez. 20. 15).[1]

The biblical spirituality of the desert, therefore, must be considered solely with respect to the gift of the promised land. Before undertaking with his people the conquest of Canaan, Yahweh must know those with whom he is dealing; thus he will test and tempt them, and the desert will become, in fact, the accepted place of temptation: "And thou shalt remember all the way through which the Lord thy God hath brought thee for forty years through the desert, to afflict thee and to prove thee, and that the things that were in thy heart might be made known, whether thou wouldst keep his commandments or no" (Deut. 8. 2). In return, Israel must blindly follow wherever God may lead, and not seek, in its destitute condition, to force his hand; Yahweh will not submit to any test and will not agree to being tried (Ps. 77. 19; 94. 9; 105. 14). The same view will be held at the time of the New Testament; for the members of the Qumrân sect, as for John the Baptist, the sojourn in the desert was but a preparatory stage, and it is in order to be tempted that Christ himself, led by the Spirit, had to go into the desert.

The ceaseless murmurings of the people against their leaders are enough to prove that the crossing of the wilderness of Sinai had no particular charm in itself: "Why have you made us come up out of Egypt, and have brought us into this wretched place which cannot be sowed, nor bringeth forth figs, nor vines, nor pomegranates: neither is there any water to drink?" (Num. 20. 5). We should not assume that these are the unedifying sentiments of insufficiently mortified people; for prophets and legists alike are almost as pessimistic in their view of the situation: "[Who] was thy leader in the great and terrible wilderness, wherein there was the serpent burning with his breath, and the scorpion and the dipsas, and no

[1] Cf. Deut. 9.28; Num. 14.16,32–33; 20.4–5; etc.

waters at all" (Deut. 8. 15). "Where is the Lord that made us
come up out of the land of Egypt? that led us through the
desert, through a land uninhabited and unpassable, through a
land of drought, and the image of death, through a land,
wherein no man walked, nor any man dwelt" (Jer. 2. 6). We
repeat, with great emphasis, for myths die hard, that the Bible
never extols the delights of life in the desert: "They wandered
in a wilderness, in a place without water: they found not
the way of a city for their habitation. They were hungry and
thirsty: their soul fainted in them" (Ps. 106. 4–5).

It is not that Israel remembers only the darkest side of the
long and arduous trek across the Sinai peninsula. Was this
not in itself a unique experience of the loving solicitude of the
God of Israel?

> And in the wilderness (as thou hast seen) the Lord thy God
> hath carried thee, as a man is wont to carry his little son, all the
> way that you have come, until you came to this place (Deut.
> 1. 31).
>
> Thy raiment, with which thou wast covered, hath not decayed
> for age, and thy foot is not worn: lo, this is the fortieth year
> (id. 8. 4; cf. 29. 4–5).
>
> He found him in a desert land, in a place of horror, and of
> vast wilderness. He led him about, and taught him: and he
> kept him as the apple of his eye (id. 32. 10).

Such experience of God's loving kindness is basically similar
to, if not identical with, that which certain prisoners and
deportees had during the last war, yet one would surely
hesitate to say that these victims would cherish the dream of
going through it all again, and that a concentration camp
should be reckoned the ideal background for all spiritual life.

The earth of mankind

The desert, in fact, appears as a completely negative world:
"Am I become a wilderness to Israel, or a lateward springing
land?" (Jer. 2. 31). It is shamelessly naked (Osee. 2. 3); it
is a mournful absence, the result of divine wrath:

> The places of the desert . . . are burnt up,
> for that there is not a man that passeth through them.
> And they have not heard the voice of the owner:
> from the fowl of the air to the beasts,
> they are gone away and departed.
> And I will make Jerusalem to be heaps of sand
> and dens of dragons:
> and I will make the cities of Juda desolate
> for want of an inhabitant (Jer. 9. 10–11).

Besides, the poetry of the desert is no more cultivated in Israel than that of the brushwood, the fallow land or waste ground, invaded by thistles, nettles and brambles (Is. 7. 23–25; Prov. 24. 31; etc.). As for a poetry of ruins, this is the shocking picture given us of the site of Babel:

> From generation to generation it shall lie waste:
> none shall pass through it for ever and ever.
> The bittern and ericius shall possess it,
> and the ibis and the raven shall dwell in it:
> and a line shall be stretched out upon it
> to bring it to nothing,
> and a plummet unto desolation . . .
> And demons and monsters shall meet,
> and the hairy ones shall cry out one to another.
> There hath the lamia lain down and found rest for herself.
> There hath the ericius had its hole
> and brought up its young ones,
> and hath dug round about and cherished them in the shadow
> thereof (Is. 34. 10–15).[1]

Here there is no affection for the desert, a wild and savage ground. The heart of Israel feels at ease only where nature has been domesticated, and bears fruit as a result of man's efforts and divine favour. There is probably no more doggedly sedentary people than the people of the Bible. In certain particularly well-known accounts there may, indeed, be heard an echo of ancient controversies aroused by the acceptance of rural and urban civilization: the story of Cain the farmer and

[1] Cf. Is. 13.20–22; Jer. 50.39; Soph. 2.13–15.

Abel the shepherd, for example, or that of the tower of Babel. The nomadic or semi-nomadic existence of the patriarchs was, in fact, scarcely ever regretted, or, at least, was not regretted for long. Those who, in spite of everything, still pined for this life, such as the Rechabites in the Book of Jeremias (ch. 35), were taken to be strangers, if not heretics.

There was never, therefore, any factual denial of the principle that the ground, with its covering of plant and animal life, has been placed at man's disposal, and that man and earth must remain united in the closest harmony: "But thou shalt have a covenant with the stones of the lands: and the beasts of the earth shall be at peace with thee" (Job 5. 23).[1] Consequently, Israel will never be carried away by the dream of great open spaces, but by that of the "earth of mankind":

> But as for you, O mountains of Israel . . . I will turn to you, and you shall be ploughed and sown . . . and the cities shall be inhabited and the ruinous places shall be repaired. And I will make you abound with men and with beasts: and they shall be multiplied and increased (Ez. 36. 8–11; cf. ib. vv. 33–35).
> And I will bring back the captivity of my people Israel:
> and they shall build the abandoned cities and inhabit them:
> and they shall plant vineyards and drink the wine of them:
> and shall make gardens and eat the fruits of them.
> And I will plant them upon their own land:
> and I will no more pluck them out of their land which I have given them (Amos 9. 14–15).

The image of the desert may, perhaps, still haunt people's imaginations, but it is with the hope of seeing it conquered, regenerated, irrigated, cultivated, vivified, inhabited:

> He hath turned a wilderness into pools of waters:
> and a dry land into water springs.
> And hath placed there the hungry:
> and they made a city for their habitation.
> And they sowed fields, and planted vineyards:
> and they yielded fruit of birth (Ps. 106. 35–37).

[1] Cf. Osee, 2.18; Is. 11.1–9; Ez. 34.25–27; etc.

For waters are broken out in the desert,
and streams in the wilderness.
And that which was dry land, shall become a pool,
and the thirsty land springs of water . . .
No lion shall be there,
nor shall any mischievous beast go up by it, nor be found
    there:
but they shall walk there that shall be delivered (Is. 35. 6–9).[1]

After twenty centuries of exile, the Jews forgetting nothing of their former dreams, will return as enthusiastic pioneers to water and sow the desert which Islam, here as everywhere else, has left behind.

Man is ennobled and strikes deep root

What conclusion can be drawn from these observations? Should we be content merely to see in this a fortuitous setting, entirely external to the essentially spiritual message of the Bible? We may certainly be permitted at least to deduce from all this the notion that the Bible unreservedly accepts the effort made by man to imprint upon the earth the mark of his passing over it; we may well say, to "humanize" the world around him. This is specially true, because the religion of Sinai did not limit its effect to bringing the Hebrews of Moses out of their nomadic existence to a sedentary state; it was able, without belying its nature, to lead the chosen people through all the stages of civilization, from the late Egyptian empire to the Graeco-Roman culture.[2] So then, the continued ascent and ennobling of human life takes place, naturally and smoothly, within the framework of the economy of revelation; it therefore in no way compromises progress in the discovery of God.

[1] Cf. Is. 32.15; 41.18–19; 43.19–20; 51.3; etc.
[2] This observation would seem to imply a good deal. All other religions, in fact, appear to be linked to a particular, well-defined type of civilization; they contribute to the development of man within the framework of a fixed mode of life, but generally prevent him from ever moving out of it. This was the case in all the religions of Antiquity, and still remains true of Hinduism, Buddhism and Islam. Only Christianity has had the power, since the twelfth century, of enabling the West to make its immense leap forward.

10

Why is it, therefore, that the Bible so often criticizes the pride of the sons of Adam, inveighing against their claim to know everything and even to wish to scale the heights of heaven (Gen. 2–3; 11. 1–9)? We must admit that it shows a certain pleasure in seeing humbled the pride of the great conquerors of the East, Sargon, Sennacherib or Nabuchodonosor:

> And thou saidst in thy heart:
> I will ascend into heaven,
> I will exalt my throne above the stars of God,
> I will sit in the mountain of the covenant,
> in the sides of the north.
> I will ascend above the height of the clouds,
> I will be like the most High.
> But yet thou shalt be brought down to hell,
> into the depth of the pit (Is. 14. 13–15).[1]

But the God of the Bible does not, in fact, protest against the human desire for greatness. What does anger him is that man should try to achieve this greatness without him, apart from or in spite of him.

Besides, if this God does never cease to inveigh against those who seek to make their way without him, this is because he claims to be alone capable of giving man his true stature. Furthermore, it is impossible to conceive of Biblical monotheism otherwise than as leading to Messianism, which is equivalent to saying that the Bible cannot think of God except in the context of his accomplishing and fulfilling history. So, from the beginning, the religion of Sinai contained in germ an aspiration for an incarnation which would be justified and realized in the New Testament. It is for this reason that we do not hesitate to reject the commonly accepted identification of Old Testament monotheism with that of Islam. The Bible shows no desire to see man prostrate; man will find God only by drawing himself up to his full height, even if, in order to do this, he has to die and then rise from the dead: "Be you therefore perfect, as also your heavenly

[1] Cf. Is. 37.24–29; Ez. 28.11–19; Dan. 4; etc.

Father is perfect" (Mat. 5. 48). Mortals will not be crushed when they meet God, but will be brought to their apotheosis by this meeting. True Christian humility, therefore, has nothing to do with a morbid contentment with weakness and failure: it consists rather in a sense of greatness which is recognized as being entirely due to God. The Magnificat of the Blessed Virgin and the proud "assurance" which the apostle Paul proclaims on every page of his epistles, lead us far from those childhood acts before communion, when we dutifully styled ourselves "miserable worms".

The attitude of the Bible towards civilization can, therefore, be regarded as an implicit recognition of the legitimacy of man's efforts to ensure his domination of the universe, in so far as this effort is undertaken in a spirit of humility for the glory of God. We may go further. Certain spiritual values seem to us to be associated with a settled rather than a nomadic mode of existence. It is a biological fact that life always seeks to become embedded more deeply in the earth in order to develop better in height and in breadth; but a deeper significance is implied by this: the higher one seeks to grow, the deeper must be the root; it is useless to hope for fruit high in the branches if the root is not deep in the soil (4 Kings 19. 30). Whence the important place which the theme of the tree occupies throughout inspired literature:[1] "And his top was elevated among the thick boughs. The waters nourished him, the deep set him up on high" (Ez. 31. 3–4). "He seemeth to have moisture before the sun cometh: and at his rising his blossom shall shoot forth. His roots shall be thick upon a heap of stones, and among the stones he shall abide" (Job 8. 16–17). To live here is to live deeply rooted; just as to die is to be torn up and blown away, like leaves, straw or dry grass:

> He will pluck thee out, and remove thee from thy dwelling place:
> and thy root out of the land of the living (Ps. 51. 7).

[1] It may, on the other hand, be asked why so little importance is attributed to the tree in Mohammedan countries.

And the enemies of the Lord, presently after they shall be
honoured and exalted,
shall come to nothing and vanish like smoke (Ps. 36. 20).
And we have all fallen as a leaf:
and our iniquities, like the wind, have taken us away (Is. 64.6).[1]

For us Christians, such a rooting consists essentially in
a rooting in charity (Eph. 3. 17); for us, to live is to live in
the Church. We do not hesitate to add, however, that this
rooting presupposes others at a lower level, that of family
and social life, for example, or geographical locality. We
may recall that the early churches were essentially "local"
in character, the bishop being bishop of a place as well as
of a community. Christian life, in fact, develops only with
difficulty in the middle of hurly-burly and bustle, and blind
migrations lacking any definite aim. So all the peoples
which have come under the influence of Christian preaching
have soon settled permanently in one spot, whereas Islam,
quite on the contrary, has often provided examples of long-
established populations, such as the Berbers, returning to a
semi-nomadic state. Let us add, conversely, that our pro-
letarian apostasy was initially associated with the sociological
phenomenon of uprooted populations. It surely cannot be
upheld that the fact of Israel's establishment in one place is
completely unrelated to the economy of biblical revelation
and that it has nothing to teach us in the matter of assuring
the happy balance of our Christian life.

To-day, humanity is claiming to make its presence felt, not
only on the earth's surface, in the air or on and under the sea,
but also in outer space, the conquest of which it has now
undertaken. So long as the heart of man remains unchanged,
this extraordinary progress and development of his technological power can no doubt be made to serve the cause of
evil as well as that of good. The discovery of metals enabled
humanity to forge swords along with ploughshares; a similar
temptation accompanies the splitting of the atom. But we
must not neglect or ignore the chance of further extending

[1] Ez. 19.10–14; Jer. 11.19; 17.8; Job 29.19; Pr. 3.18; Ps. 1; 51.10; 91.13; etc.

the Kingdom of God just because there is a darker possibility. For, the more firmly his feet are planted upon the ground as he imposes his rule over the universe, the more humus our Christian life has, the more deeply rooted it is, so much the more plentifully the sap will flow, so much the richer the fruits will be. Any new conquest by the sons of Adam enlarges the sphere of influence of God's redemptive work: are not all things, whether on earth or in heaven, to be reconciled to him through his blood shed on the cross (Col. 1. 20)?

B. THE GIFT OF THE SOIL AND ITS SPIRITUAL WEALTH[1]

Throughout the length of its troubled history, Israel gave proof of an intense love for its soil, which seems to be far removed from the poverty preached by the Gospel. The Old and New Testaments appear to diverge widely here; they would even seem to take up diametrically opposite viewpoints. In these circumstances, should we not eliminate this idea from the biblical message when we present it, or, at least, denounce it as an excessively unspiritual vision of the world, incompatible with the exacting demands of our Christian conscience?

Even if it were desirable, such an expurgation would be impossible, for the gift of the earth is an integral part of the whole development of biblical thought and the theme re-appears at each stage of the progress towards ultimate salvation. It was the promised possession of the land of Canaan which prompted Abraham to set out. If God summoned Moses, it was so that he might lead the Hebrews out of Egypt and towards the fruitful land (Ex. 3. 8) which their fathers had known as strangers only (Ex. 6. 4); and it was always with the conquest of Palestine in mind that a Covenant was agreed between Yahweh and his people; at least, none of the legislations setting out clearly the terms of this contract ever failed to link the two things (Ex. 23. 20–23; 34. 10–13; Josue 24. 1–14; Deut. 1. 7–8). In order to break off the alliance, all

[1] Article published in *La Vie spirituelle,* June 1957.

the God of Sinai had to do was to threaten his faithless people with exile: "Return ye, every one from his evil way, and from your wicked devices, and you shall dwell in the land which the Lord hath given to you and your fathers for ever and ever" (Jer. 25. 5). Finally, the very hope of a New Covenant made those who had been deported look back towards this land, now purged of all its former sin: "They shall say: This land that was untilled is become as a garden of pleasure: and the cities that were abandoned and desolate and destroyed are peopled and fenced" (Ez. 36. 35).

Indissolubly linked with the religious experience of Israel, the gift of the soil thus possesses a value which the New Testament could not deny. The Gospel of Christ will exploit, rather than reject, the spiritual wealth contained in this theme, and will invest it with a further depth of significance. Was it not by accepting the land of Canaan from the hands of Yahweh that Israel learnt to recognize that divine love was at once both gratuitous and exacting? Was it not there that the closeness of the bonds uniting the people with their God was sensed? Paradoxical as it may seem, it is in this way that they saw foreshadowed for them the poverty which was to be preached in the Gospels.

The gratuitous and exacting nature of divine love

Reflecting upon the manner in which Yahweh had placed it in control over its own territory, Israel recognized in this act the free initiative of a love upon which it was to be eternally dependent. Possession of the soil means more to Israel than a simple, isolated fact; it is reminded of a whole series of events which give evidence of God's solicitude, for the fact of possession implies a taking of possession, which in turn implies "the eviction of the previous owner in favour of the successor, and, almost always, the entering into possession of property to which one had no legal right".[1]

This certainly posed the problem in a new way, for men

[1] J. Guillet, *Thèmes bibliques. Études sur l'expression et le développement de la Révélation*, Paris, Aubier, 1950, p. 182.

rarely find any pleasure in recalling the rights of those whom they have dispossessed. People are much more apt to go back to the beginning of time in an attempt to seek justification for occupying the territory; thus the creation poem is generally recalled during the ceremonies commemorating national feasts, and at the New Year, the dedication of places of worship, and the crowning of kings. At all events, Sumerians and Accadians, Egyptians, Greeks and Romans have been only too eager to forget those who inhabited their land before them. The Bible, on the other hand, never tires of returning to the list of those who were expelled by the Hebrews under Moses and Josue: Canaanites, Hittites, Amorrhites, Hevites, etc., constantly emphasizing the fact that Israel conquered Palestine at a definite moment in time, and that other nations had previously, and lawfully, occupied these places.

It was early noted, for example, that after the children of Israel had been brought out of Egypt, Yahweh ousted the Amorrhites from Transjordania in favour of his people: "And I brought you into the land of the Amorrhite, who dwelt beyond the Jordan. And when they fought against you, I delivered them into your hands, and you possessed their land, and slew them" (Josue 24. 8).[1] This fact remained so deeply engraved in the national memory that our psalter still recalls to-day how Yahweh slew Kings Sehon and Og of Basan, in order that his people might dwell in their territory (Ps. 134. 11–12; 135. 20–2).

This particular case was soon generalized in a manner which did not reflect actual historical truth: "And he gave then the lands of the Gentiles: and they possessed the labours of the people" (Ps. 104. 44). "Thou hast brought a vineyard (Israel) out of Egypt: thou hast cast out the Gentiles and planted it . . . and it filled the land" (Ps. 79. 9–10).[2] The

---

[1] This great speech by Josue at the great gathering of the tribes at Sichem is generally ascribed to the Elohistic tradition. In it may indeed be detected an echo of Osee's preaching, while it would appear, in style, to antedate Deuteronomy.

[2] This generalization appears to be characteristic of those writings which are Deuteronomic in inspiration: Deut. 31. 3–4; Josue 23.5–9; Judges 6.9; etc.

Hebrews had not in fact seized the land of the Canaanites in so brutal a fashion. The two populations lived for a long time side by side, when they did not actually merge.[1] This distortion of historical accuracy is deeply significant; it shows the importance attached by the inspired authors to the change of ownership in the theology of the gift of the soil: is this not a way of emphasizing the positive will of God in the matter?

In this conquest of Canaan, there was, indeed, an increasing tendency to stress the divine choice and the fixed purpose governing it. According to post-Exilic priestly traditions, Moses undertook, after leading the Israelites into the desert, a general census of the tribes while they were still in the desert, in order to effect, as did Josue, a theoretical partition of Palestine. Everything seemed, therefore, to have taken place according to a set plan, and the different lots were even drawn in the presence of the priest Eleazar.[2]

In thus handing over the land of Canaan, God amply demonstrated his personal love for his people. He showed the utmost consideration in his dealing with his children. Not content with installing them in a territory which did not belong to them, he brought them into a land where preparations had been made for their welcome: large, prosperous towns which they had not built, houses that abounded in wealth which was not of their making, wells which they had not dug, vineyards and oliveyards which they had not planted.[3] Where their enemies are concerned, however, Yahweh shows himself to be relentless. Deuteronomy, in particular, condemns to *hérèm*, sacred destruction, the Canaanite populations: "[When] the Lord thy God shall have

---

[1] On this point, see: Josue 23.12–13; Judges 2; 3.1–6; Ex. 23.29–30; Deut. 7.22.

[2] Num. 32.40 reveals most clearly the thoroughly conventional character of this parcelling out which followed the conquest; here we read that "Moses gave the land of Galaad to Machir the son of Manasses, and he dwelt in it", which is simply an explanatory comment on the preceding verse: "The children of Machir, the son of Manasses, went into Galaad, and wasted it, cutting off the Amorrhites, the inhabitants thereof".

[3] Deut. 6.10–11; 9.1; Josue 24.13.

delivered them to thee, thou shalt utterly destroy them. Thou shalt make no league with them, nor shew mercy to them" (Deut. 7. 2). "Of those cities that shall be given thee, thou shalt suffer none at all to live" (ib. 20. 16). The God of Israel wants, in fact, to make a clean sweep of these nations (ib. 19. 1), even sending hornets to destroy those who remain behind as fugitives in hiding (7. 20). He does not do things by halves; his is a total giving: he places fully and squarely in the hands of his people the inheritance of the nations.

There is a definite meaning to such love. By brutally taking land away from some to hand it gently over to others, Yahweh pursues an aim which the beneficiaries themselves will have no choice but to follow. He did not, in fact, indiscriminately take away or hand over land. He would not, for example, have allowed the children of Israel to settle in the land of Moab, of Ammon or of Edom: "Take ye then good heed that you stir not against them. For I will not give you of their land so much as the step of one foot can tread upon, because I have given mount Seir to Esau, for a possession" (Deut. 2. 5). So it was natural to seek the reasons for this handing over to the Hebrews of the land of Canaan; here is the reply which Deuteronomy gives to the question: "It is not for thy justices, and the uprightness of thy heart that thou shalt go in to possess their lands. But because they have done wickedly, they are destroyed at thy coming in" (Deut. 9. 5). Whence the conclusion: "Walk not after the laws of the nations, which I will cast out before you. For they have done all these things: and therefore I abhorred them. But to you I say: Possess their land which I will give you for an inheritance" (Lev. 20. 23–24; cf. Deut. 28. 9–12).

Divine love, therefore, so tender and solicitous at first, will make heavy demands which can already be foreseen. Just as he ousted the Canaanites from their land, God can for the same reasons sweep away (3 Kings 9. 7) or banish (Josue 23. 16) Israel from their land, for they, in their turn, will have prepared the place for unknown strangers: "Mayst thou take a wife, and another sleep with her. Mayst thou build a house, and not dwell therein. Mayst thou plant a vineyard and not gather the vintage thereof . . . May a people which thou knowest not, eat the fruits of thy land, and all thy labours" (Deut. 28. 30–33). God gives freely, and freely he will take away. Other nations may adduce the fact of the creation in order to justify their right to lasting possession of their land: the Bible, on the contrary, will see in this a sign that God is quite free to choose when and where he bestows his gifts: "I made the earth and the men and the beasts that are upon the face of the earth, by my great power and by my stretched out arm: and I have given it to whom it seemed good in my eyes. And now I have given all these lands into the hand of Nabuchodonosor king of Babylon, my servant: moreover also the beasts of the field I have given him to serve him" (Jer. 27. 5–6).

Meditating thus on the possession of its land, Israel realized the extent of its indebtedness to the gratuitous yet exacting love shown by its God. But this sense of dependence did not spring solely from memories of the past; the original gift of the soil is repeated in the gift of daily bread. The corn, the wine, the fresh oil, which Israel has in abundance, all come, as Osee never ceased to recall, from Yahweh, the God of Israel since the captivity in Egypt (Osee 12. 9; 13. 4; cf. 11. 1). The Lord is at pains to tend this land of Palestine which he has given his people, watching over it from year's end to year's end (Deut. 11. 12).

There exists, therefore, a close association between the fertility of the land and the conquest of the territory. This fact explains the attempt made to link national history with the ancient feasts which characterized the cycle of pastoral or agrarian life. Thus the Passover commemorated the flight from Egypt (Ex. 12. 27; Deut. 16. 1), the feast of Tabernacles recalled the wanderings in the desert (Lev. 23. 42–43), while, later, Pentecost was to bring to mind the promulgation of the law on Sinai. With the passing of time, the most ancient rites also assumed a new significance in relation to the historic acts of the God of Israel. It was originally thought necessary, for example, to be careful not to "profane" and exhaust, as it were, the life-giving force which ensured the fertility of the soil, so the first-fruits and the last swaths of the crops were reserved for the harvest spirit.[1] The Israelites will accordingly take the first sheaf of corn to the temple, but will recite as they do so certain words which invest this archaic gesture with quite a different significance: "The Syrian pursued my father, who went down into Egypt . . . and the Lord God of our fathers . . . brought us out of Egypt with a strong hand, and a stretched-out arm . . . And brought us into this place, and gave us this land flowing with milk and honey. And therefore now I offer the first-fruits of the land which the Lord has given me" (Deut. 26. 5–10). As for the final sheaves, Leviticus will, indeed, require that they should stay where they are, but this is in order that they should feed the poor and the strangers (Lev. 19. 9–10; 23. 22), for, concludes Deuteronomy, "Remember that thou also wast a bondman in Egypt: and therefore I command thee to do this thing" (24. 22).

The soil and the benefits it brings must therefore constantly remind Israel of this gratuitous, exacting love which Yahweh shows it. Yet nothing is more difficult than to know how to appreciate God in his gifts. And the ancient Covenant will in this regard end in failure: "And my bread which I gave thee, the fine flour and oil, and honey, wherewith I fed thee, thou hast set before them (strange gods) for a sweet odour . . . thou hast not remembered the days of thy youth, when thou wast naked, and full of confusion, trodden under foot in thy own blood" (Ez. 16. 19–22). Who, in fact, does not merit this accusation which Yahweh makes against his people: "According to their pastures they were filled, and were made full: and they lifted up their heart, and have forgotten me" (Osee 13. 6)?

[1] The first and the last of a series summarize, to all intents and purposes, all the elements of a series. Whence the importance attached to the first-born or to first-fruits, as well as to the last sheaves.

Closeness of the divine Covenant

Reflecting on the way in which Yahweh had presented them
with the land of Canaan, the Israelites became aware, not
only of the depth of divine love, but also of the proximity of
their God, a God acting with them and in them. There is,
indeed, no question of comparing Yahweh to a baal, a god
and master of the soil who, without sharing personally in
human affairs, yields a life interest in territory of which
he remains the eternal owner. Coming from Sinai, the God
of Israel conquers the land of Canaan with his people, fights
in their ranks and places his invincible power at the disposal
of his armies. This God does not remain a stranger to the
effort of his elect, he co-operates in their action in order to
implement the power which he gives them over the universe.
The conquered world can thus be considered by man to
have been truly inherited by him from his God.

Yahweh, we are told, delivered into the hands of Israel the
land of Canaan. This expression "delivered into the hands
of" means "gave power over", "placed at the disposal of",
the hand being considered as the mainspring of human
action.[1] Applied first to persons,[2] this expression is then
extended to cover towns which have been captured and their
territory: "Behold I have given into thy hands Jericho, and
the king thereof" (Josue 6. 2). "Behold I have delivered into
thy hand the king thereof (of Hai), and the people, and the
city, and the land" (ib. 8. 1).[3] Finally, it will be applied
directly to the conquest of the earth itself: "The Lord will
deliver the place to us, in which there is no want of anything
that groweth on the earth" (Judges 18. 10; cf. Josue 2. 24).

This expression "delivered into the hands of" merits our
especial attention, because it tends to define the conquest
as a work undertaken by God and man in common. Yahweh
hands over to the Hebrews the ground which their feet shall

[1] P. Dhorme, *L'Emploi métaphorique des noms et des parties du corps en hébreu et en accadien,* Paris, 1923, p. 144.
[2] See, for example: Judges 4.7; 11.9,30; 12.3; 1 Kings 17.46.
[3] See further: Num. 21.34; Deut. 2.24,31; 3.2.

tread upon (Josue 1. 3), that is, the ground which they themselves will take over in person. But this is not to say that he will do no more than bless their victory *post eventum*: this victory is entirely his. He has fought for Israel (Deut. 3. 22; Josue 23. 3) and marched at the head of Israel's armies (Deut. 1. 30): "And forty thousand fighting men by their troops, and bands, marched through the plains and fields of the city of Jericho in the sight of Yahweh" (Josue 4. 13 Hebrew). We no longer have the text of the book of Yahweh's battles (Num. 21. 14), but we know from other sources what powerful weapons he had at his disposal to hurry to the support of his chosen people: storms, earthquakes, hailstorms, etc. We should, however, note that his action generally remains more discreet, without being any the less effective. He acts through his very presence in the middle of his troops, giving them an enthusiasm, a mysterious power which makes them invincible: "And then the Lord God will take away before your eyes nations that are great and very strong, and no man shall be able to resist you. One of you shall chase a thousand men of the enemies: because the Lord your God himself will fight for you, as he hath promised" (Josue 23. 9–10); without this help, on the contrary, the most heroic efforts will prove to be in vain: "Go not up, and fight not, for I am not with you" (Deut. 1. 42; cf. Num. 14. 39–45). In short, the Hebrews learnt, in this conquest of Canaan, that in their midst was beyond all doubt a "living God" (Josue 3. 10).

If God assumes responsibility for bringing to a successful conclusion the affairs of men, the sole courage of the warriors loses much of its importance. Should his servants raise as an objection the insignificance of their family, as Gedeon did, or again, like Moses, their lack of eloquence, Yahweh has but one reply: "I will be with thee" (Judges 6. 15–16; Ex. 4. 10–12). Nothing, in fact, prevents Yahweh from effecting salvation through a large or a small number (1 Kings 14. 6), and, so that Israel should make no mistake about it, he can on occasion refuse to lend the help of too large a troop: "And the the Lord said to Gedeon: The people that are with thee are many, and Madian shall not be delivered into their hands: lest Israel should glory against me, and say: I was delivered by my own strength" (Judges 7. 2).[1] Thus psalmist and sage can conclude: "For they got not the possession of the land by their own sword: neither did their own arm save them. But thy right hand and thy arm . . ." (Ps. 43. 4). "The horse is prepared for the day of battle: but the Lord giveth safety" (Prov. 21. 31).

The whole merit of the operation, therefore, comes back to God, and perhaps it is basically in this collaboration between the human and the divine that man becomes most deeply aware of his nothingness. Christian humility is, indeed, not to be confused with a simple sense of impotence; it implies experience of divine omnipotence at the heart of our human weakness: "The weak things of the world hath God chosen, that he may confound the strong . . . That no flesh should glory in his sight" (1 Cor. 1. 27–29).

So Yahweh has not just once and once only rendered fruitful through his omnipotence the actions of his children: after conquering with them the land, does he not daily bless the work of their hands?[2] Since the continued gift of rain and vegetation prolongs the original gift of the land, the divine blessing guarantees that work in the fields will always have the constant collaboration of the God who handed over the soil. This blessing is, in fact, like a mysterious potentiality which God has placed in the heart of all living things in order that they may come to their fullness of being; for mortal men it is a pledge of success, of an exceptionally happy issue to all their enterprises.[3] And this blessing may be acknowledged in the same way as was the entry into possession of the promised land; when God co-operates thus with the effort of man, it is the divine influence which is supreme: "The blessing of the Lord maketh men rich: neither shall affliction be joined to them" (Prov. 10. 22).

[1] For the same idea, cf. Deut. 8.17–18; Amos 6.14; Is. 10.13.
[2] Deut. 2.7; 14.29; 15.18; 16.15; 28.12; Job 1.10.
[3] Pedersen, *Israel, its Life and Culture,* Copenhagen and Oxford, 1947, I–II, pp. 181–212.

The earth, therefore, does not come between man and God; on the contrary, it unites them in a common enterprise of conquest and development. We need hardly recall here the well-known definition of mutual love, which is not looking at each other but looking each in the same direction. It is in this close collaboration that Israel became fully aware of its divine sonship; the land conquered under the protection of divine power was in very ancient texts[1] known as "Yahweh's inheritance": "So he brought them to that holy land of his, the mountain slopes he took, with his own right hand for title; so he drove out the heathen at their onset, parcelled out the land to them by lot, to each his own inheritance, bidding the tribes of Israel dwell where the heathen had dwelt before them" (Ps. 77. 54–55).[2]

Israel's grounds for believing itself to be the son of its God are the same as the successor of David's, namely its dominion over a land which it had inherited (Ps. 2. 7–8). Man is said to be created in the image of God, precisely because he is God's associate in the government of the world, when, for example, arrayed in the majestic glory of the Almighty, he sees the universe lying submissive at his feet (Ps. 8. 6–7). When about to create man, God paused as if to reflect and take counsel: "Let us make man to our image and likeness: and let him have dominion over the fishes of the sea, and the fowls of the air, and the beasts, and the whole earth, and every creeping creature that moveth upon the earth" (Gen. 1. 26). It is through this work carried out together that was to be established between God and man the close intimacy of a truly loving relationship: "For all are yours. And you are Christ's. And Christ is God's" (1 Cor. 3. 22–23).

A foreshadowing of the poverty of the Gospels

Israel loves its land with a fervent love, hardly compatible, it would seem, with the detachment preached and practised

[1] 1 Kings 26.19; 2 Kings 20.19; 21.3; Ps. 46.5.
[2] (Translator's note: Knox version).

by Christ. Evangelic poverty, however, is not the poverty of
Diogenes, is not to be confused with a sort of experiment in
proving that a vacuum is possible; on the contrary, we may
say that it leads positively towards a just appreciation of divine
love through God's gifts. Israel is attached to its land because
it constitutes a visible sign of Yahweh's paternal solicitude
for his people. Besides, in order to have a right to God's
favour, Israel had to prove that it was prepared to place
itself entirely in God's hands, to accept in advance the utter
deprivation of the desert; thus, paradoxical as it may seem,
the gift of the soil, far from turning the hearts of the Israelites
towards the enjoyment of material benefits, taught them to
love the Lord and only him.

For the entry into the promised land, the Old Testament
demands the same gesture of self-surrender, the same leap
into the unknown that Christ will require from his disciples:
"Leaving all things, they followed him" (Luke 5. 11, 28).
"Go forth out of thy country, and from thy kindred, and
out of thy father's house, and come into the land which I
shall shew thee" (Gen. 12. 1). Abraham, therefore, with his
eyes fixed on the divine promises, will forsake everything;
but events do not seem to follow out the divine purpose, and
the plans of the patriarch are frustrated one after the other.
He first surrenders to his nephew Lot the best portion of his
land in order to move as a guest and a stranger (Gen. 13.
7–11; 22. 15ff.; cf. Ex. 6. 4) over a territory which his descendants alone would be able to inherit. Here again everything
tends relentlessly towards the destruction of his dreams:
the risks to Sara at the court of the foreign kings, her barrenness,
the long migrations away from Israel, the sacrifice of Isaac—
all these things seemed to challenge more and more effectively,
after each new surge of hope, the realization of the divine
plan. Finally, the adventure reaches its climax with complete
failure: the forefathers of Israel have to give up their territory.
However, when the whole affair appears to be utterly
jeopardized, God reiterates his promise, claiming that they
should continue to trust in him: "Fear not, go down into

Egypt, for I will make a great nation of thee there. I will go down with thee thither, and will bring thee back again from thence" (Gen. 46. 3–4).

The entry into the promised land implies therefore this faith which seems to run counter to all hope, and which St Paul considered to be the model for the faith of Christians. God gives only when one gives oneself entirely to him.

Complete destitution will similarly precede the taking over of the land. Israel will start with nothing in order to understand that it owes everything to its God. Yahweh will meet his people in an abandonment like that of grapes out in the desert (Osee 9. 10), or of a new-born baby, uncared for and weltering in its blood (Ez. 16. 4–6). It is in these fearful desert spaces (Deut. 32. 10) that he will summon Israel for judgement face to face (Ez. 20. 35–38), and that he will talk with them heart to heart (Osee 2. 14): "I have remembered thee, pitying thy youth and the love of thy espousals, when thou followedst me in the desert, in a land that is not sown" (Jer. 2. 2).

Never, indeed, did the chosen people feel more completely in God's hands than at this time. They take pleasure in repeating that, from the Exodus out of Egypt to the entry into Palestine (Josue 5. 12), Yahweh nourished them with his own manna (Deut. 8. 3) and caused water to spring from the hard rock. It was here that he gave proof of his fatherly care for Israel: "The Lord thy God dwelling with thee, knoweth thy journey: how thou hast passed through this great wilderness, for forty years, and thou hast wanted nothing" (Deut. 2. 7). "He hath brought you forty years through the desert. Your garments are not worn out, neither are the shoes of your feet consumed with age. You have not eaten bread, nor have you drunk wine or strong drink: that you might know that I am the Lord your God" (ib. 29. 5–6; cf. 8. 2).

In the heart of the Israelite who remembered the desert from which God had rescued him, this reflexion from Ecclesiastes must have awakened many echoes: "For every man that eateth and drinketh, and seeth good of his labour, this is the gift of God" (3. 13).

11

Possession of the land, which the Israelites undertook as an act of faith after the ordeal in the desert, did not tie them to the search for material benefits: without taking their eyes off their God, the chosen people will gratefully accept what the Lord has to give them. The same religion, therefore, will allow them to possess God and to possess the land.[1] A people would not, in fact, even aspire to the notion of possessing God unless it had already experienced the gift of territory. Thus the tribe of Levi was dedicated to the service of Yahweh only after having accidentally lost its land.[2] The tribe of Moses, which had, at Beelphegor, proved faithful to the God of the Covenant (Num. 25; Ps. 105. 28–31), then received as an inheritance, not territory, but a share in the sacrifices reserved for the priests who lived off the offerings made to Yahweh: "But to the tribe of Levi he gave no possession: but the sacrifices and victims of the Lord God of Israel, are his inheritance, as he spoke to him" (Josue 13. 14; cf. 18. 7).[3] For them it became a title of honour to have no inheritance in Israel: "And they shall receive nothing else of the possession of their brethren: for the Lord himself is their inheritance, as he hath said to them" (Deut. 18. 2; cf. 10. 9).

This example is sufficient to show how God takes the place of his gifts, becoming himself the inheritance of his elect, the only good that they have to desire. When, after the Exile, the Levites were reduced to the status of mere assistants to the priests, they considered themselves as being offered to the Lord in the place of the first-born,[4] transforming their humble condition into a choice situation. Do not those who spend so much time in the sanctuary enjoy every day close communion with God? It is certainly they who composed the finest hymns of self-surrender and confidence in our psalter: "The Lord is the portion of my inheritance and of my

[1] Guillet, *op. cit.*, p. 195.

[2] The eponymous narration of the raid against Sichem by the sons of Jacob (Gen. 34) appears to indicate that the tribe of Levi was decimated following a premature assault against the Canaanite fortress.

[3] This privilege passed to the Aaronite priests when they had acquired the exclusive monopoly of the priesthood: Num. 18.20; Ez. 44.28–31; Ecclus 45.27.

[4] Num. 3.11–13,40–45; 8.16–18.

cup: it is thou that wilt restore my inheritance to me. The lines are fallen unto me in goodly places: for my inheritance is goodly to me" (Ps. 15. 5–6).

The experience of this tribe, at one and the same time sacrificed and yet privileged, spread to the whole community; all Israel was finally brought to consider Yahweh as its inheritance (Jer. 10. 16; 51. 19); simple laymen made God their choice portion,[1] placing his love above all created good: "Thou hast given gladness in my heart. By the fruit of their corn, their wine, and oil, they are multiplied" (Ps. 4. 7–8).

It is the gift of the promised land, rather than a premature discovery of the realities of the beyond, that prepared the human heart to love God with a supreme love, and to love him alone. If Christianity is to be considered as a "spiritual force", it will not be on the grounds that it represents an escapist force; for it is not the religion of Christ that one can reproach with being "the opium of the people". The only genuine spiritual forces are, in fact, those which enable one to understand and to dominate the world, and any religious system which does not include this initial experience of the gift of the soil, will inevitably decline into a more or less Manichaean dualism, or lead to the enjoyment of material things purely and simply—and that is the worst possible form of materialism.

---

[1] Lam. 3.24; Ps. 72.26; 118.57; 141.6.

V

THE UNIVERSE FOLLOWING IN THE WAKE OF HISTORY

A TOKEN and an implement of the God of history, an inheritance of the children of the Covenant, the universe is summoned to share intimately in the religious adventure of humanity; this adventure becomes that of the universe itself, so much so that the sons of Adam commit by their acceptance or refusal the whole work of the Creator, so much so that their failure or their success can involve the failure or success of the whole of creation. Whereas up till now we have examined the world from the outside, speaking of cosmos, visible universe and material realities, we must now see how the world is intimately associated with our destiny, how we are, as it were, woven out of its very substance.

But here our language betrays us and scarcely allows us any longer to enter directly into the intuition of our inspired authors. For to-day we instinctively isolate the living being from the environment in which he is placed, whereas the Bible, on the other hand, never looks at the world without considering mankind which has assumed responsibility for its affairs, any more than it looks at mankind apart from the world which maintains it in existence. The universe, for the Bible, always includes a human presence, and man's life is of necessity involved in material realities. It is true that God's message is addressed essentially to the sons of Adam, but these sons of Adam are "in the universe", to which they are mysteriously bound by inseparable links.

The idea brought to light here is expressed, therefore, in a language which is not ours, it is associated with a particular manner, no longer our own, of envisaging our situation in this world. However, that is no reason for denying it all value or refusing to take it into consideration. We shall devote, then, the first part of this chapter to a study of this language and this "poetic vision" of nature; not that we wish to extol unduly an adventitious, debatable representation of the universe; but we shall try and discover, behind certain modes of expression destined to pass out of use, a mode of thought which is not to alter.

For there is no question here of mere poetic construction without theological significance or relevance to our daily Christian life. The very aim of all our spiritual struggle is at stake; the seriousness of man's choice is, indeed, particularly heightened if he is held to be responsible for the universe. Is it really possible for us to involve nobody and nothing but ourselves? Do we not risk compromising the whole work of the Creator? Such is the problem to be discussed. Now Christ did not come only to save souls or even mankind; he came to save the world: "And I, if I be lifted up from the earth, will draw all things to myself" (John 12. 32).

A. THE POETIC SENSE OF NATURE AND BIBLICAL LANGUAGE[1]

A preliminary question which would seem to arise from the fact that the Bible associates the material world with the drama of salvation, is: What value should be attributed to its language in this field? For the Greeks have taught us to make a clear distinction between spirit and matter. It is indeed accepted to-day that the latter has meaning and significance, but, outside the realm of art and poetry, it is difficult to believe that it has a soul. The Semites had fewer scruples on the subject; they had no difficulty in attributing to the world about them the same ebb and flow of life and emotion they discovered in themselves, and they called upon the world to share their disappointments and successes.

[1] Article published in *Bible et Vie chrétienne*, No. 11, Sept., 1955, under the title "Poésie et sens de la nature dans la Bible".

Obviously, we must here discriminate between a mode of expression which bears the stamp of its period and the eternal substance of a message.

It must be admitted that the problem has hitherto been resolved in a rather negative fashion; the texts which we shall use as illustrations in this chapter have generally, in fact, been passed over without any attempt to take them very seriously. Yet these are texts which do mean something, and something quite precise; they have been too lightly touched upon, the pretext being that only the human, the strictly spiritual, drama merits our attention. Yet it is exceedingly difficult to consign to the realm of poetic fantasy all those passages which bring in the realities of nature, for the language of the Bible is realistic and concrete; and, if it is poetic, this is not because it evokes for us a magic sort of universe, but rather because there is in it a keen sense of movement and life. It is quite natural for this universe to come to life, to become personified when it has to play its part in the history of mankind.

A factual language, a sense of life and of movement, and an instinctive personification of everything that is familiar to man, these are the characteristics of the poetic sense of nature in the Bible. If once we accept this, we shall have no difficulty in entering into the logic of the sacred writers to share intimately in their thought without the risk of distorting any part of it.

The realism of biblical language

The reader who is unaccustomed to the language of the Bible will certainly feel somewhat baffled at first by a series of images which are completely foreign to his customary world of thought. In order to reassure him and help him on his way, well-intentioned commentators hasten to remind him now and again, in accompanying notes, that these are merely "poetic" exaggerations. This sort of commentary, however, occurs too frequently, especially when cosmic Messianism is involved, and it causes some embarrassment. Is it not sometimes a neat way of dismissing certain texts which do not seem to tally with our present-day conception of the world? For those with minds inured to the discipline of the positive sciences, this adjective "poetic" suggests the notion of inconsistency and unreality: "Such is the instinctive poetry of the human mind that it has a tendency to gain from facts an impression which is keener and deeper than the facts themselves."[1] And so it is: it is particularly misleading to speak of poetry in this sense, when referring to biblical language; for the Bible never takes us out of the world of reality into a universe of fiction where we can dream; with the Bible, we remain in the realm of concrete reality, of observed phenomena.

Furthermore, here as in all the writings of the ancients, there is a tendency to invest the word with the same reality as the object itself. The word receives something of the essence, the quality, of the object, to such an extent that to know the name of something amounts to the possession of an advantage, a hold over it, or to a knowledge of its secret;[2] one can therefore understand why Adam begins by giving a name to the animals in the garden, and why, conversely, the Jews avoided uttering the divine name from the third century onwards, since man could lay no claim to appropriate to himself, in any way whatever, the power of the God of Sinai.

But the name represents one particular case only; it possesses, in fact, the efficiency attributed in general to any word, be it oracle, advice, curse or blessing. Are not the poor in the psalter obsessed by the fear of evil words which their enemies may utter against them? As for blessings and curses, they are pictured as irresistible emanations penetrating people and things: "This is the curse that goeth forth over the face of the earth . . . I will bring it forth, saith the Lord of hosts: and it shall come to the house of the thief and to the house of him that sweareth falsely by my name: and it shall remain in the midst of his house, and shall consume it, with

---

[1] Guizot, *Histoire de la Civilisation en France*, 8ᵉ leçon; quoted in Littré, *Dictionnaire de la langue française*, article "Poésie", col. 1182.

[2] Cf. Contenau, *La Magie chez les Assyro-Babyloniens*, Paris, 1947; ch. III, "La doctrine du Nom", pp. 127 ff.

the timber thereof, and the stones thereof" (Zach. 5. 3–4). What has been said thus cannot be taken back, as the patriarch Isaac explains to his unfortunate elder son, whose brother had obtained through deceit his father's blessing: "And I have blessed him, and he shall be blessed" (Gen. 27. 33). To counter the effect of a curse which is in operation, there is no course open but to have a more powerful blessing pronounced in a contrary sense.[1] We may also recall the rôle played in royal court circles by those who give advice or bear messages, like Chusai, whom David had to send to Absalom with the express purpose of foiling the wily designs of Achitophel (2 Kings 15. 34). Let us merely point out how the message is embodied in the man who brings it, to such an extent that the character of the messenger shares in the essential quality of his message. When, at the time of Absalom's revolt, David, remaining in Mahanaim, awaits at the gates of the city news of the battle, he is finally informed by the watchman, who has perceived a runner, that it is Achimaas, son of Sadoc, whereupon the king exclaims: "He is a good man; and cometh with good news" (2 Kings 18. 27).[2]

But it is the oracle of the prophet which, more than any other word, is considered to be particularly efficacious. Thus, before setting out on a campaign, kings are anxious for favourable assurances from the divinity, imposing silence where necessary upon those men of Yahweh who would venture to express predictions contrary to their plans (3 Kings 22. 17–18). If so much trust had not been placed in the irreparably baleful influence of oracles presaging misfortune, there would never have been such bitter campaigns against such prophets as Amos, Osee, Isaias and Jeremias, who accompanied the words with gestures thus giving them a tenfold efficacy. For example, Eliseus, lying sick, said to king Joas: "Bring a bow and arrows . . . put thy hand upon the bow . . . Open the window to the east . . . Shoot an arrow . . . The arrow of the Lord's deliverance, and the arrow of the deliverance from Syria: and thou

[1] Ex. 12.32–6; Deut. 29.18–19; Judges 17.2; 2 Kings 21.3.
[2] Cf. 2 Kings 4.10; Prov. 12.17; 17.11; 25.13.

shalt strike the Syrians in Ephec, till thou consume them."
Then again: "Strike with an arrow upon the ground"; but
here the king struck only three times, which provoked the
prophet to anger: "If thou hadst smitten five or six or seven
times, thou hadst smitten Syria even to utter destruction; but
now three times shalt thou smite it" (4 Kings 13. 15–19).
And here again it is impossible to counteract the effect of a
prophetic gesture or oracle, except by the propagation of a
new message. When Hananias had broken the yoke from off
the neck of Jeremias, saying: "Even so will I break the yoke
of Nabuchodonosor the king of Babylon after two full years
from off the neck of all the nations" (Jer. 28. 11), the great
prophet of Anathoth had to go on his way very shamefaced;
but next day, after a night's reflexion, he returned, bearing a
yoke of iron, and, regaining the advantage, was able to exclaim:
"Thus saith the Lord: Thou hast broken chains of wood, and
thou shalt make for them chains of iron" (Jer. 28. 13).

The efficacy of word and gesture springs from the fact that
they are thought to contain in themselves the reality to which
they give expression. For it is not the mind of man which
creates the relationship between the token and the thing
signified; this relationship pertains to the object, even when it
seems to be a purely formal one, even when we can see
nothing but a play on words: "What seest thou, Amos? And
I said: A hook to draw down fruit (*qāyis*). And the Lord said
to me: The end (*qēs*) is come upon my people Israel" (Amos
8. 2). Similarly, in the Book of Jeremias, we read: "And the
word of the Lord came to me, saying: What seest thou,
Jeremias? And I said: I see a rod watching (a branch of almond
blossom—*shāqēd*). And the Lord said to me: Thou hast seen
well, for I will watch over (*shōqēd*) my word to perform it"
(Jer. 1. 11–12).

A comparison, therefore, will not appear to be merely the
result of any author's poetic fancy; it forms part of the thing
seen; everything springs from this objective reality which, at
the first impact of sensation, compels recognition in the
observer, to such an extent that Renan wrote: "What dis-

tinguishes the Semitic family is that the primitive close relationship between sensation and idea has always been maintained, that one of the two terms has never excluded the other, that, in a word, the process of idealization has never fully operated; so much so that, in each word, can be heard, as it were, an echo of the primitive sensations which determined the choice of the earliest appellations."[1]

Our biblical language, therefore, is inapt to serve a free, creative imagination; it is intended to express only things which have been actually experienced. This does not, of course, mean that it is never artificial, as when the sacred authors indulge too freely in clichés or exaggerate beyond measure accepted figures of speech. They do not, in fact, feel the need to be always creating a new expression, but are quite content to recall the image, for example, of a hidden lion as it lies in wait for its prey, or that of a starving bear, deprived of its cubs. In order to meet new situations, they will simply take up old themes, to which they will give unexpected proportions; thus the apocalypses will construct rambling edifices with borrowed materials; an examination of the detail of their background will, fundamentally, reveal nothing but simple, traditional images: storm, thunder, earthquake, darkened skies.[2] This disjointedness is evidence of a lack, rather than an excess, of imagination. Thus, even when it is inflated, the language of the Bible remains close to concrete reality and never turns into a language of escape. It is created by a reality from which it is unable to break away and over which it claims to have control.

The poetry of movement and life

If the word "poetry" is to evoke the idea of fantasy and unreality, the adjective "poetic" is unsuitable to qualify a language as factual as that of the Bible. But it is impossible to deny that Holy Writ has a true poetic sense, arising out of

---

[1] *Histoire générale et système comparé des langues sémitiques,* Paris, 1863, pp. 23–24.

[2] See chapter III above: A. The Theophanies of the God of history, an intervention that moves heaven and earth, p. 91.

a spontaneous perception of movement and of life. For the Semitic genius is more easily inspired by the life and vitality of the universe than by the harmony of its forms and colours. One will here seek in vain colourful, romantic pages, inspired by the sight of a sunrise or sunset, a starry night or the moon rising over a dark mountain-top; nor will one hear the gentle murmur of a clear spring, or the rustle of forests. Ben Sira, for example, when evoking the sun, moon, stars and rainbow (Ecclus 43. 1–12), does not seem to discern any colour; he is unaware of hues or tonalities, perceives only violent contrasts; for him, everything shines and dazzles. As for the psalmist, he is reminded by the sunrise of an exulting runner who sees the track before him, or of a bridegroom coming from his bed in triumph; but of its majestic clearing of the horizon, the author retains nothing more than an impression of growing heat: "His going out is from the end of heaven. And his circuit even to the end thereof: and there is no one that can hide himself from his heat" (Ps. 18. 7).

In nature, therefore, the sacred writers are sensitive only to movement. If they have any notion of a possible communion between the universe and the destiny of mankind, it is because they are aware of a common life and rhythm in both. So they will not waste time contemplating the harmony of forms, the splendour or the melancholy of outlines, but will derive their most frequent images from realities which move, change, are born and die: the wind bursting forth, the clouds scudding away, the fire burning up, the water flowing and swallowing up, the withered flower swept away by the storm: "Therefore they shall be as a morning cloud, and as the early dew that passeth away, as the dust that is driven with a whirlwind out of the floor, and as the smoke out of the chimney" (Osee 13. 3). So it is in the evocation of this vitality in things that the reader can discover the poetry of a new and powerful mode of expression; when, for example, he reads of the felled tree which "hath hope . . . If its root be old in the earth, and its stock be dead in the dust: at the scent of water, it shall spring, and bring forth leaves" (Job 14. 8–9), or of a thread of tow scorched by fire (Judges 16. 9).

The originality of this poetic sense, compared with our own, is evident in many details. For example, it will be noted that though we may use the same metaphors, we do not attribute exactly the same significance to them. We refer to the "break" of dawn as to a phenomenon which is worthy of retaining our attention by the variable play of its colours—the famous "rosy-fingered dawn"—whereas the prophet will be aware only of the coming invasion of light: "A numerous and strong people as the morning spread among the mountains" (Joel 2. 2). And whereas, for us, a shadow suggests the image of a vague presence, the Bible envisages it as the image of something which flees without ever pausing in one place, something after which one runs in vain,[1] something which goes on ahead, with no chance of turning back save by special intervention of God (4 Kings 20. 10–11); it appears here as a "fugitive shadow", whilst for us it is rather a "faint shadow". It is quite understandable that some translators of the Bible should have been mistaken in the matter, as when the original Crampon Bible reads: "*Et tous mes membres ne sont plus qu'une ombre*" (Job 17. 7)[2]—a reminiscence, perhaps, of the line of Horace: "*pulvis et umbra sumus*"—instead of: "My limbs are vanishing like a shadow".[3]

This poetic genius, it will readily be seen, displays itself to fullest advantage in the depiction of the animal world. Few inspired pages are not peopled with the fauna of land, sea and air: startled deer (Is. 13. 14), heifers treading out corn (Osee 10. 11), scattered sheep, etc. Here, the eagle glides through the air, the swallow soars aloft (Prov. 26. 2), the sparrow fusses about on the roof-top (Ps. 101. 8), the dove

---

[1] Job 8.9; 14.2; Eccl. 7.1; 8.13; Wisdom 2.5; Ps. 101.12; 108.23; 143.4.

[2] (Translator's note: "And my limbs are now no more than a shadow").

[3] Dhorme, *Job, Études bibliques, ad locum*. The "Bible de Jérusalem" translates: "*Mes membres s'évanouissent comme l'ombre*" (Translator's note: "My limbs are fading away like a shadow"), which gives little help as to the exact meaning of the image. (Translator's note: A comparison of a few English versions is not altogether encouraging. Douai has: "My limbs are brought as it were to nothing"; Knox: "My whole frame wasted away"; AV: "All my members are as a shadow"; RSV: "All my members are like a shadow").

circles without knowing where to alight (Osee 7. 11); there, the snared bird escapes from the net (Ps. 123. 7) and the locusts spread their wings (Nahum 3. 17). It is of "beasts, and of fowls, and of creeping things, and of fishes" that Solomon will discourse (3 Kings 4. 33), as he learns to look at the noble animals of creation: "There are three things which go well, and the fourth that walketh happily: a lion, the strongest of beasts, who hath no fear of any thing he meeteth: a cock girded about the loins: and a ram: and a king, whom none can resist" (Prov. 30. 29–30), as well as the tiny creatures, wiser than the wise: "The ants, a feeble people, which provide themselves food in the harvest: the rabbit, a weak people, which maketh its bed in the rock; the locust which hath no king, yet they all go out by their bands: the stellio which supporteth itself on hands, and dwelleth in kings' houses" (ib. 25–8).

This animal world, therefore, so well understood and so well loved, provides the Bible with its finest source of poetic inspiration. Let us just recall here the brilliant and striking portrait of the horse, taken from the Book of Job. God reveals himself to be not a little proud of having created such an animal, all nobility and dashing courage:

> Wilt thou give strength to the horse,
> or clothe his neck with neighing?
> Wilt thou lift him up like the locusts?
> The glory of his nostrils is terror.
> He breaketh up the earth with his hoof,
> he pranceth boldly, he goeth forward to meet armed men.
> He despiseth fear,
> he turneth not his back to the sword.
> Above him shall the quiver rattle,
> the spear and shield shall glitter.
> Chasing and raging he swalloweth the ground,
> neither doth he make account when the noise of the trumpet soundeth.
> When he heareth the trumpet he saith: Ha, ha.
> He smelleth the battle afar off,
> the encouraging of the captains,
> and the shouting of the army (Job 39. 19–25).

Personification of familiar beings

Possessing instinctively a sense of movement and of life, the sons of Israel will be prompt to endow with a soul the realities which surround them, in the midst of which their destiny is played out. It is a universally recognized tendency of primitive man in general to attribute human characteristics to the external world and to project upon it his own image: "It is in conformity with a general law that the names of the different parts of the body are applied to animals, plants, inanimate objects, even sometimes to abstractions. In this manner, man can project an external image of himself just as when he ascribes his own sentiments and emotions to the creatures which surround him."[1] Is there any need, however, to go to the extent of saying, in connexion with the Bible: "The close relation between the country and the life of the people is only possible because earth itself is alive. We know that the Israelites do not acknowledge the distinction between the psychic and the corporeal. Earth and stones are alive, imbued with a soul, and therefore able to receive mental subject-matter and bear the impress of it."[2] This view seems to us to be an overstatement of the case; there are, in fact, but few traces of such "animism" in the Bible, and those there are, are to be found in the oldest texts: the hymn to the well (Num. 21. 17–18), the incantation to the sun (Josue 10. 12), the image of the earth opening its mouth to swallow up Dathan and Abiron (Num. 16. 32), to drink in Abel's blood (Gen. 4. 11). Generally speaking, nature only appears to be capable of replying to man's summons, and vibrating in sympathy with the rhythm of man's destiny, for the simple reason that, without possessing living being, that is, an independent personality, it has the power of coming to life when brought into contact with the men and peoples which live surrounded by it.

The Bible shows, in fact, no tendency to personify indiscriminately all realities external to man; only that which

[1] Dhorme, *L'emploi métaphorique,* p. 161.
[2] Pedersen, *Israel,* I–II, p. 479.

directly concerns the drama of salvation is personified, e.g., the divine attributes presiding over history: the Justice and Fidelity of Yahweh,[1] his Wisdom (Prov. 1–9), the creative Word (Ps. 118, 89), etc. And if dawn takes on a human countenance, it is only in so far as it has come to prepare the advent of justice, holding and shaking the extremities of the earth in order to expel the ungodly: "From the wicked their light shall be taken away: and the high arm shall be broken" (Job 38. 12–15). But it is, above all, the nations and cities that we shall see brought to life in order to share in the joy and the troubles of mortals:

> Judea hath mourned,
> and the gates thereof are fallen
> and are become obscure on the ground,
> and the cry of Jerusalem is gone up (Jer. 14. 2).
> And her gates shall lament and mourn:
> and she shall sit desolate on the ground (Is. 3. 26).
> How doth the city sit solitary that was full of people!
> How is the mistress of the Gentiles become as a widow
> (Lam. 1. 1).

Bold as such images may be, they nevertheless do evoke very concrete realities; the land, with its geographical features, is here present in the minds of the inspired writers, quite as much as the people in their social and political organization: "Egypt riseth up like a flood,[2] and the waves thereof shall be moved as rivers. And he shall say: I will go up and will cover the earth. I will destroy the city and its inhabitants" (Jer. 46. 8). We should not speak glibly here of a use of metonymy; nations and cities are not brought in as a substitute for the inhabitants: both realities are quite distinct, and there is a clear passage of thought from one to the other, from what contains to what is contained. Just as reference is made to "the earth and the fulness thereof",[3] "the sea and the fulness

---

[1] Ps. 35.6; 70.18–19; 84.11–12; 88.15; 107.5.

[2] (Translator's note: i.e. the Nile).

[3] Ps. 23.1; 49.12; 88.12; Deut. 33.16; Is.34.1; Jer. 8.16; 47.2; Ez. 19.7; 30.12; Mich. 1.2.

thereof", [1] the prophet exclaims: "Because thou hast spoiled many nations, all that shall be left of the people shall spoil thee: because of men's blood, and for the iniquity of the land, of the city, and of all that dwell therein" (Hab. 2. 8).

The external world alone may sometimes hold the attention: "The ways of Sion mourn, because there are none that come to the solemn feast" (Lam. 1. 4), but, even here, the sacred authors are interested in the external world only because of the people inhabiting it; they never assume that it has any particular, independent personality. The earth comes to life only in its relations with the men who live on it: against the sinner, it will rise in revolt (Job 20. 27), it will yield its fruit no longer to Abel's murderer (Gen. 4. 10–12), its wine shall disown the wanton, Israel (Osee 9. 2); stones and timbers cry out for vengeance (Hab. 2. 11) and, finally, the land vomits out its inhabitants (Lev. 18. 25, 28): "If my land cry against me, and with it the furrows thereof mourn: if I have eaten the fruits thereof without money" (Job 31. 38–9).

So we should not be surprised to see the earth summoned to hear God's judgement: "O earth, earth, earth, hear the word of the Lord" (Jer. 22. 29; cf. 6. 18). "Let the earth hear, and all that is therein, the world, and every thing that cometh forth from it" (Is. 34. 1); nor should we find it strange that the earth should applaud the triumph of the elect: "Let the heavens rejoice, and let the earth be glad, let the sea be moved, and the fulness thereof: the fields and all things that are in them shall be joyful. Then shall all the trees of the world rejoice" (Ps. 95. 11–12).

It is surely by now clear that these inspired texts ought not to be considered as mere poetic flights of fancy; their aim is rather to evoke for us a very real communion between the earth and the men who live on it; and we have no right to reject *a priori* this idea. Perhaps we have, in the past, been too quick to dissociate, in an unreasonably conclusive and arbitrary manner, the religious drama of humanity from the universe on which it is staged. Could we not, even to-day—

[1] Ps. 95.11; 97.7; Is. 42.10; etc.

without, of course, taking to the writing of fables—imagine
a concrete union between the life of nature and the life of
history?

B. THE COSMIC REPERCUSSIONS OF THE DRAMA OF SALVATION[1]

For the expectation of the creature waiteth for the revelation
of the sons of God. For the creature was made subject to
vanity: not willingly, but by reason of him that made it subject,
in hope. Because the creature also itself shall be delivered from
the servitude of corruption, into the liberty of the glory of the
children of God. For we know that every creature groaneth
and travaileth in pain, even till now.   *Rom. 8. 19-22.*

"This passage of St Paul," comments Fr Huby,[2] "in which
is so clearly set out the participation of the universe in the
destinies of man, is one of the most noteworthy passages in
the whole of Pauline doctrine for the scope and depth of the
views it contains. It is furthermore one of the passages which
surprise even Christians, to the point of disconcerting them.
The immense perspective that St Paul sees before him is above
their comprehension, because they are not sufficiently aware
of the place that mankind occupies in total creation, and
imagine that the human world is shut in upon itself. For
the Apostle, Christ did not assume an abstract nature, utterly
remote from the bonds which unite man and creation. His
work of redemption extends throughout the whole of creation,
and all is marked with the seal of the Cross."
Perhaps we may be permitted to add that such a point of
view is not, fundamentally, peculiar to St Paul. It has been
prepared and elaborated by the whole of the Old Testament,
in response to a deep desire which mankind has never ceased
to express; for the world resists the ascendancy of a humanity
which seeks to subject everything to its own rhythm, whereas
man seems always to have dreamed of this unity in the
anthroposphere which Marx expressed in his definition: "Man

---

[1] Article in *La Vie spirituelle*, Dec. 1957.
[2] Huby, *Épître aux Romains*, Coll "Verbum Salutis", Paris, 1950, pp. 297-298.

12

is his action upon the world". In the earliest settled civilizations, the liturgies of expiation and regeneration made an
attempt to narrow the differences between the forces of life
and the ambitions of men. Taking as its starting-point a
similar intuition, the Bible, for its part, considers that the
restoration of complete harmony in creation will ultimately
result from man's return to favour with his God. Here,
man and his earth form an entity. When the God of Israel
comes to punish or to rescue, his hand falls not only upon the
sons of Adam, but also on the whole environment in which
their existence is plunged. Evil, then, wrecks the whole order
in nature; man's sin and his salvation involve the whole realm
of creation.

Man and his earth

The notion of an external world appears to be a modern
abstraction, unknown, at all events, to the inspired authors.
The Bible cannot isolate container from contents, or, conversely, the living being from his environment. Thus, for
example, time will be defined by the events which constitute
it, and so we find expressions such as the day of Madian, or
the day of Gedeon, or the day of Yahweh. Space, in a similar
way, never appears like an inert, lifeless box; it is always the
sea where the fish swim, the water whose surface is streaked
by sea-birds, the ground trodden upon by the beasts of the
fields, or the land belonging to such and such a people.

Life, therefore, cannot be isolated from the ground that
sustains it, in which it remains of necessity rooted. It is on
the land of the living that one walks in the presence of God
(Ps. 114. 9), enjoying there his goodness (Ps. 26. 13). But the
deletion, or the uprooting, of the living from the earth, or their
extirpation from beneath the heavens,[1] is equivalent to sentence
of death, which will be complete the day the very memory of
the man is effaced from this earth (Ps. 108. 15): "If one swallow
him up out of his place, he shall deny him, and shall say:
I know thee not" (Job 8. 18).

[1] Gen. 6.7; 2 Kings 4.11; Ps. 118.87; Jer. 11.19; Lam. 3.66; etc.

Every human community possesses its piece of land outside which it ceases to exist, a place that knows us and is known by us (Jer. 17. 4). Thus the land of Palestine is an integral part of the unique destiny of Israel. An inheritance occupied on the terms of the Covenant (Jer. 17. 4), it is here that Yahweh has chosen to dwell among his children (Num. 35. 34) and here alone that worship of him seems possible: "How shall we sing the song of the Lord in a strange land?" (Ps. 136. 4). To abandon this familiar earth which surrounds our existence and harbours like a mother in her womb the corpse which death has rendered completely helpless,[1] is equivalent to being flung alive into the emptiness and horror of the unknown. Hence we can appreciate the harshness of the message given by Jeremias: "As you have forsaken me and served a strange god in your own land, so shall you serve strangers in a land that is not your own" (Jer. 5. 19).

* * *

Any land constitutes, together with its inhabitants, a single, living reality; the land of Israel, however, by virtue of the Covenant, acquires particular dignity: it shares in the consecration of the elect. Their gaze constantly directed towards this land, which they considered to be the only pure soil (Amos 7. 17; Osee 9. 3–4), the exiles even dream of altering its physical structure in order to render it more holy.[2] A few centuries later, an apocalyptic passage from the Book of Zacharias will announce a complete hallowing of the land, to come at the end of time: "In that day that which is upon the bridle of the horse shall be holy to the Lord: and the caldrons in the house of the Lord shall be as the phials before the altar.

[1] We have no space here to insist upon the importance attached to burial; we can merely refer readers to: Deut. 28.26; 1 Kings 17.44,46; 3 Kings 14.11; 16.4; 21.24; Ps. 78.2; Jer. 7.33; 16.4; 19.7; 22.19; 34.20.

[2] This concerns especially chapter 48 of the Book of Ezechiel. Through a curious oversight which may be explained by his long absence, the prophet seems to have lost the sense of a third dimension; he sees nothing but flat surfaces anywhere, and this doubtless renders in concrete form, in space, his notion of holiness. This holiness moreover, is for the most part a purely ritual one, and it may be noted that the phrase "holy land" is not met until very late, and then twice only in the Old Testament: Zach. 2.12; 2 Mac. 1.7.

And every caldron in Jerusalem and Juda shall be sanctified to the Lord of hosts: and all that sacrifice shall come, and take of them and shall seethe in them: and the merchant shall be no more in the house of the Lord of hosts in that day" (Zach. 14. 20–21).

This consecration of the land, however, remains conditional upon the fidelity of Israel; for the sin of the chosen people will lead them into exile, that is, will involve a cessation of worship in Jerusalem and the profanation of the land: "I will give it into the hands of strangers for spoil and to the wicked of the earth for a prey: and they shall defile it. And I will turn away my face from them, and they shall violate my secret place: and robbers shall enter into it and defile it" (Ez. 7. 21–2). This desecration is not, however, merely the result of the chosen people's departure; the impurity of man appears to have been communicated to the earth, like an emanation which makes its way from persons to things: "For all these detestable things the inhabitants of the land have done, that were before you, and have defiled it. Beware then, lest in like manner, it vomit you also out, if you do the like things: as it vomited out the nation that was before you" (Lev. 18. 27–8). Initially, it was a mere matter of ritual transgressions, but, with the development of the moral conscience, the sad privilege of defiling the land was extended to the sins and infidelities of Israel, so that Jeremias will be able to accuse the elect of having profaned the land by "the facility of (their) fornication" (Jer. 3. 9).

Directly affected by the wickedness of its inhabitants, the land will then rise up against the sinner (Job 20. 27), refusing its fruit to the killer of Abel, for example (Gen. 4. 10–12). In the shame of its defilement, the soil will even go so far as to vomit forth those it has borne, or devour them: "Because they say of you: Thou art a devourer of men and one that suffocatest thy nation" (Ez. 36. 13).

*   *   *

Linked so intimately with the life of its inhabitants, the land cannot fail to share their destiny, and threats and promises are directed towards country as well as citizens: "I will forsake you and the city which I gave to you and to your fathers" (Jer. 23. 39). It is indeed tempting to see in this passage merely an example of metonymy. But to do so would certainly not be doing justice to the thought of the inspired writers; for the allusion is here to the land itself as land. Besides, it frequently happens that the vision of the cursed land is by itself alone sufficient to provoke the prophet's indictment of it:

> For the mountains I will take up weeping and lamentation,
> and for the beautiful places of the desert, mourning:
> because they are burnt up,
> for that there is not a man that passeth through them.
> And they have not heard the voice of the owner:
> from the fowl of the air to the beasts,
> they are gone away and departed.
> And I will make Jerusalem to be heaps of sand
> and dens of dragons:
> and I will make the cities of Juda desolate
> for want of an inhabitant (Jer. 9. 10–11).

Later, Ezechiel and the Second Isaias will not hesitate to deliver to this same land quite a different message, that of salvation:

> Ye mountains of Israel, hear the word of the Lord . . . I am for you and I will turn to you, and you shall be ploughed and sown. And I will multiply men upon you and all the house of Israel: and the cities shall be inhabited and the ruinous places shall be repaired. And I will make you abound with men and with beasts: and they shall be multiplied and increased. And I will settle you as from the beginning and will give you greater gifts than you had from the beginning. And you shall know that I am the Lord (Ez. 36. 1–15).

The inhabitants, therefore, leave on their land the imprint of their destiny, and the soil of Palestine was for a long time to bear the signs of the great dramatic history of Israel. Is it not, in fact, in the ground itself that historical continuity is given concrete expression? Various generations may come and go, but the land remains, retaining the memory of both triumphs and disasters experienced by its inhabitants. The earth, mother of all (Job 1. 21; Ecclus 40. 1), envelops indissolubly in her womb the life and the drama of mankind.

The deeds of God as far-reaching as the universe

Since earth and man form an inseparable unity, divine action cannot isolate the creature, lifting him out of his environment in order to reach and affect him alone. The dialogue with God is of necessity held in the world and implicates the world.

*   *   *

Although the divine word is written in men's hearts (Deut. 30. 14), it is not whispered in the ear, as if it were a piece of private news. The earth and the heavens are there to act as witnesses: "Hear, O ye heavens, and give ear, O earth, for the Lord hath spoken" (Is. 1. 2).[1] Once again, we must not see in this a mere poetic image. The fact is noted in a perfectly concrete fashion, the anguished waiting of the universe, on the announcement of God's judgement, being compared with the heavy anxiety weighing over all beings after the first rumble of thunder: "Thou hast caused judgment to be heard from heaven: the earth trembled and was still" (Ps. 75. 9). It might be said that for the whole world the hour of the great liturgical silence has now come: "Let all the earth keep silence before him" (Hab. 2. 20).[2]

These witnesses are anything but indifferent spectators: "Be astonished, O ye heavens, at this: and ye gates thereof, be very desolate, saith the Lord. For my people have done two evils" (Jer. 2. 12–13); their shuddering is like that of simple mortals; it is an attack of giddiness, a loss of balance: "The Lord hath reigned, let the people be angry: he that

[1] Cf. Deut. 4.26; 30.19; 31.28; Is. 34.1; Micheas 1.2; 6.2; Jer. 2.12; 6.19; 22.29.

[2] Cf. Soph. 1.7; Zach. 2.13; Apoc. 8.1.

sitteth on the cherubims, let the earth be moved" (Ps. 98. 1).
"At his wrath the earth shall tremble, and the nations shall
not be able to abide his threatening" (Jer. 10. 10). Yet, if
divine anger shakes the whole world from the seabed to the
mountain-top (Ps. 113. 3–7), the sin of mankind is alone
responsible for it: "Was thy wrath upon the rivers? Or thy
indignation in the sea? . . . In thy anger thou wilt tread the
earth under foot: in thy wrath thou wilt astonish the nations"
(Hab. 3. 8–12).

*   *   *

Admittedly, the universe is not only a witness in the affair,
it also shares in the punishment directed against men: "I will
stretch forth my hand upon them: and I will make the land
desolate and abandoned, from the desert of Deblatha, in all
their dwelling places" (Ez. 6. 14). "Behold my wrath and my
indignation is enkindled against this place, upon man and
upon beasts, and upon the trees of the field, and upon the
fruits of the land, and it shall burn and shall not be quenched"
(Jer. 7. 20). "He stretched out his hand over the sea: he
troubled kingdoms" (Is. 23. 11).

Divine action, indeed, appears to be incapable of stopping
short at the boundaries of the human domain; it penetrates
directly into a whole milieu of life:

> Behold, the day of the Lord shall come, a cruel day,
> and full of indignation and of wrath and fury,
> to lay the land desolate,
> and to destroy the sinners thereof out of it.
> For the stars of heaven and their brightness
> shall not display their light:
> the sun shall be darkened in his rising,
> and the moon shall not shine with her light.
> And I will visit the evils of the world,
> and against the wicked for their iniquity (Is. 13. 9–11).

And in order to come and chastise mortals, Yahweh overwhelms and destroys everything, hills, rocks, the fish in the sea,
the birds of the air, the beasts of the field and all the creeping

things of earth: "I will gather together all things from off the face of the land, saith the Lord: I will gather man and beast: I will gather the birds of the air and the fishes of the sea. And the ungodly shall meet with ruin" (Soph. 1. 2–3).[1]

This cosmic upheaval, it should be noted, is on the same scale as the judgement concerning history. Before the Exile, for example, the prophets scarcely mentioned anything that was to occur beyond the frontiers of Palestine, for the drama essentially affected an Israel grouped together in its own territory:

> I beheld the earth, and lo it was void and nothing:
> and the heavens, and there was no light in them.
> I looked upon the mountains, and behold they trembled:
> and all the hills were troubled.
> I beheld, and lo there was no man:
> and all the birds of the air were gone.
> I looked, and behold Carmel was a wilderness:
> and all its cities were destroyed
> at the presence of the Lord, and at the presence of the wrath
> of his indignation (Jer. 4. 23–6).

But an intervention by God against the whole of humanity will have repercussions throughout the universe, endangering its very stability: "I will move both heaven and earth. And I will overthrow the throne of kingdoms" (Aggeus 2. 22–3; cf. 2. 7–8); and here we have, as seen above, the origin of those generalized catastrophes which the apocalyptic writers have heralded for the end of time. In his determination to chastise kings, Yahweh will shatter the earth (Is. 24. 12–13) and will roll up the heavens like a scroll (Is. 34. 2–4).

The hand of God makes no distinction between man and his environment: it affects external nature at the same time and as thoroughly as it does history.

*   *   *

Obviously, the external world will have a right to something more than the bare "privilege" of suffering from Yahweh's acts of vengeance; it will also have its share in the happiness

[1] Cf. Ez. 38.20.

which he reserves for the elect. For the God of Israel is Most High over all the earth, which will, by this very fact, be filled with his mercy and his glory: "For the earth is filled with the knowledge of the Lord, as the covering waters of the sea" (Is. 11. 9; Hab. 2. 14).[1]

Here again, one might be tempted to speak of metonymy; thus, for example, in the verse: "That we may know thy way upon earth: thy salvation in all nations" (Ps. 66. 3), the terms "earth" and "nations" might be considered as synonymous. But, treated thus, the fairest thoughts soon become shockingly trite. We do not think that the statement: "Truth is sprung out of the earth: and justice hath looked down from heaven" (Ps. 84. 12) means "The inhabitants of the earth shall become faithful and the God of heaven shall exercise his justice". Truth and justice are here two divine attributes pervading the whole domain of creation, from the depths of the earth to the heights of heaven.[2]

Besides, a good many texts are available to confirm this interpretation: "Thy power, and thy justice, O God, even to the highest great things thou hast done" (Ps. 70. 18–19). "O Lord, thy mercy is in heaven: and thy truth reacheth even to the clouds" (Ps. 35. 6; 107. 5). Similarly, a well known prophecy in the Book of Isaias gives praise to God's salvation and love which spread throughout the universe:

Drop down dew, ye heavens, from above:
and let the clouds rain the just.
Let the earth be opened
and bud forth a saviour:
and let justice spring up to together.
I the Lord have created him (Is. 45. 8).

Here, as with the effects of divine wrath, we have an extension to the whole of nature of the mercy shown to men: "Surely

[1] Ps. 118.64; Is. 4; Num. 14.21.

[2] The interpretation of this verse has been falsified by the exegesis usually given of the preceding verse. We think both the niphals should be understood in a vaguer manner, and should read: "Encounter of Mercy and Truth, embrace of Justice and Peace". See: "L'Heure d'une réconciliation universelle", in *Bible et Vie chrétienne*, 24, Dec. 1958, p. 75, note 14, and pp. 77–9.

his salvation is near to them that fear him: that glory may dwell in our land" (Ps. 84. 10).

*   *   *

Sharing in the salvation of men, the universe will also share in their joy:

> For you shall go out with joy
> and be led forth with peace.
> The mountains and the hills shall sing praise before you:
> and all the trees of the country shall clap their hands (Is. 55.12).

And, in speaking thus, the prophet certainly means to give his words a concrete value:

> Instead of the shrub, shall come up the fir-tree,
> and instead of the nettle, shall come up the myrtle-tree
> (Is. 55. 13).
> The land that was desolate and impassable shall be glad:
> and the wilderness shall rejoice and shall flourish like the lily.
> It shall bud forth and blossom,
> and shall rejoice with joy and praise (Is. 35. 1–2).

Here, more than anywhere else, we must insist upon the fact that such cosmic exultation is essentially an association of nature with the exultation of redeemed man. Thus the famous verse: "The heavens shew forth the glory of God: and the firmament declareth the work of his hands" (Ps. 18. 2), sings far less of the magnificence of creation in itself than of the gift of faith which will be symbolized by the majestic appearance of the blazing sun. For it is always in this way that things are presented to us:[1]

> Give praise, O ye heavens, for the Lord hath shewn mercy:
> shout with joy, ye ends of the earth.
> Ye mountains, resound with praise,
> thou, O forest, and every tree therein:

[1] In the Book of Job, one does, indeed, hear of stars singing together on the day of the earth's appearing (38.7). Here the stars form Yahweh's court; it is their role to utter the customary acclamation when the foundation-stone of a temple is laid (1 Esd. 3; Zach. 4.7).

for the Lord hath redeemed Jacob,
and Israel shall be glorified (Is. 44. 23).
Give praise, O ye heavens, and rejoice, O earth;
ye mountains, give praise with jubilation:
because the Lord hath comforted his people
and will have mercy on his poor ones (Is. 49. 13).

We need only to read Psalm 148 in order to realize that the point is the salvation of mankind and not the fact of the creation alone. In this psalm, all the works of God are invited to give praise to the Lord, following the order of their creation: the establishment of the heavens, the separation of the waters, the uprising of the mountains, the emergence of life, the appearance of human beings of all ages. And it is only at the end that we are given the reason for this enthusiasm which is to fire the whole universe: Yahweh has assured the triumph of his people: "The praise of him is above heaven and earth: and he hath exalted the horn of his people. A hymn to all his saints: to the children of Israel, a people approaching to him" (Ps. 148. 14).

In this intuition of a close communing of the universe with the joy of our salvation, will be found the key to many passages about which the reader often feels uncertain. Without drawing any further theological conclusions from this, let us merely emphasize the fact that these inspired texts can, in this manner, be immediately restored to their natural and obvious meaning, without any attempts at arbitrary spiritualization or allegorical transposition.

Degradation and redemption of the universe

Nature and man form an entity which God never dissociates when he acts. But alas! the closeness of their relationship has been disturbed by sin, for peace between man and the world necessarily implies peace between man and God.

*　　*　　*

All settled races, it seems, have nourished a dream of complete harmony between themselves and the soil they occupy. Unfortunately, life in nature periodically dies away, as if opposing control by mortals. But, with the return of the new year, the accession of a king, the dedication of a temple, we see hope revive in a superabundant rising of the sap: "Towards the sky, a wind of water shall proclaim it; from the sky shall come abundance; the land with abundance shall overflow. From my temple, when the foundations are laid, let abundance come! The plain (lit. the vast field) shall yield thee much produce. The rivers shall press against their banks: under the earth, water which used not to come out, will, for thee, appear. In the land of Shumer, oil shall be poured out; (the land) in abundance of wool shall be covered".[1]

Israel did not fail to make specially applicable to itself this dream, which is common to all peoples. With the Israelites, even more than elsewhere, the presence of the temple amounts to a pledge of life and prosperity for the nation.[2] For heaven and earth will answer to the desires of man in as far as Yahweh is there to achieve a total harmony in creation: "I will hear the heavens. And they shall hear the earth. And the earth shall hear the corn and the wine and the oil. And these shall hear Jezrahel"[3] (Osee 2. 21–2). "For the Lord will give goodness: and our earth shall yield her fruit" (Ps. 84. 13). And, each time a successor of David takes his place on the throne, one gets the impression that the God of Israel is regaining control of his territory, giving an indication of the coming total regeneration of the forces of nature: "And there shall be a firmament on the earth on the tops of mountains: above Libanus shall the fruit thereof be exalted. And they of the city shall flourish like the grass of the earth" (Ps. 71. 16).

Civilization had in the most primitive times appeared as a victory of man over the wild animals. This is one of the major themes of the epic legend of Gilgamesh, which the Bible did not fail to exploit. Everyone will, of course, know the passage in Genesis where Adam gives names to the various animals in the Garden of Eden (Gen. 2. 20):

---

[1] From the famous inscription *Gudea Patesi* of Lagash, quoted in Podechard, *Le Psautier*, Lyons, 1949, p. 312.
[2] Ez. 47; Joel 3.18 (=4.18); Zach. 14.8.
[3] The prophetic name of the renewed Israel: "seed of God".

Thou hast set him over the works of thy hands.
Thou hast subjected all things under his feet:
all sheep and oxen,
moreover the beasts also of the fields.
The birds of the air, and the fishes of the sea
that pass through the paths of the sea (Ps. 8. 7–9).

But many other texts echo these familiar verses:

And in that day I will make a covenant with them,
with the beasts of the field and with the fowls of the air
and with the creeping things of the earth (Osee 2. 18).
In destruction and famine thou shalt laugh:
and thou shalt not be afraid of the beasts of the earth.
But thou shalt have a covenant with the stones of the lands:
and the beasts of the earth shall be at peace with thee (Job
5. 22–23).
Thou shalt walk upon the asp and the basilisk:[1]
and thou shalt trample under foot the lion and the dragon
(Ps. 90. 13).

Furthermore, this submissiveness of the animal world to man
fits admirably into the vistas of peace of which the Covenant
gives hope:

And I will make a covenant of peace with them and will
cause the evil beasts to cease out of the land: and they that dwell
in the wilderness shall sleep secure in the forests. And I will
make them a blessing round about my hill and I will send
down the rain in its season: there shall be showers of blessing.
And the tree of the field shall yield its fruit and the earth shall
yield her increase and they shall be in their land without fear
(Ez. 34. 25–7).
I will give peace in your coasts: you shall sleep, and there
shall be none to make you afraid (Lev. 26. 6).

This is a noble dream which will, in fact, grow with the expectation of the Messianic kingdom. When God made his
covenant with Noe, he did indeed allow people to eat meat,
but this was merely a concession to a degenerate universe,

[1] Here, the serpent, as in Genesis, typifies a world treacherously hostile to
man.

riddled with sin (Gen. 9. 3); originally, it was not intended that the work of the Creator should be stained with blood, and the entire animal world was subject to a strictly vegetarian diet (Gen. 1. 29–30), and here is the prophet Isaias foreseeing how, for the advent of the Messias-King, the whole of nature will recover its pristine state of absolute purity:

> The wolf shall dwell with the lamb:
> and the leopard shall lie down with the kid.
> The calf and the lion and the sheep shall abide together:
> and a little child shall lead them.
> The calf and the bear shall feed,
> their young ones shall rest together:
> and the lion shall eat straw like the ox.
> And the sucking child shall play on the hole of the asp:
> and the weaned child shall thrust his hand into the den of the basilisk.

The inspired author will then conclude:

> They shall not hurt, nor shall they kill
> in all my holy mountain (Is. 11. 6–9).

*   *   *

Such a dream was, alas, to be constantly frustrated by fact. But the responsibility for failure lies, not with the organization of things, it lies with man himself: "Nothing upon earth is done without a cause: and sorrow doth not spring out of the ground. Man is born to labour, and the bird to fly" (Job 5. 6–7). And it is his sin that disturbs the harmony of creation:

> There is no truth, and there is no mercy,
> and there is no knowledge of God in the land.
> Cursing and lying and killing and theft
> and adultery have overflowed:
> and blood hath touched blood.
> Therefore shall the land mourn
> and every one that dwelleth in it shall languish,
> with the beasts of the field and with the fowls of the air:
> yea, the fishes of the sea shall also be gathered together (Osee 4. 1–3).

In fact, through his sin, man makes himself an enemy of the universe, at the same time as he cuts himself off from God and shatters the unity of his species (Gen. 11. 1–9): "Cursed is the earth in thy work; with labour and toil shalt thou eat thereof all the days of thy life. Thorns and thistles shall it bring forth to thee; and thou shalt eat the herbs of the earth" (Gen. 3. 17–18). We should see in this a consequence of sin in general, and not solely of original sin, for a few pages further on Yahweh cries to the murderer of Abel: "What hast thou done? The voice of thy brother's blood crieth to me from the earth. Now, therefore, cursed shalt thou be upon the earth, which hath opened her mouth, and received the blood of thy brother at thy hand. When thou shalt till it, it shall not yield to thee its fruit: a fugitive and a vagabond shalt thou be upon the earth" (Gen. 4. 10–12). A veiled hostility will henceforth exist between man and his soil. Sin has estranged him from the universe which surrounds him, and the animal world will similarly war with him:

> Wherefore a lion out of the wood hath slain them,
> a wolf in the evening hath spoiled them,
> a leopard watcheth for their cities:
> every one that shall go out thence shall be taken,
> because their transgressions are multiplied,
> their rebellions are strengthened (Jer. 5. 6).

The ancients believed they could, with the aid of periodical liturgies of purification, put right this decomposition of the cosmos. They could see the sun rising triumphantly over the line of the horizon each new day. Every year, life reappeared on the face of the earth after apparently dying. But the grace of Yahweh does not obey the laws of an indefinitely renewable cycle. It is on the day and at the hour chosen by him that nature will be reborn with her power increased tenfold:

> Behold the days come, saith the Lord,
> when the ploughman shall overtake the reaper
> and the treader of grapes him that soweth seed:
> and the mountains shall drop sweetness
> and every hill shall be tilled (Amos 9. 13).

And it shall come to pass in that day,
that the mountains shall drop down sweetness
and the hills shall flow with milk:
and waters shall flow through all the rivers of Juda (Joel
3. 18) (=4. 18).

And this restored nature[1] will be much more beautiful than
before. Instead of Adam, a child shall be master of the world,
according to the prophecy of Isaias. The apocalyptic writers
will even hail the dawn of an entirely new universe, for the
old world will have to die together with the sin which has
corrupted it: "For behold I create new heavens and a new
earth: and the former things shall not be in remembrance"
(Is. 65. 17). "*Ecce nova facio omnia*—Behold, I make all things
new" (Apoc. 21. 5).

*   *   *

The passages quoted above may seem strange at first sight,
but they do express, nevertheless, an intuition which is as
simple as it is profound: the universe is completely in tune
with the destiny of man, and it will find its fulfilment only in
the salvation of man.

Although he views things in a different light, the man of
to-day, like the ancients, cannot think of his own destiny
without associating it closely with the general organization
of the cosmos. It is therefore useful to emphasize that Christ
came not only for the redemption of souls, nor for the liberation
of humanity, but for the salvation of the entire world. The
Christian message means little in certain quarters given up
to technology and science. This is because the real message
has been unconsciously mutilated and emasculated till it
appears totally irrelevant to the lives of those who are absorbed
in their effort to dominate nature.

Such cosmic vistas do, in fact, pertain to a genuine spiritual
life. The Canticle to Brother Sun is no accidental trait in the
holiness of Francis of Assisi. We have to look at the world

[1] The idea has been put forward that this is a mere question of allegory.
There is nothing, in our opinion, to justify this hypothesis.

not solely in order to discover the munificence of the Creator, but also to find in it a keener awareness of the splendour of our vocation. With us lies the responsibility of completing the work of creation by the manifestation of our charity.   This charity of the sons of God is no secondary phenomenon on the surface of the universe, but the keystone whereby the whole acquires significance and cohesion.

Following the Old and the New Testaments, we must associate in our eucharist this cosmos which, from the planning of the atom to the emergence of life itself, has prepared and awaited our coming. As members of Christ, we are associated in this fullness of the Godhead (Col. 2. 9) of which the Apostle speaks at such length: "Because in him, it hath well-pleased the Father that all fulness should dwell: and through him to reconcile all things unto himself, making peace through the blood of his cross" (Col. 1. 19–20).

CONCLUSION

THE UNIVERSE AND THE SPIRITUAL LIFE
OF CHRISTIANS

For many, the spiritual life of man is completely contained within the framework of his intimate, personal relationship with God; no emphasis is placed on the fact that total submission to the will of God must change the behaviour of man in the universe. And yet, every effort towards perfection must of necessity be expressed in a new attitude towards others and towards the world; this attitude, unlike mystical elevations, is never misleading. Such has been the judgement of the Church, which has ever made charity the true criterion of holiness: "If any man say: I love God, and hateth his brother; he is a liar" (1 John 4. 20). Now, this humanity which love brings together has deep roots in the heart of the material universe, which is itself an extension of our body and which can be utilized in order either to kill or to make live; thus the universe, too, awaits impatiently "for the revelation of the sons of God", in order to "be delivered . . . into the liberty of the glory of the children of God" (Rom. 8. 19–21). Can one really be said to have known the Father when one has not discovered in nature the visible sign of his love, when one has not come to offer God the fruit of a work by which the work of creation is consummated? For want of attributing to this vision of the world the importance it merits, one overrates too frequently the significance of many religious texts which are perhaps scarcely more than mere words. It is by the observable attitude of the believer in given circumstances and not by lofty expressions of poetic or philosophical thought that one must appreciate the genuineness of his understanding of God.

By allowing us to participate in the dialogue between God

and his people, the Bible suggests to us a certain manner of observing the world, of using it, of exercising an action upon it. The humanity which God takes in hand is no interplanetary humanity, as it were, but it is deeply rooted in this earth "Man is his action upon the world," said Marx, and the man moulded and brought to completion by the God of Sinai, is precisely a man who wields his influence over the world, together with all the present and past bonds which link him indissolubly with the cosmos.

The history of man linked with the movement of the universe

By proclaiming the summons of a transcendent God, the Bible unites, in a manner never before experienced, the movement of the universe with the momentum of history. The people chosen by God will, in fact, never be strangers in the midst of a hostile world; everything, on the other hand, will be friendly and familiar. For example, Israel will be able to discern, in the unfolding of the work of creation, an indication of its own drama, whilst the ordinary, daily natural phenomena will reveal the loving presence of the One who works for its salvation. Thus Israel will find all around it evidence of faithful attentiveness and triumphant love. But mere looking is not enough; action too is necessary; this world which reveals the Father is the "inheritance" of the sons; they will, therefore, have to bear responsibility for it, and their shoulders will feel the weight of a creation yet to be completed. A voice from beyond has called upon the universe to serve in the wake of history: everything that really exists has found its place within the limits of a single, unique design.

No religious or philosophical system ever offered such a coherent vision of the whole of creation. Polytheism might have been expected to reveal a principle of unity in those realities of nature amongst which man plays out his destiny, and tries to enlist the support of the powers of the sea, of the air, and of life on earth; but man found that he had to negotiate separately with each of these, and always he lay at the mercy of some outburst of ill humour on the part of an unknown god who had been momentarily neglected. No doubt the universe had assumed a human countenance, but it remained multiple, and the divinities, caught in the selfish game of the passions attributed to them, finally remained indifferent to the drama of the sons of Adam. Man thought he had found allies, accomplices; as a matter of fact, he had no loving hand to guide him, to take responsibility for his destiny, to put him completely at ease in the bosom of the universe.[1]

Even with the coming of Greek thought and philosophy, a satisfactory solution to the problem of human drama and its place in the development of the cosmos was scarcely brought any nearer. Energies were stimulated by new ideals—virtue, reason, beauty—which encouraged men to place their ambitions on a higher plane than that of the world of the senses, but it became impossible to resolve the matter–spirit dichotomy, and so, in his search for a doctrine of salvation, the Greek merely evolved a type of mystical escapism, such as the mystery religions or Neoplatonism. Perhaps we may be allowed to recall a few aspects of the history of Greek philosophy. Plato, for instance, was an idealist "for whom virtue represents a thrust towards the divinity, and who, in reply to man's earnest and persistent questioning of the universe, provides the soothing reply that the soul, separated from the imperfect body which is governed by the senses, is able to find in death alone, an opportunity to soar towards a superior world".[2] Or we have Stoic pantheism, the most optimistic of the then current philosophical systems, since it sees man as a microcosm in perfect harmony with the universe, the one being animated with a soul, an igneous breath endowed with intelligence, the other actuated by a divine principle emanating from a primordial fire; as far as the practical issue is concerned, its programme of "living according to the dictates

---

[1] There seems to be no need here to mention the attempts most of the ancient peoples made to arrive at some unity in their particular representation of the divinity. Many see in this a rough draft of primitive monotheism; in fact, the God in favour of whom unity is achieved remains a cosmic reality, as, for example, Akhen-Aton, Amenophis IV's disc of the sun.

[2] *L'Orient et la Grèce* (Coll. Histoire générale des civilisations), Paris, 1953, p. 368.

of nature" brings us back, paradoxically, to a dualistic solution; we have to despise suffering, feeling, all tangible good, and reject an inferior world which we feel incapable of assuming. Although the expressions used are largely the same, there is an irreconcilable difference between the Stoic who is rich in his poverty, free in his slavery, happy in sickness, torture and death, and the Christian apostle who is thought to be sorrowful whereas he is always rejoicing, to have nothing when he possesses all things (2 Cor. 6. 10). With St Paul, there is no longer any attempt at denial or rejection; there exists no trace of any moral outlook suggesting resentment; suffering and death are faced squarely, overcome and transfigured.

Perhaps we may be luckier with the poets. For is it not in its Greek bucolic poetry that Antiquity learnt its love of nature? The contemplation of nature proposed for us here is scarcely, however, of a kind to stimulate our energies; rather than an appeal to action, its voice comes to us as a weary cry:

> Waste not thy flesh, O man, with journeying, wandering endlessly,
> on from land unto land, on without rest, without aim:
> Waste not thy flesh, if only a cabin ungarnish'd may shelter thee,
> Comforted, spite of storms, by a fitful flicker of flame . . .[1]

Besides, this type of poetry appears to be a late product of universal literature. Is it not after failure, after frustrating experiences and betrayed ambitions, that man generally turns to the beauty of surrounding landscapes, like a child who runs to hide his tears in his mother's apron? In any case, it was when Athens had seen the collapse of its dreams of hegemony, when it had had to learn to endure in silence the insolent Macedonian domination, that on Greek soil sprang up this slight and subtle poetry of the tired man seeking peace and consolation in nature: "I Hermes, stand here at the cross-roads by the wind-beaten orchard, near the hoary-grey coast; And

[1] Leonidas of Tarentum, "The Wanderer's Regrets" in *Poems,* translated by Edwyn Bevan, Oxford, 1931.

I keep a resting-place for weary men. And the cool stainless spring gushes out."[1] Representing thus a mere rest, a halt for sleep and oblivion, a confidant, in short, of our disappointments, the external world is not here a genuine companion of the human adventure as in the Bible; one could not imagine this world applauding the successes of the sons of Adam: "Give praise, O ye heavens, and rejoice, O earth; ye mountains, give praise with jubilation: because the Lord hath comforted his people and will have mercy on his poor ones" (Is. 49. 13).

If we pursued our investigation further, we should doubtless be fairly soon convinced that the moderns have been scarcely more successful than the ancients in attuning their history to the life of the universe. We ought, in particular, to pause for a moment to look at the synthesis Marxism proposes on this subject. Should we be obliged to concede here that Hegelianism as re-interpreted by Marx is, in fact, a satisfactory attempt at harmonizing human thought and activity on the one hand, and the movement of the cosmos on the other? Here at last, we find ourselves in the presence of a man freed from myth and no longer alienated, self-sufficient in himself, in his future history, in his action upon the world. It appears to us, however, that with or without dialectic the dilemma remains: either the movement of history prolongs the movement of the universe, and, by drawing ahead, breaks away from it altogether, or else, always immanent, becomes completely absorbed in it. If history is to continue the forward momentum of the cosmos and remain faithful to it, it seems impossible not to postulate a point of reference external to both, a pole of attraction inducing them to unite at some stage beyond their present position.

In our opinion, only the Bible has been able to offer an harmonious vision of total reality, in which the destiny of man is perfectly situated in the organization of the surrounding world. Nowhere else has the voice of God been heard calling mankind to resurrection and, at the same time, the heavens and earth to a new creation (Apoc. 21. 1).

---

[1] Anyte of Tegea, *Poems,* trans. by Richard Aldington, London, n.d., p. 5.

Dependence on the universe and ascent towards God

This balanced vision which the Bible reveals, in which our history is associated so closely with the very respiration of the world, may appear to have been seriously called in question by the ideal of sanctity which the Church proposes to us Christians. Are we not always hearing about detachment, renunciation, preparation for a better world, for a life beyond? Does not our language of mysticism, in short, reveal a fond yearning for escape? There are, undoubtedly, many truly religious people who, in their search for God, set out deliberately to lose all possible contact with earthly realities, who think of their spiritual ascension as a sort of Plotinian way of purification leading from the multiple to the One. With such people and their ideals, Marxism, we may note, would find it easy to come to a compromise: "You look after your heaven, and we will get on with putting the world in order." We should, however, take into account the fact that mystical language is necessarily equivocal. The expressions we find over and over again in our manuals of piety are intended merely to develop our Lord's command that we should be in the world but not of the world. A genuine Christian spirituality teaches us to look at the universe in a different fashion rather than to escape from it; for our closeness to the Lord throws new light upon our relations with others and with the world in which we live. Here, as in the Covenant of Yahweh with Israel, God's friendship seals the peace treaty between the chosen people and cosmic realities.

Furthermore, rather than linger over certain expressions which may easily be little more than facile slogans on the lips of ill-advised preachers, we shall doubtless do better to go back to the history of Christian spirituality throughout the ages. To mention only certain characteristic aspects of the question, neither the longing for martyrdom during the first two centuries, nor eastern monasticism, nor the urge of many to pursue an ideal of utter poverty which has shaken the Latin Church so often since the eleventh century, can ever be taken to be evidence of a *mystique* of escapism. To judge by the most authoritative representatives of the primitive spirituality of martyrdom, the Apocalypse of St John the Divine, the epistles of St Ignatius, the letter of the Christians of Lyons, it cannot be suggested that the disciples of Christ ever desired to flee from a bad world in order to go in search of a better one. The author of the Apocalypse, the Bishop of Antioch, the priests and faithful of the great Church of Gaul reveal, on the contrary, the deepest solicitude for the spread of the Church itself and the diffusion of its charity here on earth. Besides, it is clearly understood that one ought not to rush headlong into martyrdom; one should prepare, in all humility, for a struggle which offers a chance of triumph with the risen Christ. This conviction of a total, final victory over a persecuting world is diametrically opposed to an attitude of abandonment and withdrawal, or even of mere haughty disdain; it could find no place in the categories of a Stoic emperor such as Marcus Aurelius.

The same prospect of a victorious combat induced St Anthony and the early anchorites, two centuries later, to go into the desert and encounter Satan. As it developed, the movement no doubt frequently acquired questionable forms; nor should the whole of eastern monasticism be judged solely by the Fathers of the desert; and we should give greater prominence to the reaction of Basilian spirituality. The fact remains that the massive departure towards the scorched wilderness of Egypt is providentially associated with the conversion of the empire. In the retreats of Nitria and the Thebaid, the Church breathed in the pure air which enabled her henceforth to assume responsibility for the Graeco-Roman world, to absorb its essential values and yet not be engulfed by it. And since then there has never been any relaxation of tension between these two opposing forces, compelling her on the one hand towards a reaching out to higher things, and on the other hand towards an assumption of temporal realities; the more the Church had to take part in the contingencies of history, the more clearly affirmed was her effort towards disengagement. The whole equilibrium of her life depends on these two contradictory as well as complementary pressures; were one of the two suppressed in favour of the other, then there would be no outcome but death.

Moreover, this same effort towards disengagement which always accompanied the Church's assumption of the realities of this world is in no way to be confused with a temptation to escapism. To be convinced of this, we have but to consider for a moment the movement in favour of poverty which, from the end of the eleventh century, gradually grew in intensity as western civilization developed. The early Cistercians, for example, choosing the wildest and most uncultivated regions for their retreat, inaugurated an age of forest-clearance which was rapidly to alter the face of the French countryside. Here, poverty instinctively joined forces with a love of nature—was it not said of Stephen Harding that he liked "the rule and the place",[1] evidence of which is still furnished by many names which were then created. Merely to hear the pleasant sounds of these names, a chronicler disclosed,[2] gave one an immediate desire to go and taste the joy which they evoked. Happiness at having found God had, as it were, completely impregnated these areas conquered by the work of the White Monks: Bonport, Saint-Port, Port-Salut, Repos-Notre-Dame, Beaubec, Beaulieu, Beaupré, Beauvin, Bellecombe, Bellevaux, Belmont, Bonlieu, Bonnecombe, Bonneval, Bonnefont, Bonnefontaine, Bellaigue, Belleau, Aiguebelle, Bonnaigue, etc.,—or these, henceforth bathed in light: Clairvaux, Vauclair, Clairmont, Vauluisant, Netlieu, Candeil (Candelium), Clarté-Dieu, Lume-Dieu, Aubepierre, Auberive, Clairefontaine, etc.,—totally consecrated to God: Lieu-Dieu, Loc-Dieu, Theuley (Theolocus), la Part-Dieu, la Cour-Dieu. These lands, which were formerly lying waste had become blessed territories: Benoîte-vaux, Laval-Bénite, Le Breuil-Benoît, Chambenoît, Prébenoît,

[1] Quoted by Marie-Anselme Didier, *Clarté, Paix et Joie*. Les Beaux Noms des monastères de Cîteaux en France, Lyons, p. 12. The proper names mentioned below are all from this evocative little book.

[2] "Quibus auditores solo nominis nectare invitantur festinanter experiri quanta sit ibi beatitudo quae tam speciali denotetur vocabulo." Odericus Vitalis, *Historia Ecclesiastica*, VIII, 25.

Sauvebenoît, la Bonté-Dieu, l'Abondance-Dieu, la Grâce-Dieu, la Piété-Dieu.[1]

May we be permitted, in this connexion, to dwell at somewhat greater length upon the Franciscan movement? Everyone knows the story of the Christmas at Greccio and the influence of this Franciscan cult for the poverty of the crib on the piety and the art of the Middle Ages. Rather less known, however, is the relationship between this devotion and another, equally Franciscan, that of Christ the King. Now, for St Francis, poverty never appears otherwise than as a condition for a sound and complete mastery over the world—*cuius imperium super humerum eius*, as the liturgy sings—, a mastery which nothing can restrict, which nothing can break, which reaches out to the depths of the universe, which unites all things in love. Thus the Hymn to Lady Poverty naturally finishes with the *Laudes Creaturarum*, the canticle in praise of the Creation. If these two complementary aspects of the message of Assisi are not maintained intact and indissoluble, Franciscan spirituality disintegrates into an endless series of devotions, no doubt excellent in themselves, but which, by their length and redundancy, offer no more interest than the endless round of foolish ideas circulating in the world without any conscious direction.

It must not be thought that there are two Saint Francises, the one of the ascetics and the one of the poets; that there is on the one hand the tragic monk portrayed by Zurbaran, inspirer of spiritual treatises, rather tiresome, it has to be admitted, as are all great figures who have been subject to the tactless treatment of the mediocre; and on the other hand, the troubadour, the preacher to the birds, the hero of Liszt's pilgrimages or of Axel Munthe's, *The Story of San Michele*. These two images are, are after all, utterly false if they remain isolated, if they do not support one another, serving interchangeably as obverse and reverse. The persistent refusal of the saint to allow any form of appropriation is not to be

---

[1] Cf. in Britain such names as: Beaulieu, Dieulacres, Grace Dieu, Strata Florida, Valle Crucis.

interpreted as evidence of his scorn for creation, but is rather a mark of his love of creation; it seems to him that ruthless possession of the world is a threat to the liberty of nature, at least as great, perhaps, as its threat to the liberty of man himself, for the master of a thing soon becomes its slave. There is no question of denying that the Creator placed the universe at the disposal of the sons of Adam, but Francis dreams that, in our dealings with the beings of nature, we should always display that chivalrous courteousness by which he himself was always obsessed: my brother the wolf, my sister the water; he would wish that his brothers, realizing that nothing is their due, should marvel at every gift of the Creator. In short, a great wind of cosmic peace and liberty blows through this cult of poverty: "And in that day I will make a covenant with them, with the beasts of the field, and with the fowls of the air, and with the creeping things of the earth" (Osee 2. 18).

Such a pure, respectful and fraternal attitude remains the fruit of a severe ascetic effort, of a constant striving after detachment. Thus it is to the Saint of Assisi much more than to the elegiac poets of Ancient Greece that may fittingly be applied this definition by Fr Festugière of a man "who begins to look at nature, no longer to derive some advantage from it, nor even to learn its secrets, but simply to look at it and because he has pleasure in looking at it, because his gaze is now pure enough, his heart sufficiently free of all lucrative considerations, to find his perfect happiness in peaceful contemplation."[1] For this purity of gaze is achieved in the experience of Christ's Cross: "And I, if I be lifted up from the earth, will draw all things to myself" (John 12. 32). Then it is that man, maintaining that he has no other point of reference but God alone, free from the weight and the attraction of material things, is able to admire all things with a feeling that the world has been given to him quite gratuitously; no longer will he crush beneath his heavy and clumsy steps the delicate flowers strewn in his path by the Creator.

Thus the Church has never invited the best of her children

[1] *L'Enfant d'Agrigente*, pp. 152–3.

to go in search of God in the barrel of Diogenes; she has never set forth as an ideal some escapist *mystique*, spreading lotus flowers beneath man's steps in order to preserve him from contact with an impure soil. She has remained faithful to the fullness of the biblical vision of creation, in which are indissolubly united, in the same loving purpose, the urge of history and the life of the universe. The Christian, therefore, will never forget that far from God, he remains far from everything:

> J'écoute les bruits de la ville
> et prisonnier sans horizon
> je ne vois rien qu'un ciel hostile
> et les murs nus de ma prison,[1]

and that only a state of grace will reveal to him the true significance of creation:

> Pour l'élever plus que toi-même, ô nature,
> tu lui parles au coeur, de ta voix grave et pure;
> devant cet orbe en feu, disparaissant là-bas,
> il rêve d'un soleil qui ne se couche pas;
> et doucement, avant que la clarté ne meure,
> il bénit et l'espace et la raison et l'heure,[2]

and in the same eucharist he will give thanks to God "for having created the world and delivered us from evil".[3]

---

[1] Guillaume Apollinaire, *Alcools*. (Translator's note: "I can hear the sounds from the town, and, a prisoner with no horizon, I can see nothing but a hostile sky and the bare walls of my prison").

[2] Louis le Cardonnel, *Assisium, Carmina Sacra*. (Translator's note: "In order to raise him higher than yourself, O nature, you speak, in your grave and pure voice, to his heart; as this fiery orb is swallowed up yonder, he dreams of a sun that never sets; and softly, before the light fades, he blesses space, and reason, and time").

[3] St Justin, *Dialogue with Trypho*, XLI, 1.

BIBLIOGRAPHY

I—GENERAL WORKS

Albright, W. F., *Archaeology and the Religion of Israel*, Baltimore, 1941, Oxford, 1953.
Bertholet, A., *Histoire de la civilisation d'Israël*, Paris, 1929.
Dhorme, É., *Évolution religieuse d'Israël*. I: La Religion des Hébreux nomades, Brussels, 1937.
Eerdmans, B.D., *The Religion of Israël*, Leyden, 1947.
Eichrodt, W., *Theologie des Alten Testaments, I–III*, Leipzig 1933–1939.
Gelin, A., *Les Idées maîtresses de l'Ancien Testament*, Paris, 1948.
Guillet, J., *Thèmes bibliques*, Paris, 1950.
Imschoot, D. van, *Théologie de l'Ancien Testament*, Paris-Tournai, 1954.
Jacob, E., *Théologie de l'Ancien Testament*, Neuchâtel, 1955.
Koehler, L., *Theologie des Alten Testaments*, Tübingen, 1936.
Pedersen, J., *Israel, its Life and Culture, I–II*, Copenhagen and Oxford, 1947.
Procksch, O., *Theologie des Alten Testaments*, Gütersloh, 1950.
Rad, G. von, *Theologie des Alten Testaments, I*, Munich, 1958.
Rowley, H. H., *The Biblical Doctrine of Election*, London, 1950.
—— *The Unity of the Bible*, London, 1953, Philadelphia, 1955.
—— *The Faith of Israel*, London, 1956, Philadelphia, 1957.
Tresmontant, C., *Étude de métaphysique biblique*, Paris, 1955.
Vaux, R. de, "La Religion de l'Ancien Testament" in *Initiation biblique*, Paris, 1948.
—— *Les Institutions de l'Ancien Testament, I*, Paris, 1958. *Ancient Israel: Its Life and Institutions*, London, 1961.
Vincent, A., *La Religion des Judéo-Araméens d'Éléphantine*, Paris, 1937.
Vriezen, T. C., *Theologie des Alten Testaments in Grundzügen*, 1956. *An Outline of Old Testament Theology*, Oxford, 1958.

II—PARTICULAR QUESTIONS

Aalen, S., *Die Begriffe "Licht" und "Finsternis" im Alten Testament*, in Skrifter utgitt av det Norske Videnskaps-Akademi i Oslo, 1951, No. 1.
Bentzen, A., "King Ideology", "Urmensch", "Troonbestijgingsfeest", in *Studia Theologica*, Lund, 1951, pp. 143–57.
Buber, M., *Das Königtum Gottes*, Berlin, 1932.
Dhorme, P., *L'Emploi métaphorique des noms de parties du corps, en hébreu et en accadien*, Paris, 1923.
Ehrlich, E. L., *Kultsymbolik im Alten Testament und im nachbiblischen Judentum*, Stuttgart, 1959.
Fraine, J. de, *L'Aspect religieux de la Royauté israélite. L'Institution monarchique dans l'A. T. et dans les textes mésopotamiens*, Rome, 1954.
Frazer, J. G., "Études d'Anthropologie biblique", in *Revue d'Histoire et de Philosophie Religieuse*, No. 15, 1935, pp. 43 ff.
Gross, H., *Die Idee des ewigen und allgemeinen Weltfriedens im Alten Orient und im Alten Testament*, Trier, 1956.

187

Guglielmo, De, "The Fertility of the Land in the Messianic Prophecies", in *Catholic Biblical Quarterly*, 1957, pp. 306–11.

Gunkel, H., *Schöpfung und Chaos in Urzeit und Endzeit*, Göttingen, 1922.

Hempel, J., "Glaube, Mythos und Geschichte im A. T.", in *Zeitschrift für die alttestamentliche Wissenschaft*, N.F. 24, 1954, pp. 109 ff.

Herner, S., *Die Natur im A. T.*, Lund, 1941.

Hooke, Edited by, *Myth, Ritual and Kingship*, London and New York, 1958.

Johnson, A. R., *Sacral Kingship in Ancient Israel*, Cardiff, 1955.

Kraus, H. J., *Die Königsherrschaft Gottes im Alten Testament*, Tübingen, 1951.

Lambert, G., "La Création dans la Bible", in *Nouvelle Revue théologique*, 1953, pp. 252 ff.

Mackenzie, J. L., "God and Nature in the Old Testament", in *Catholic Biblical Quarterly*, XIV, 1952, pp. 18–39; 124–45.

Mengers, E. T., *The Idea of Creation in the Old Testament*, Boston, 1957.

Mowinckel, S., "Urmensch und 'Königsideologie' ", in *Studia Biblica*, Lund, 1948, pp. 71–89.

——   *Religion und Kultus*, Göttingen, 1953.

——   *He that Cometh*, Oxford, 1956.

Reymond, P., 'L'Eau, sa vie et sa signification dans l'A.T. (Supplement to *Vetus Testamentum VI*), Leyden, 1958.

Rowley, H. H., "The Meaning of Sacrifice in the Old Testament", in *Bulletin of the John Rylands Library*, 23, 1950, pp. 74 ff.

Snaith, N. H., "Sacrifices in the Old Testament", in *Vetus Testamentum*, 1957, pp. 307 ff.

Speiser, E. A., "The Biblical Idea of History in its Common Near-Eastern Setting", in *Israel Exploration Journal*, 1957, pp. 201–16.

Weiser, A., "Die Darstellung der Theophanie in den Psalmen und im Festkult", in *Festschrift für Bertholet*, 1950, pp. 513 ff.

Widengren, G., *Sakrales Königtum im Alten Testament und im Judentum*, Stuttgart, 1955.

III—COMPARATIVE STUDIES

Baumgartner, W., "Ugaritische Probleme und ihre Tragweite für das Alte Testament", in *Theologische Zeitschrift*, III, 1947, pp. 81 ff.

Dentan, Edited by, *The Idea of History in the Ancient Near East*, 1955.

Dhorme, É., *Les Religions de Babylonie et d'Assyrie*, Paris, 1949.

Eliade, M., *The Myth of the Eternal Return*, New York, 1954, London, 1955.

——   *Patterns in Comparative Religion*, London and New York 1958.

Engnell, *Studies in Divine Kingship in the Ancient Near East*, Uppsala, 1943.

Falkenstein, A., "La Cité-Temple sumérienne", in *Cahiers d'histoire mondiale*, 1954, pp. 784–814.

Fish, T., "Some Aspects of Kingship in the Sumerian City and Kingdom of Ur", in *Bulletin of the John Rylands Library*, 1951–1952, pp. 37–43.

Frankfort, H., *Kingship and the Gods*, Chicago, 1948.

Gadd, C. J., *Ideas of Divine Rule in the Ancient Near Eastern Religions*, London, 1948.

Gaster, T. H., *Thespis: Ritual, Myth and Drama in the Ancient Near East*, New York, 1950.

James, E. O., *Myth and Ritual in the Ancient Near East*, London and New York, 1958.

Kramer, S. N., *Sumerian Mythology*, Philadelphia, 1944.

Labat, R., *Le caractère religieux de le Royauté assyro-babylonienne*, Paris, 1939.

Langhe, R. de, *Les textes de Ras Shamra Ugarit et leurs rapports avec le milieu de l'A.T.*, Paris, 1945.

INDEX OF BIBLICAL TEXTS

14